KW-550-666

HARBRACE VOCABULARY GUIDE

THIRD EDITION

BEAR
STUDENT STORES
USED

HARBRACE VOCABULARY GUIDE

THIRD EDITION

DONALD W. LEE
Late of University of Houston

KATHLEEN G. ROUSSEAU
West Virginia University

HARCOURT BRACE

HARCOURT BRACE COLLEGE PUBLISHERS

Fort Worth Philadelphia San Diego New York Orlando Austin San Antonio
Toronto Montreal London Sydney Tokyo

Publisher Ted Buchholz
Acquisitions Editor Stephen T. Jordan
Senior Developmental Editor Sarah Helyar Smith
Project Editor Nancy Lombardi
Production Manager Erin Gregg
Senior Art Director Don Fujimoto
Electronic Publishing Coordinator Jill Stubblefield
Electronic Publishing Supervisor Mike Beaupré

Copyright © 1994, 1970, 1956 by Harcourt Brace & Company
Copyright renewed 1984 by Doris A. Lee, Eric C. Lee, Davis H. Lee and Donald A. Lee

All rights reserved. No part of this publication may be reproduced or transmitted in any form or by any means, electronic or mechanical, including photocopy, recording, or any information storage and retrieval system, without permission in writing from the publisher.

Permission is hereby granted to reproduce the Chapter Exercises and Tests in this publication in complete pages, with the copyright notice, for instructional use and not for resale by any teacher using classroom quantities of the related student textbook.

Address for Editorial Correspondence:
Harcourt Brace College Publishers, 301 Commerce Street, Suite 3700, Fort Worth, TX 76102

Address for Orders:
Harcourt Brace & Company, 6277 Sea Harbor Drive, Orlando, FL 32887
1-800-782-4479, or 1-800-433-0001 (in Florida)

ISBN: 0-15-500855-2

Library of Congress Catalog Card Number: 93-78320

Printed in the United States of America

3 4 5 6 7 8 9 0 1 2 066 9 8 7 6 5 4 3 2 1

Preface

More scholarly than most vocabulary textbooks, the *Harbrace Vocabulary Guide* is designed for those who wish to enhance their vocabularies. It is suitable for composition, reading, and vocabulary courses.

The vocabulary of the 1990s is far more technologically based than that of the 1970s, and the Third Edition reflects that evolution. Featuring many new words, each chapter begins with a germane quotation; provides simpler, more lucid, and more euphonious explanations; and concludes with exercises that encourage articulation. To reflect the changing language, former chapters 8 and 9 are now combined and special attention has been given to chapter 4 so that its assignments support scientific and technical terminology. To counterbalance the technical coverage, the exercises in context in chapter 12 are expanded and amended to include excerpts from selected great works of literature. Students can check their retention of words in cumulative exercises placed periodically throughout the book.

An inadequate vocabulary is distressing to both the possessor and the listener. Of all the disciplines, it is *avid reading* that leads to precise, erudite, colorful, and fascinating vocabulary. A well-developed vocabulary enables a person to speak persuasively and to write concisely, lucidly, and euphoniously. As Francis Bacon explained, "Reading maketh a full man; conference a ready man; and writing an exact man." Students can attain and perfect these forms of communication only by being profoundly aware of language; such an awareness is the focus of the *Harbrace Vocabulary Guide,* Third Edition.

KATHLEEN G. ROUSSEAU

To the Student

In today's world the scope of a person's vocabulary is often regarded as a good indication of his or her overall intelligence and general knowledge. Universities and professional schools commonly use vocabulary tests as part of their admissions and placement procedures. Industrial and commercial firms and branches of the armed services often use vocabulary tests to screen or rate people. Therefore, increasing your vocabulary now may be very valuable to you later. More important than expediting your future success, however, is the fact that the survival of democracy depends on the existence of a well-informed electorate, and members of such an electorate need a wide vocabulary in order to read and listen with perception and intelligence.

How can you enlarge your vocabulary? There is no one single way. Certainly there is no one simple easy way. In this book, we recommend three general procedures: (1) use of a dictionary; (2) analysis, which we will later call morphemic analysis, of words; and (3) use of content and context clues. The book begins with a chapter on the dictionary, explains analysis, the body of the book, and ends with considering context. Constant attention, constant interest, and constant curiosity about words will help you more, perhaps, than the specific comments in this book.

Contents

Preface v
To the Student vii
Preliminary Vocabulary Test 1 1
Preliminary Vocabulary Test 2 3
Preliminary Vocabulary Test 3 5

1 IMPORTANCE OF THE DICTIONARY AND ITS USAGE 9
Seeing words correctly, syllabification, meanings, variant forms, pronunciation

2 NATIVE AND BORROWED WORDS 25
Sources of borrowed words, frequency, pronunciation, plural forms, meanings

3 WORD ANALYSIS: PREFIXES 41
Root or morpheme words, separating prefix from root, recognizing and using prefixes

CUMULATIVE TEST 1 57

4 WORD ANALYSIS: GREEK ROOTS 61
Greek roots—finding, analyzing, meanings

5 WORD ANALYSIS: LATIN ROOTS I 81
Latin roots—finding, analyzing, prefixes and roots, meanings

CUMULATIVE TEST 2 93

CUMULATIVE TEST 3 96

CUMULATIVE TEST 4 97

6 WORD ANALYSIS: LATIN ROOTS II 99
Latin roots—defining, analyzing, meanings

7 WORD ANALYSIS: SUFFIXES 113
Recognizing and forming suffixes

8 WORD ANALYSIS: 125
A. RESERVATIONS
Unusual roots, common roots in pairs, and groups of words
B. SEMANTIC CHANGE
Original meanings, words derived from names of persons or places, original root meanings, archaic uses, semantic changes

CUMULATIVE TEST 5 135

9 FIGURATIVE LANGUAGE 139
Varieties of figures of speech, figurative words in historic writings, uncommon figurative expressions, meanings

10 SYNONYMS 145
Finding, contexts, connotations, antonyms

11 DESCRIPTIVE LABELS 157
Usage labels, formal and informal words, slang, dialectal, archaic, and literary words

12 READING AND LISTENING 163
Exercises in Context: Language, politics, literature

CUMULATIVE TEST 6A 171

CUMULATIVE TEST 6B 174

CUMULATIVE TEST 6C 177

CUMULATIVE TEST 6D 178

CHAPTER WORD LIST 181

SUPPLEMENT:
Vocabulary Test 1 **197**
Vocabulary Test 2 **199**
Vocabulary Test 3 **201**

NAME ______________________ SECTION __________ DATE __________

PRELIMINARY VOCABULARY TEST 1: The words in the following test are "thirteenth grade" words—that is, they should be in the vocabulary of a college freshman. Choose the word or expression closest in meaning to the italicized word and print its number in the blank.

1. an *abstruse* subject: 1 unimportant 2 theological 3 complex and difficult — 1. ______
2. feelings of *antipathy:* 1 deep respect 2 piqued interest 3 dislike — 2. ______
3. an *assiduous* student: 1 affected and silly 2 careful and industrious 3 mediocre — 3. ______
4. his *benign* appearance: 1 kindly and mild 2 eccentric 3 weak and infirm — 4. ______
5. a *captious* critic: 1 fault-finding 2 quite influential 3 kind and sympathetic — 5. ______
6. a lawyer's *chicanery:* 1 trickery and fraud 2 cleverness 3 delaying tactics — 6. ______
7. a fearful *chimera:* 1 grotesque fantasy 2 cancer 3 murderous attack — 7. ______
8. a *clandestine* meeting: 1 furtively secret 2 illegal 3 unimportant — 8. ______
9. a *commodious* room: 1 littered and dirty 2 fashionable 3 ample and spacious — 9. ______
10. the surfing *coterie:* 1 closed group 2 spectators 3 opponents — 10. ______
11. to *denigrate* a reputation: 1 protect 2 blacken and defame 3 overlook — 11. ______
12. to *deprecate* her skill: 1 praise 2 try to copy 3 disapprove or slight — 12. ______
13. his *dilatory* procedures: 1 crude and insulting 2 delaying 3 scrupulous — 13. ______
14. *disparities* between stories: 1 correspondences 2 dissimilarities 3 relationships — 14. ______
15. *dissembling* her anger: 1 soothing 2 concealing 3 showing or proclaiming — 15. ______
16. an *effete* society: 1 worn out and strengthless 2 polished 3 aristocratic — 16. ______
17. an *encomium* for the chief: 1 speech of praise 2 award 3 promotion — 17. ______
18. an *enervated* patient: 1 encouraged and cheerful 2 weakened 3 chronic — 18. ______
19. an *erudite* professor: 1 very learned 2 quite dull 3 wry and sarcastic — 19. ______
20. *euphonious* sounds: 1 rough and discordant 2 imperceptible 3 pleasant — 20. ______
21. *forensic* activities: relevant to 1 sports 2 narcotics 3 speech and debate — 21. ______
22. marked by *hyperbole:* 1 grotesque curves 2 exaggeration 3 doubt and anger — 22. ______
23. an *imminent* fate: 1 impending 2 cruel 3 ironic — 23. ______
24. *indigent* applicants: 1 well-qualified 2 eagerly zealous 3 impoverished — 24. ______
25. an *innocuous* drug: 1 poisonous 2 extremely expensive 3 harmless — 25. ______
26. *insentient* things: 1 without senses or life 2 dangerous 3 expensive — 26. ______
27. tropical *lassitude:* 1 weary languor 2 discomfort 3 rich lushness — 27. ______
28. to *mitigate* the offense: 1 record 2 punish 3 lessen the seriousness of — 28. ______
29. meeting his *nemesis:* 1 faithful ally 2 agent of retribution 3 healer — 29. ______
30. a *palpable* truth: 1 recently discovered 2 quite obvious 3 immortal — 30. ______
31. delivered a *panegyric:* 1 accusation 2 eulogy 3 universal curse — 31. ______
32. a *pernicious* tendency: 1 beneficial 2 unexpectedly sudden 3 harmful — 32. ______
33. skilled at *persiflage:* 1 concealment 2 interpretation 3 light banter — 33. ______
34. a *precursor* of the new era: 1 opponent 2 forerunner 3 prophet — 34. ______

Copyright © 1994 by Harcourt Brace & Company. All rights reserved.

35. the *progeny* of the pioneers: 1 heritage 2 offspring 3 leaders 35. ________

36. a *rapacious* old man: 1 infirm 2 covetous 3 vigorous 36. ________

37. a *salubrious* climate: 1 varied 2 weakening 3 healthful 37. ________

38. a *sententious* observation: 1 profane 2 trite and puffed up 3 ungrammatical 38. ________

39. *specious* reasoning: 1 deceptively plausible 2 profound 3 inclusive 39. ________

40. a *stentorian* voice: 1 extremely loud 2 musical 3 quivering 40. ________

41. a *strident* tone: 1 harsh and shrill 2 pathetic 3 wavering 41. ________

42. a *taciturn* mountaineer: 1 daring 2 threatening 3 silent and reserved 42. ________

43. *thalassic* studies: pertaining to 1 heat energy 2 seas 3 mythology 43. ________

44. *torpid* animals: 1 diseased 2 uncommon 3 inactive and sluggish 44. ________

45. to *traduce* her character: 1 examine 2 defame 3 protect 45. ________

46. a *trenchant* comment: 1 keen and cutting 2 demanding 3 unsuitable 46. ________

47. the *vagaries* of fate: 1 whims and fancies 2 fixed decrees 3 principles 47. ________

48. a reputation for *veracity:* 1 truthfulness 2 craftiness 3 stubbornness 48. ________

49. to *vitiate* his conclusion: 1 invalidate 2 reinforce 3 ignore 49. ________

50. a *vitriolic* answer: 1 placating 2 angry and caustic 3 unnoticed 50. ________

Copyright © 1994 by Harcourt Brace & Company. All rights reserved.

NAME ______________________ SECTION ________ DATE __________

PRELIMINARY VOCABULARY TEST 2: The words in the following test have been taken from recent issues of newspapers and magazines with large national circulations. Choose the word or expression closest in meaning to the italicized word and print the number of that word or expression in the blank.

1. the dean's *admonitory* note: 1 complimentary 2 prompt 3 cautionary 1. ________
2. to *alleviate* the distress: 1 intensify 2 ignore 3 relieve 2. ________
3. *animosities* aroused by the talk: 1 discussions 2 enmities 3 answers 3. ________
4. an *anomalous* development: 1 gratifying 2 abnormal 3 preliminary 4. ________
5. *apothegms* about thrift: 1 maxims 2 precautions 3 instances of neglect 5. ________
6. an *arduous* task: 1 laborious 2 unexpected 3 easily overlooked 6. ________
7. the *banality* of the speech: 1 triteness 2 suitability 3 effectiveness 7. ________
8. *coerced* to follow: 1 persuaded 2 compelled by force 3 directed 8. ________
9. treated with *derision:* 1 veneration 2 ridicule 3 reluctant consent 9. ________
10. into *discrete* divisions: 1 unclear 2 separate and distinct 3 uneven 10. ________
11. opposed by the *dissident* group: 1 militant 2 dissenting 3 radical 11. ________
12. an *ebullient* person: 1 mournful 2 unhealthy 3 enthusiastic and excited 12. ________
13. *emulous* of his brother: 1 contemptuous 2 eager to equal or beat 3 loving 13. ________
14. an *enigmatic* suggestion: 1 improper 2 appropriate 3 puzzling 14. ________
15. aroused *ephemeral* interest: 1 short-lived 2 enthusiastic 3 prurient 15. ________
16. to *eschew* more talk: 1 speed up 2 shun or avoid 3 consider 16. ________
17. *ethnic* studies: pertaining to 1 morals 2 peoples and races 3 money 17. ________
18. answered with *fatuity:* 1 emphasis 2 utter foolishness 3 tenderness 18. ________
19. *inhibiting* the operations: 1 showing 2 approving 3 hindering or stopping 19. ________
20. a person of *integrity:* 1 honest character 2 wide reputation 3 great wealth 20. ________
21. *internecine* conflicts: 1 minor 2 covert 3 bloody or deadly 21. ________
22. an *intransigent* enemy: 1 temporary 2 unimportant 3 uncompromising 22. ________
23. a *lucrative* contract: 1 very profitable 2 unfortunate 3 illegal 23. ________
24. a *lugubrious* expression: 1 laughably mournful 2 noncommittal 3 fierce 24. ________
25. a *mandatory* order: 1 obligatory 2 trivial 3 wild and rash 25. ________
26. the character's *metamorphosis:* 1 identity 2 complete change 3 outward appearance 26. ________
27. a *nominal* debt: 1 trivial 2 pressing 3 legal but unjust 27. ________
28. *occult* practices: 1 secret and supernatural 2 criminal 3 hurtful 28. ________
29. an *opulent* display: showing 1 lavish wealth 2 bad taste 3 pitiful need 29. ________
30. Yeltsin's *partisans:* 1 zealous followers 2 relatives 3 spies and saboteurs 30. ________
31. a *pastoral* background: 1 religious 2 rural 3 fierce and barbarous 31. ________
32. a *peccant* husband: 1 cruel and oppressive 2 submissive 3 sinning 32. ________
33. a *penchant* for mathematics: 1 inability 2 liking and inclination 3 dislike 33. ________
34. *proliferation* of taxes: 1 collection 2 rapid multiplication 3 hatred 34. ________

Copyright © 1994 by Harcourt Brace & Company. All rights reserved.

35. to *reiterate* an objection: 1 repeat 2 withdraw 3 apologize for 35. ________
36. *restive* natives: 1 lethargic 2 unruly 3 stupid and naive 36. ________
37. *sinuous* motions: 1 lustful 2 difficult to see 3 winding and curving 37. ________
38. *sporadic* cases of the disease: 1 fatal 2 unexpected 3 found here and there 38. ________
39. a limited *stipend:* 1 grant or allowance 2 obligation 3 time limit 39. ________
40. *subliminal* propaganda: below 1 dignity 2 conscious perception 3 truth 40. ________
41. a *succinct* account: 1 lurid and colorful 2 terse 3 slanderous 41. ________
42. a *sumptuous* table: 1 rich and lavish 2 bare and scant 3 mediocre 42. ________
43. *sycophantic* followers: 1 weak and irresolute 2 flattering 3 determined 43. ________
44. a *tortuous* path: 1 steep and narrow 2 twisting irregularly 3 almost unknown 44. ________
45. a *traumatic* effect: marked by 1 illusion 2 misfortune 3 shock and injury 45. ________
46. his *travail* ended: 1 toil and pain 2 voyaging 3 horseback riding 46. ________
47. a *ubiquitous* insect: 1 dangerous 2 present everywhere 3 harmful to crops 47. ________
48. answered with *unction:* 1 rudeness 2 oily slickness 3 self-deprecation 48. ________
49. the *verbosity* of the essay: 1 wordiness 2 persuasiveness 3 smooth style 49. ________
50. a *vitreous* substance: 1 glassy 2 unanalyzable 3 steely and firm 50. ________

Copyright © 1994 by Harcourt Brace & Company. All rights reserved.

NAME ______________________ SECTION ________ DATE __________

PRELIMINARY VOCABULARY TEST 3: The words in the following test are taken from a word frequency list. The most common are from the 10,000–11,000 bracket, the least common from the 19,000–20,000 bracket. A score of 75 might be interpreted as an indication of a vocabulary of 15,000 words (although this figure is probably low). Choose the word closest in meaning to the italicized word and print its number in the blank.

1. to *abdicate* the throne: 1 claim 2 renounce 3 occupy — 1. ________
2. the *aborigines* of the land: 1 rivers 2 natives 3 animals — 2. ________
3. a pact *abrogated* by consent: 1 drawn up 2 endorsed 3 abolished — 3. ________
4. to *accentuate* this point: 1 emphasize 2 contradict 3 consider — 4. ________
5. an *acrimonious* argument: 1 sharp and bitter 2 trivial 3 endless — 5. ________
6. an *adroit* worker: 1 bungling 2 dissatisfied 3 skillful — 6. ________
7. under the club's *aegis:* 1 protesting 2 sponsoring 3 planning — 7. ________
8. a man of *affluence:* 1 notoriety 2 position 3 wealth — 8. ________
9. to *ameliorate* conditions: 1 investigate 2 worsen 3 improve — 9. ________
10. his *asinine* comments: 1 foolish 2 sarcastic 3 determined — 10. ________
11. an *atrocious* crime: 1 mysterious 2 sordid 3 cruel and beastlike — 11. ________
12. under *auspicious* circumstances: 1 difficult 2 doubtful 3 favorable — 12. ________
13. Russian *autocrats:* 1 ideologies 2 absolute rulers 3 satellite states — 13. ________
14. *belligerent* nations: 1 bankrupt 2 densely populated 3 warlike — 14. ________
15. a *bestial* action: 1 foolhardy 2 secret 3 beastly — 15. ________
16. a foolish *braggart:* 1 fanatic 2 boaster 3 apprentice — 16. ________
17. *bucolic* surroundings: 1 frightening 2 rural 3 congested — 17. ________
18. to *buttress* an assertion: 1 support 2 explain 3 refute — 18. ________
19. a *buxom* woman: 1 fashionable 2 well-loved 3 plump — 19. ________
20. a *callow* youth: 1 immature 2 excitable 3 adventurous — 20. ________
21. the *candor* of her answer: 1 honest frankness 2 hesitation 3 abruptness — 21. ________
22. the editor's *captious* ways: 1 careful 2 faultfinding 3 angry — 22. ________
23. a *carmine* color: 1 deep 2 unattractive 3 reddish — 23. ________
24. a *choleric* temperament: 1 placid 2 dull 3 hotheaded — 24. ________
25. *a chromatic* chart: pertaining to 1 chemicals 2 colors 3 weather — 25. ________
26. a *clement* judge: 1 dishonest 2 mild and lenient 3 learned — 26. ________
27. *cogent* suggestions: 1 irrelevant 2 feeble 3 strong and convincing — 27. ________
28. *cognizant* of danger: 1 aware of 2 unhappy about 3 careless of — 28. ________
29. a *colloquy* on the question: 1 argument 2 talk 3 sudden silence — 29. ________
30. a *complaisant* welcome: 1 boisterous 2 sullen and rude 3 pleasing — 30. ________
31. to *concoct* an excuse: 1 deny 2 ignore 3 cook up, make up — 31. ________
32. to *conduce* to peace: 1 lead to 2 think about 3 work against — 32. ________

Copyright © 1994 by Harcourt Brace & Company. All rights reserved.

33. a *conflagration* downtown: 1 big fire 2 riot 3 epidemic — 33. ________
34. a *decrepit* old house: 1 broken down 2 beautiful 3 cheap — 34. ________
35. old and *desiccated:* 1 weakened 2 confused 3 dried out — 35. ________
36. the *disruption* of his plan: 1 breaking 2 culminating 3 ending — 36. ________
37. planning *drastic* measures: 1 unusual 2 routine 3 quite severe — 37. ________
38. a poetic *effusion:* 1 temperament 2 vision 3 outpouring — 38. ________
39. an *elongated* pattern: 1 intricate 2 lengthened 3 old-fashioned — 39. ________
40. to *expedite* the deal: 1 investigate 2 cancel 3 speed up — 40. ________
41. gave a *fillip* to the party: 1 pause 2 stimulus 3 alarm — 41. ________
42. trained in *fiscal* matters: 1 financial 2 administrative 3 fishing — 42. ________
43. the play's *flamboyant* style: 1 showy 2 baffling 3 trite and old — 43. ________
44. *friable* rock: 1 volcanic 2 easily crumbled 3 multicolored — 44. ________
45. a *garbled* story: 1 confused 2 prejudiced 3 very brief — 45. ________
46. a *gossamer* fabric: 1 synthetic 2 rough and durable 3 filmy — 46. ________
47. the *habitat* of fur-bearing animals: 1 diet 2 dwelling area 3 sanctuary — 47. ________
48. a *hermetic* closure: 1 airtight 2 temporary 3 insecure — 48. ________
49. sorting *homogeneous* things: 1 similar 2 miscellaneous 3 dangerous — 49. ________
50. an *immutable* law: 1 extremely just 2 changeless 3 imperfect — 50. ________
51. seeing the devil *incarnate:* 1 alone 2 in the flesh 3 on earth — 51. ________
52. an *incongruous* costume: 1 inappropriate 2 cheap 3 modest — 52. ________
53. heard the news with *incredulity:* 1 disbelief 2 calm 3 fright — 53. ________
54. an *indigenous* plant: 1 edible 2 native 3 very large — 54. ________
55. an *irascible* teacher: 1 angry 2 unpopular 3 severe — 55. ________
56. the *itinerary* of the candidate: 1 travel route 2 endurance 3 knowledge — 56. ________
57. a *lacteal* solution: 1 colorful 2 poisonous 3 milky — 57. ________
58. a space-age *lexicon:* 1 education 2 outlook 3 word list — 58. ________
59. explaining with *lucidity:* 1 evasion 2 lightheartedness 3 clarity — 59. ________
60. to *mediate* the dispute: 1 arbitrate 2 prolong 3 intensify — 60. ________
61. a *menial* position: 1 uncomfortable 2 grotesque 3 lowly and undignified — 61. ________
62. a *mercurial* temperament: 1 sympathetic 2 morose 3 quickly changing — 62. ________
63. *meretricious* advertising: 1 effective 2 falsely showy 3 detailed — 63. ________
64. *misconstruing* his intent: 1 forgetting 2 misinterpreting 3 perceiving — 64. ________
65. of *momentous* significance: 1 short-lived 2 quite important 3 uncertain — 65. ________
66. *monitions* about their conduct: 1 arguments 2 hints 3 warnings — 66. ________
67. a *moot* question: 1 important 2 arguable 3 ridiculous — 67. ________
68. *nefarious* activities: 1 wicked 2 profitable 3 adolescent — 68. ________
69. a person showing *obesity:* 1 bad manners 2 fatness 3 laziness — 69. ________

Copyright © 1994 by Harcourt Brace & Company. All rights reserved.

NAME ______________________________ SECTION ________ DATE ________

70. an *obtruding* brace: 1 supporting 2 thrusting out 3 sagging 70. ________

71. the *olfactory* nerves: pertaining to 1 reflexes 2 taste 3 smell 71. ________

72. *onerous* wartime duties: 1 honorable 2 burdensome 3 secret 72. ________

73. the monks' *orisins:* 1 costumes 2 rituals 3 prayers 73. ________

74. the *oscillating* marker: 1 sinking 2 flaming 3 vibrating 74. ________

75. *ossified* tissue: 1 healed 2 turned to bone 3 deadened 75. ________

76. the *ostentation* of the display: 1 taste 2 showiness 3 smartness 76. ________

77. viewed with *overt* suspicion: 1 unjust 2 unconcealed 3 ill-based 77. ________

78. *parrying* awkward questions: 1 warding off 2 answering 3 ignoring 78. ________

79. saved by a *penurious* relative: 1 stingy 2 eccentric 3 foresighted 79. ________

80. interested in *philology:* 1 word study 2 stamp collecting 3 dramatics 80. ________

81. a *pliant* material: 1 sturdy 2 synthetic 3 flexible 81. ________

82. *precluding* any discussion: 1 waiving 2 requiring 3 shutting off 82. ________

83. taking a new *pseudonym:* 1 assumed name 2 disguise 3 assignment 83. ________

84. acting with *rectitude:* 1 rightness 2 caution 3 wide knowledge 84. ________

85. tending to *regress:* 1 stand still 2 turn aside 3 go backward 85. ________

86. a complete *renovation:* 1 abandonment 2 renewing 3 cleaning 86. ________

87. a *replica* of the ship: 1 picture 2 blueprint plan 3 copy 87. ________

88. some lengthy *rigmarole:* 1 nonsense 2 explanation 3 protest 88. ________

89. a *sacerdotal* custom: 1 primitive 2 priestly 3 harmful 89. ________

90. *scurrilous* rumors: 1 vulgar and abusive 2 widespread 3 fearful 90. ________

91. a *senile* condition: 1 convalescent 2 old and enfeebled 3 venerable 91. ________

92. to *simulate* desire: 1 pretend 2 extinguish 3 fulfill 92. ________

93. to *stultify* development: 1 quicken 2 prevent 3 await 93. ________

94. a *thermal* unit: pertaining to 1 weight 2 moisture 3 heat 94. ________

95. to *transcribe* the laws: 1 study 2 violate 3 copy 95. ________

96. a *truculent* answer: 1 fiercely assertive 2 respectful 3 candid 96. ________

97. the *turpitude* of the court: 1 extravagance 2 immorality 3 disloyalty 97. ________

98. an *unkempt* appearance: 1 fastidious 2 feverish 3 untidy 98. ________

99. the pup was a *waif:* 1 mongrel 2 stray 3 runt 99. ________

100. playing the *zany:* 1 clown 2 coward 3 lieutenant 100. ________

Copyright © 1994 by Harcourt Brace & Company. All rights reserved.

Dictionaries are like watches; the worst is better than none, and the best cannot be expected to go quite true.

Samuel Johnson

1 Importance of the Dictionary and Its Usage

Because of the numerous, various, and diversified dictionaries that are at our command, an exceedingly great length of time would be required to explain differences in editorial policies and procedures among even the most important ones; such, however, is not the task of this text, and therefore the text will make no attempt to delve into those matters. It is, however, important to point out that one should use an up-to-date dictionary because the English language is constantly changing. Dictionaries should not be discarded because of age; rather they should be retained as a history of people and language, and should be used as a reference for words of the past that have undergone neither semantic nor spelling changes. Some of the best and most widely used dictionaries are the following:

American College Dictionary

American Heritage Dictionary

The Random House Dictionary

Standard College Dictionary

Webster's New World Dictionary

Webster's Tenth Edition Collegiate Dictionary

One prerequisite to using a dictionary is a thorough scrutiny of printed forms of words. There is a difference between *funeral* and *funereal,* and between *corporal* and *corporeal,* for example. Accordingly, a desultory use of the dictionary will do little to enhance one's vocabulary. Often a word is heard that has not been read, and this will lead to difficulty in locating the word in a dictionary. For example, if you hear a word that sounds like "bay-lee-wick," with the first syllable most strongly stressed, it will not be too difficult for you to try to find this word under *ba-,* perhaps more specifically under the sounds or spelling of *bai-,* or *bay-*, with a chance of *bei-* as a possibility. If you hear something like "nar-siss-izm," it would be natural for you to look under *nar-*, with *gnar-,* or *knar-* as bare possibilities. From the sounds, however, *bailiwick* and *narcissism* would not be very difficult to find.

Suppose that you hear a word that sounds like "uh-ful-jint." This would be more difficult. But you are at this point at least somewhat familiar with the variations and vagaries of English spellings. You can use either your knowledge or your intuition to find what you are after. You know that this word that you have just heard probably starts with a vowel followed by *f* or *ff,* although *ph* is a possibility. You know that words beginning with *if-, iff-, iph-, uf-, uff-,* and *uph-* are not really very common. You know that you have seen several words beginning with *af-, aff-, ef-, eff-, of-*, and *off-*. You may make some false starts, but before long you will locate the word *effulgent.* As another example, suppose you hear a word sounding like "uhb-stet-rick." Your familiarity with the language tells you that there are rather few words beginning with *eb-* (despite *ebony* and *ebullient*), with *ib-* (despite *ibidem* and *ibis*), or with *ub-* (despite *ubiquitous*). Your obvious choices for finding this word are sections in *ab-* or *ob-,* and without much loss of time you can find *obstetric.*

Approximately the same procedure—that is, familiarity with the language and linguistic intuition—applies when you are not sure of the second letter of a word that you have heard but not seen. Imagine that you have heard something that sounds like "duh-mot-ik," with the main stress or accent on the second syllable. This could be spelled with *da-* (like *daguerreotype*), *di-* (like *didactic, diffusion, diminutive*), *do-* (like *domestic, dominion*), *du-* (like *dubiety*), or even *dy-* (like *dynamic*), but you will probably sense almost at once that it is likely to be *de-,* and you may rather quickly find the word *demotic* in your dictionary. Imagine that you hear a word sounding like "kuh-layt" or "kuh-late," with the accent on the second syllable. The word might begin with *k,* but words beginning with *c* are more

Copyright © 1994 by Harcourt Brace & Company. All rights reserved.

common, and "kuh-layt" sounds as though it might be like *colloid, collude, and collide.* The chances are that you will have no great trouble finding the word *collate.* For such matters, the treatment of prefixes in Chapter 3 may be of considerable assistance.

Tracking down words in this fashion is admittedly not always easy. Suppose you hear something that sounds like "sigh-an" or "sin-till-layt," the accent of each being on the first syllable. You will certainly have trouble trying to find these under *si-* or under *s-* and another vowel. Maybe in time you will remember that *scene, scent,* and *science* begin with the *s* sound but have no *k* sound following, even though they are spelled with *sc-,* not just *s-*. You might then find *scion* and *scintillate,* along with *scenario* and *sciatica.* At this point it may be useful to refresh your memory about some variations in spellings of initial sounds in English words:

Sound		**Variation in Spelling**
f	*(five)*	*ph (phalanx, pharynx, philanthropy,* and so on)
t	*(ten)*	*th (thyme, Thames,* and so on); *pt (ptomaine, ptarmigan,* and so on)
k	*(kiss)*	*c,* especially before *a, o, u; ch (chemistry, chimera, choir,* and so on); *kh (khaki, khan,* and so on)
g	*(get)*	*gh (ghetto, ghoul,* and so on); *gu (guile, guise,* and so on)
s	*(set)*	*sc (scintillate, scion,* and so on); *c* before *e* and *i; sch (schism,* and so on); *ps (psalm, pseudonym,* and so on)
z	*(zest)*	*x (xylophone,* and so on)
sh	*(ship)*	*ch (chagrin, chamois,* and so on); *sch (schist,* and so on)
zh	*(azure)*	*g* in some pronunciations of *gendarme, genre,* and so on, and *j* in some pronunciations of *jalousie* and *jejune,* and so on
ch	*(chin)*	*c (cello,* and so on); *cz (Czech)*
j	*(just)*	*g* before *e* and *i* often
n	*(noon)*	*kn (know, knight,* and so on); *gn (gnat, gnaw,* and so on); *pn (pneumonia,* and so on)
r	*(rose)*	*wr (wrap, wrong,* and so on); *rh (rhapsody, rhythm,* and so on)
h	*(hay)*	*j* in some pronunciations of *jai alai* and *junta,* and so on

The list of possibly difficult situations given above is suggestive only and by no means complete. We could have included such freakish words as *bdellium,* pronounced with an initial *d* sound, or *phthisis,* with an initial *t* sound. This list deals only with initial elements that may cause you difficulty in finding words in dictionaries. For that reason it does not indicate, for instance, that *ss* may be pronounced as *sh* in such words as *issue.*

All dictionaries follow alphabetical order in arranging word entries. There is little else to be said about the alphabetizing principle. Strange-looking words like *Tlingit* and *phthisis* are to be found where you would expect them, as are acronym words (words made of initials) such as *WAC, UNESCO, AWOL,* and odd combinations such as *X-ray; Rh-factor,* and *CT-Scan.*

One of the most important differences between two main kinds of dictionaries is between those that use a "one-index" listing and those that present a variety of matters in supplements. Those in the first group, such as the *Standard College Dictionary (SCD),* include in the body of the work both ordinary words and abbreviations, geographical names, biographical names, and similar items. In *SCD* one will find, for instance, entries in order for the following: *ma, Ma, MA, M.A., ma'am, Maas, Maastricht, Mab, Mabinogion, Mac-, macabre,* and *Macao.* In using such a dictionary one looks in the main body of the work for the birth date of John Masefield or the length of the Mississippi River. On the other hand, some dictionaries, such as *Webster's New Collegiate Dictionary (WNCD),* give abbreviations, names of persons, names of geographical features, and so on in special supplements after the *z* section of the main work. Near the beginning of *m, WNCD* lists the following: *ma, ma'am, Mab, mac, macabre,* and *macadam.* Abbreviations such as *M.A.,* names of geographical features such as *Maas* and *Maastricht,* names of persons, and so on are to be found in special supplements. Proofreaders' marks, special symbols, and lists of colleges and universities are

Copyright © 1994 by Harcourt Brace & Company. All rights reserved.

customarily given in supplements in all dictionaries. By all means find out what items are given in the body of your dictionary and what items in special supplements.

Perhaps you will not always be able to find in your dictionary a word or term you are seeking. It may be that the word is obsolete—one no longer used in Modern English. There are special dictionaries to which you can turn in such a situation. Perhaps the word is so new that it could not have been listed in your dictionary, despite heroic efforts by the lexicographer to keep up to date. It would be absurd to expect the word *sputnik* to be in a dictionary of 1950 or *psychedelic* in one of 1955. It is important that your reference books be up to date. Perhaps the word is scientific or technical—too much so for inclusion in a general desk dictionary. No desk dictionary can make even a pretense at listing the whole vocabulary of chemistry, antibiotics, aeronautics, space activities, photography, or any of a large number of similarly technical studies or pursuits. It is probable that your library will have a fair number of specialized dictionaries and lexicons to help you. Or maybe you are seeking information about a word in use in Ireland, Canada, South Africa, or elsewhere outside the United States. It would be impossible for a contemporary American desk dictionary to give full coverage on such matters. All in all there are, as you see, a number of reasons why you may be unable to find a particular word. In this connection you should notice one important fact: *absence of a word from a dictionary emphatically does not mean that the word does not exist or that there is something wrong with it if it does exist.* No given dictionary could or should contain all the words, or all the acceptable words, in a language.

Once you find the entry for which you are looking, it is possible that you will not immediately perceive or understand all the information that the dictionary tries to convey. You may welcome some of the explanations that follow.

I. THE FORM OR FORMS OF THE WORD

A. Syllabification. The boldface (that is, heavy type) entry word set far to the left in a dictionary column (usually one or two spaces to the left of the margin used on other lines of the entry) shows the acceptable printing or writing syllabification of the word. This syllabification is usually indicated by dots or raised periods between syllables; thus for *fumigate* and *funeral* you are likely to find *fu·mi·gate* and *fu·ner·al.* This means of course that when these words are broken at the end of a line of printing or writing, one may satisfactorily break them thus: *fu-migate* or *fumi-gate, fu-neral* or *funer-al.* Occasionally an older dictionary will try to indicate both the printing or writing syllabification and also the position of main accents or stresses in the pronunciation of the word. A printing such as *fu'mi·gate* or *fu'mi͵gate* would indicate both the syllabification to be followed in writing or printing and also the stressing on the first syllable in the pronunciation. This procedure, never very satisfactory, is now largely being given up.

B. Single word, hyphenated compound, combination of separate words. English of course has thousands of expressions made by putting together two or more words to express a specific meaning. *Handball* is not just any kind of ball game played with the hands, and *hot dog* hardly means a dog that is hot. If you think of the various expressions that you can make up ending in *ball* or *man* or beginning with *dog* or *sun,* this comment will not need further explanation. Under *bear,* for instance, you will find *bearbaiting, bearberry, bear garden, bear grass,* and *bearskin,* and under *water* you will find *water beetle, water blister, water boy, water clock, watercolor, water-cool, watercress, water dog,* and so on. In this last series some expressions, of course, are printed as single words, one *(water-cool)* as a hyphenated compound, others as two-word combinations with the elements printed separately. Lexicographers, faced with the printing problem involved, do not try to list all possible satisfactory ways of treating these expressions; what they do is suggest to you one way found to be common—very probably most common—and therefore safe and satisfactory for your use. Moreover, lexicographers do not mean that another treatment, like *bear-baiting* or *bear baiting* or *bear-skin* or *bear skin* would necessarily be wrong.

C. Capitalization. Most desk dictionaries are likely to print a boldface capital letter initially in each proper noun or adjective and initially in most verbs formed from such nouns and adjectives. You are likely to find such entry words, with capitals, as *Melpomene, Memnon, Memorial Day, Mendelian,*

Copyright © 1994 by Harcourt Brace & Company. All rights reserved.

Mendelism, Mendel's Law, Menelaus, Mennonite, and *Menshevik.* This procedure is clear enough. Some words, however, are capitalized in some senses and not capitalized in others. The words *Democrat* and *democrat* and *Catholic* and *catholic* will probably be familiar to you. In such situations a dictionary is likely to use the tag *cap* in italics before the senses in question. In your dictionary, for instance, you may find the word *calypso* given with two or three different meanings. The definition giving the name for the sea nymph in the *Odyssey* may be prefaced by the expression *cap* in italics or perhaps with a *C-*. Definitions of *calypso* as a bog orchid or an impromptu ballad will lack such indications, and you will consequently know that the lowercase (that is, small-letter) form of the word is used in such senses. The word *capuchin* may have the designation *cap* before the definition concerning the Order of Friars, Minor Capuchin, but it may have no indication before the definitions concerning hooded cloaks or South American monkeys. This latter fact indicates that the word is not capped but is lowercased in these meanings. Sometimes the tag *often cap* is used. In the entry for ^{2}*continental* in *WNCD,* for instance, one finds this tag introducing the definition concerning an American Revolutionary War soldier. The tag *sometimes cap* is also used. On the other hand, if most of the definitions refer to senses for which a given word is capitalized, the tag *l.c.* or perhaps simply a small letter printed by itself may be used before definitions of meanings commonly used without caps. Sometimes dictionaries try to make different entries for a word capped on the one hand, lowercased on the other. You may find in your dictionary one entry for *Echo,* another for *echo.* When lexicographers treat capitalization, they often try to tell you simply what has frequently been done with the word or form in question. They do no attempt to tell you that you are necessarily wrong in using a procedure different from the one indicated. Before using your dictionary to any considerable extent, find out how it treats capitalizing and lowercasing.

D. Apostrophes. In some compounds of two or more words, the first or second may be a possessive noun in form. In such situations an apostrophe may be regarded as an essential part of the spelling. Notice, for instance, how your dictionary treats such items as *calf's-foot jelly, cat's cradle, cat's-eye, Charles's Wain, Christ's thorn, corporal's guard,* and *Cushing's disease.* The apostrophe is of course ignored in alphabetizing, but compounds of this kind are entered with the *s* being counted in the alphabetical arrangement. One finds *calf's-foot jelly* after *calf love* and before *calfskin.* In at least some situations the lexicographer does not attempt to say, when giving a form with an apostrophe, that omitting the apostrophe would necessarily be wrong.

E. Italics. During the first part of this century it was quite usual for printers to print a foreign word in italics—a word still felt to be French or German or Italian or Latin or something else not felt to be English. Notice the insistence on "feeling" in the sentence just preceding; it was and is hard to devise objective tests for such matters. One used to find *faux pas* and *smorgasbord* and *panzer* and *intelligentsia* in italics. But to an increasing degree writers, copy editors, and printers seem to be becoming impatient with this practice, and a good many words and phrases that would formerly have appeared in italics are now printed in ordinary roman. As a result, some dictionaries, notably *WNCD,* adopt the opinion that if a word is English it should be entered in the dictionary, printed in roman both in the dictionary and elsewhere, and regarded like any other English word, but if a word is foreign, it does not belong in an English dictionary in the first place. Dictionaries like *WNCD* do not notice italicizing at all. Other dictionaries, notably *SCD,* print outside the etymology and before the first (or only) definition the name of a language, such as *French, German,* or *Latin.* Thus *SCD* has for *café noir* the entry "*French.* Black coffee." This dictionary regards *café noir* as still French rather than English and by implication at least directs the user of the word to italicize it. Other dictionaries treat such words by a variety of devices, for instance double daggers (‡).

F. Variants. The great majority of English words do not have variants. If you open your dictionary at random and scan a column, you will probably find only one form given for each word in that column. Some, however, may have variant forms; you may meet with *axe* or *ax, gray* or *grey, wagon* or *waggon, whisky* or *whiskey, tabu* or *taboo.* Each word in a pair like these is a variant. Dictionaries differ widely in their treatments of such variants. The *WNCD* prints the second variant in boldface, like the first, separating it from the first with either *or* or *also* in italics: **louver** *or* **louvre, woolly** *also* **wooly.** Variants joined by *or* are usually given with the first form coming before the second form in alphabetical order. Such variants are equal in use; no preference is expressed by the lexicographer; the user may choose freely between the two. Thus the choice between *louver* and *louvre* depends entirely on the

Copyright © 1994 by Harcourt Brace & Company. All rights reserved.

user's own personal preference. When lexicographers use *also* between variants, they are trying to tell the consultant that the second form may be somewhat less common than the first but that the second form is also quite satisfactory. From the entry **woolly** *also* **wooly,** we learn that *woolly* is perhaps more common but not necessarily preferred. A variant form separated from another, at which etymology and definition are given and located in the finished dictionary more than one column of type away, may be simply glossed as *var of* . . . ("variant of . . . "). Thus for *esthete* one finds *var of aesthete.* Other dictionaries treat the problem of variants in different ways. The *SCD* is apt to print the variant spelling at the end of the whole entry, after definitions and usage notes, in boldface and preceded by the notation *also.* After the definitions for *whisky* one finds the note "*also* whiskey," and after the definition for *leery* the note "*also spelled* leary." If a distinguishing label for the variant will help the consultant, the lexicographer will supply it. Both *WNCD* and *SCD* indicate that *defence* as a variant of *defense* is more British than American. Incidentally, most American dictionaries try to record American forms mainly and regard British or purely English forms as existent variants but not as standards for American usage. Before we leave the subject of variants, we should be reminded to discern between variants—such as *sulfide* and *sulphide* or *whimsy* and *whimsey*—and pairs of words similar in form but really totally different words—such as *council* and *counsel, advice* and *advise, extent* and *extant,* and *hoard* and *horde.*

G. Run-ons. From time to time a lexicographer may presume on your knowledge of regular suffix patterns and similar devices in English and use what is called a *run-on.* A run-on is a word obviously related to a main entry word and inserted in the dictionary after the definition of the entry word. A run-on is usually left undefined, the definition being felt to be unnecessary; there is usually an indication of pronunciation for a run-on, and there is always a part-of-speech label. Thus in *WNWD* one will find as run-ons *feigner* after *feign, felicitation* and *felicitator* after *felicitate, felicitously* and *felicitousness* after *felicitous,* and so on. Some dictionaries, notably *Webster's New World Dictionary (WNWD),* pride themselves on using no run-ons at all, but most dictionaries do use the device.

The run-on can cause some problems and calls for some discussion here. For one thing, the run-on may, strictly speaking, appear out of alphabetical order in a dictionary. At *improve* in *WNCD,* for instance, one finds the run-on *improver,* given thus before the following entry word *improvement.* At *monitor* one finds as a run-on the form *monitress,* with *monitory* given as an entry word later. You are advised not to jump to the conclusion that a certain word does not appear in your dictionary until you have checked the possibility of its appearing as a run-on after a main entry word. Remember that a run-on form should never be looked on as an important word. A run-on is inserted in the dictionary simply to indicate that it does exist (or has existed) in the language, but the lexicographer's treatment of it shows its relative insignificance. When you find both a main entry word and a run-on that seem to have the same meaning and function, the former is always more important and should be preferred to the latter unless there is some specific reason to do otherwise. It is safe, for instance, in using *WNCD* to prefer *complication,* a main entry word, to *complicatedness,* a mere run-on at *complicated,* and to prefer *dreamy,* a main entry word, to *dreamful,* a run-on after *dream.* (In exercises in this book never use a run-on in preference to a main entry word; prefer *legislative,* for instance, to *legislatorial.*)

II. PRONUNCIATION

It is usual dictionary practice to give the pronunciation of the word being treated immediately after the printing of that word in boldface as an entry word. Many dictionaries give the pronunciation within parentheses: (. . .), some dictionaries between reversed virgules or slant lines: \ . . .\ . The material enclosed within such indicators concerns only pronunciation and nothing else. A statement that *case* is pronounced as *kās* or *cask* as *kask* or *kăsk* has nothing whatever to do with the spelling. In general, pronunciation transcription is the most difficult and the most controversial aspect of dictionary making. Perhaps pronunciation transcription is more commonly misunderstood than any other part of a typical dictionary entry. Unfortunately, this book would be too long and expensive if we gave details about this subject. We must, then, be content with a few comments.

One very important aspect of the pronunciation of a word of more than one syllable is the position of the main stress or accent. If we put the heavier stress on the first syllable of *entrance* and let the second syllable trail off with lighter enunciation, we will have the noun meaning "way of entering." If we

Copyright © 1994 by Harcourt Brace & Company. All rights reserved.

change and stress the second syllable, we will have a verb meaning "to enchant or captivate." *Refuse* with the accent on the first syllable is a noun, with the accent on the second syllable a verb. Some dictionaries, notably *WNCD,* place a raised mark *before* the syllable to be stressed and, when necessary, a lowered mark before a syllable receiving secondary but perceptible stress. Thus the pronunciation of *barbarism* is given as ˈbär-bə-ˌriz-əm and *barbecue* as ˈbär-bi-ˌkyü. This practice accords with that used now by most linguists and phoneticians, and it may well become quite general in the future. Other dictionaries place syllabic accent or stress marks *after* stressed syllables; they give transcriptions such as bär′bə-riz,-əm and bär′bə-kyo͞o,. Be sure that you know which procedure your dictionary uses.

The specific sounds of the vowels and consonants are usually given in a pronunciation key, even if an abridged one, at the bottom of each odd-numbered page in a desk dictionary, and there is sure to be a full explanation of all symbols either in the preface of the book or in a supplement. Inside cover pages are also frequently used to give pronunciation keys. Dictionary makers generally try to use familiar and easily understood symbols. Thus, in most transcriptions such letters as *b, d, f, g, h, j, k, l,* and *m* have the values that they most commonly have in ordinary English words. But the transcriptions of the sounds of *ng* in *sing, ch* in *check, sh* in *shop, th* in *the* and also *th* in *thing, z* in *azure* or *s* in *leisure,* and others may be treated in various ways. With the vowel sounds there is always likely to be at least a degree of variation in various dictionaries. You may find the *a* sound of *father* transcribed as *ä, ȧ,* or *a,* the *a* sound of *cat* as *a, ă,* or perhaps *ae.* Always be sure that you know the meaning of the pronunciation symbols used before consulting any dictionary extensively. Almost all contemporary dictionaries are now using the symbol ə (called *shwa* or *schwa*) for the relatively unclear central sound of vowels in unstressed syllables—for *a* in *about, e* in *oven, i* in *satin, o* in *correct, u* in *bonus.*

If a word has more than one common pronunciation your dictionary will indicate this fact. Note the treatment in your dictionary for *either, route, greasy,* or *tomato.* Different pronunciations given with *or* inserted in italics between them or with no wording between them may be regarded as equal in the lexicographer's eyes; there is no preference. A less common pronunciation may be prefaced by *also* in italics. If the pronunciations are different for different senses of a word, the dictionary will call this to your attention. See, for instance, how your dictionary treats the word *gallant.* Some dictionaries use parentheses to indicate optional sounds in pronunciation; your dictionary may have something like *(w)* in the pronunciation of *continuous* to show that you may or may not have this sound between the sound of the first *u* and the sound of the *ous.* The fact that a certain pronunciation is not listed in a dictionary should not be interpreted as an indication that that pronunciation is necessarily incorrect, although it is likely that that pronunciation is uncommon. It is impossible for an ordinary desk dictionary to record all possible regional dialect forms; no desk dictionary editor would try to do so. And there are some words for which there are too many possible pronunciations to list them all. The word *praline* is a good illustration. The whole subject of pronunciation is important and fascinating, and you might enjoy taking some courses in it.

III. PART-OF-SPEECH LABELS

In most dictionaries the pronunciation is followed by a part-of-speech or form-class label: *n., adj., adv.,* and so on. Most of the time these labels are easily understood, and usually you will find that the dictionary labels fit in pretty well with whatever form of English grammar you have previously learned. For complete understanding, however, read the definitions given in the dictionary itself for *noun, verb, adjective,* and so on; the definitions will probably differ a bit from those you have previously learned. In assigning part-of-speech labels the dictionary will be consistent with its own grammatical definitions. In verb entries, *v.t.* or *vt* means "transitive verb," *v.i.* or *vi* "intransitive verb." The fact that some verbs or verb definitions are labeled only *v.t.* or *vt* should not be taken as an indication that intransitive uses are impossible. By tradition, transitive uses are often defined first. If a single word has two or more grammatical functions, such as *cheat, check,* and *cheer* (each of which may be either noun or verb), these different uses may be presented in the same main entry or presented as different homographs (words identical in spelling but different in origin, meaning, and sometimes in pronunciation). See how your dictionary treats these words. Less common part-of-speech designations may be used to label auxiliary verbs, impersonal verbs, imperative verbs, and so on. For information about such matters check the

Copyright © 1994 by Harcourt Brace & Company. All rights reserved.

introduction or preface to your dictionary. An uncommon grammatical usage may be noticed in a run-on. The fact that a dictionary does not list a word in a certain grammatical function should not be interpreted as meaning that the usage does not exist. Sometimes the use exists, although it is not very common. Sometimes, on the other hand, it is so common that it is taken for granted and not listed. For instance, most dictionaries will not bother to enter adjective definitions for *auto* in "an auto mechanic," *table* in "a table leg," and *state* in "a state tax." The *WNCD* indicates awareness of such usages by frequently using the tag *often attrib,* that is, often used before a noun so as to modify that noun.

IV. INFLECTIONS

An inflection is any variation in the form of a word to show a grammatical property such as number, case, person, tense, mood, voice, or degree of comparison. The addition of *-s* to *rat* and the change from *ou* in *mouse* to *i* in *mice* are inflections, as are the addition of *-ed* to *turn* and the change of *o* in *grow* to *e* in *grew.* A noun is customarily entered in a dictionary in its singular form. Nouns plural in form but singular in meaning, such as *news* or *mumps* or *economics,* may be described by tags such as *n pl but sing in const* ("noun plural [in form] but singular in construction"). If a plural form is made up regularly it is usually not entered; it would be pointless to swell the size of the dictionary and to increase the cost to the consumer by including perfectly regular forms. Most dictionaries indicate after the part-of-speech label any irregular or unusual plural forms of nouns. Thus after the label *n* at *basis* you are likely to find something like *pl BASES.* Sometimes such a designation is "cut back," that is, given incompletely, as *pl -SES. Bacillus* will be followed by the notation *pl BACILLI* or by a cut-back form of this plural. If there are two different plural forms with no discoverable preference between them, the dictionary will so indicate by printing both forms without comments or by joining them with *or.* For *bus* you may find *pl BUSES, BUSSES* or *pl BUSES or BUSSES.* A more common form may be given first, a less common second after the word *also.* Thus at *criterion* in *WNCD* one finds *pl CRITERIA* ... also *CRITERIONS.* Often plurals may be given in cut-back form. Syllabification of plurals is indicated, as is pronunciation. Thus at *index* you may find *pl IN-DEX-ES or IN-DI-CES* \-də-ˌsēz\. Sometimes in one meaning a word will have one plural, in another meaning another plural. Notice in your dictionary the different notations about *stamens* and *stamina* at *stamen* and those about *stigmas* and *stigmata* at *stigma.* If there is a plural form expressing a meaning not expressed by a singular, the dictionary will indicate this fact, often by giving the meaning in question with a notation such as *pl* before it or with a note such as *usually in the plural* after it. Look up *facing* and *fall* in your dictionary and notice the definitions involving trimmings on a military coat and waterfall or cascade.

An adjective is entered in its positive form; comparative and superlative forms are given only if there could be some question or problem about them. The entry for *bright* in your dictionary is unlikely to give *brighter* and *brightest;* it is presumed that anyone with a knowledge of English could make up these forms. But you are likely to find *fatter* and *fattest* in the entry for *fat* because there might be some question about doubling the *t,* and you will almost certainly find *farther* and *further* at *far.* If a dictionary does give *-er* and *-est* forms for a two-syllable adjective, this does not mean that forms with *more* and *most* are not used.

A verb is entered in its present infinitive form (without the *to*) or in the first person, present tense, singular form. (These two are, of course, always the same except for *to be.*) Dictionaries list past tense and past participle forms if there is any problem about them. You are unlikely to find *helped* or *turned* or *walked* at *help, turn,* or *walk* in your dictionary, but you will certainly find *rode* and *ridden* at *ride* because *ride* is irregular, and you are likely to find *batted* at *bat* to remind you that the *t* is doubled. With many dictionaries the user must be careful to note which form is past tense and which is past participle; procedures for listing these forms are not always consistent and not always clear. There is an increasing tendency to list the present participle forms—the *-ing* forms, such as *running, receiving*—among the principal parts. See how your dictionary treats the forms of *ride, cleave, awake, begin, buy, dig, grind, melt, shrink, weave, travel, bevel, defer,* and *omit.* Some dictionaries use the cut-back principle in giving forms of two-syllable and longer verbs; thus for the forms of *ridicule,* for instance, you may find only *-culed* (for *ridiculed*) and *-culing* (for *ridiculing*).

Copyright © 1994 by Harcourt Brace & Company. All rights reserved.

V. ETYMOLOGY

Because understanding of etymologies is dependent on at least elementary knowledge of the history of the English language, this book will explain dictionary etymologies in the next chapter on "Native and Borrowed Words."

VI. DEFINITIONS

Dictionaries differ widely in the order of presentation of definitions for words having two or more meanings. Some dictionaries use historical order; that is, they give the meanings in the order (insofar as it can be determined) in which they developed in the history of the English language. If four definitions are given in such a dictionary, the first may take care of the meaning of the word in its first recorded use in English, let us say perhaps in 800. The second may apply to a meaning developing around 1100, the third to one from around 1400, the last to one from around 1700. The *WNCD* treats the word *diplomatic* by giving first a definition having to do with ancient writing; second, one having to do with international affairs; and third, one meaning "tactful, conciliatory." This arrangement accords with the historical development of the various meanings. For *magazine WNCD* gives in order the following definitions concerning warehouses: powder stores, gun chambers, accumulations of munitions, and finally printed periodicals. Other dictionaries prefer different arrangements. *The American Heritage Dictionary,* for instance, prefers to give first the most common meanings in twentieth-century English and to give less common meanings later. In this dictionary, for example, one is likely to find definitions given in about the following order: *magazine:* 1. a printed periodical; 2. a powder storeroom; 3. a munitions supply building; 4. a collection of munitions. The general meaning of *storehouse* might be given seventh and last. Other dictionaries may attempt a midway treatment between these two policies. Find out what procedure your own dictionary uses. You may be interested to realize that nothing happens just by accident in the writing or arranging of a dictionary entry.

In general, definitions are so written that the word being defined can be equated with any one unit in the definition, any one defining word or phrase. The definition of *salute* as "to address with kind wishes or friendly greetings; to greet" indicates that *salute* equals in meaning either "to address with . . . greetings" or "to greet." It does not indicate that *salute* has all the meanings of the word *address* without the modifiers used in the definition. If a meaning is expressed in terms of synonyms alone, these synonyms are separated by commas. You may find *hardy* defined as "bold, brave." For the most part, however, different definitions are separated by semicolons (if not by numbers). The definition is the whole unit within semicolons. At *heroic* you may find "of, pertaining to, or like heroes." This of course does not mean that *heroic* simply means "of" or "pertaining to." One naturally uses the definition that fits the context in which one encounters the word. If one looks up *express* in connection with "an express train," one naturally notices the meaning "going at high speed and making few stops" rather than such meanings as "explicit" and "specific."

No desk dictionary could list all meanings for multisense words. Some meanings are omitted because they are obvious to any native user of English. Thus most dictionaries will define *carafe* as "a glass water bottle," but few will add the further definition "the contents of a carafe" (as in "he drank the whole carafe"), since few native users of English will need this definition. Many times other meanings are omitted because they are too infrequent to justify use of the space needed for including them. If a particular sense of a word is not given in your dictionary, you should not conclude from that fact alone that the word in question never expresses that sense or that there is anything necessarily wrong with that sense.

VII. SPECIAL LABELS

Dictionaries attach special labels to certain words to show some peculiarity in their connotation or use. These labels in general fall into two main groups: status labels and diction labels. Status labels may indicate temporal or time considerations. A word no longer used in English but at one time used with

Copyright © 1994 by Harcourt Brace & Company. All rights reserved.

at least a degree of frequency may be labeled—in italics before the definition or definitions—*obs* or *obsolete.* (*Obsol* might be taken to mean "obsolescent," meaning "not entirely obsolete but evidently becoming so"; this label is now rarely used.) A word used only in writing about older periods may be labeled *arch* or *archaic.* Words whose usage suggests speech of a nonprestige group and that are therefore uncommon or nonexistent in formal English may be labeled *substandard, nonstandard,* or *slang.* The term *colloquial,* often abbreviated as *col* or *colloq,* was once commonly used but is now falling out of fashion. *Informal* sometimes takes its place. A third kind of label refers to area or locale for usage of the word. A number of labels, of which *dial* (for *dialect*) is probably the most common, show that words are restricted to limited areas and are not common throughout the whole English-speaking world.

Another kind of label, subject labels, are italicized guide words indicating the special activity in which the words being defined, or special meanings of those words, are used. Accompanying the definition for the chemical use of the word *formula* may be an introductory label or phrase such as *chem, chemistry,* or *in chemistry.* If you think of the widely different meanings in athletics of the word *foul,* you will be able to appreciate how much subject labels such as *baseball, basketball,* and *boxing* may help the consultant.

VIII. SYNONYMIES

English contains a great many synonyms, words that have the same or about the same general meanings. Dictionaries often add after definitions synonymy paragraphs—paragraphs explaining differences among various synonyms in specific meaning, connotation, implication, area of use. You may find that your dictionary contains paragraphs explaining differences between *kingly* and *royal, thrifty* and *economical, finish* and *conclude, rise* and *ascend, rebellion* and *insurrection,* and *volume* and *tome.* For a synonymy see *WNCD* at *incur* or SCD at *insanity.* Words treated in synonymies after other words are followed by cross-references—usually with **syn** or **Syn** in boldface, the word *see* in roman, and then in small caps the word at which the synonymy paragraph is to be found.

Copyright © 1994 by Harcourt Brace & Company. All rights reserved.

NAME ______________________ SECTION __________ DATE __________

CHAPTER 1

EXERCISE 1: One must look closely at words to find them in the dictionary. In the second column below write the correct form of the word given in the first column. In the third column write a brief statement of the first meaning in your dictionary.

	Correct Form	Meaning
1. abyssmal	______________	______________
2. acquamarine	______________	______________
3. beastial	______________	______________
4. colerik	______________	______________
5. dias	______________	______________
6. dissimiliar	______________	______________
7. haitus	______________	______________
8. postumous	______________	______________
9. sizmatic	______________	______________
10. tendancy	______________	______________

EXERCISE 2: Sometimes words sound like the following when they are heard. In the second column write the correct forms of the written words; in the third column write a brief statement of the first meaning given in your dictionary.

	Written Form	Meaning
1. bi′nīn	______________	______________
2. kuh′dă-ver	______________	______________
3. kah′dū-sē-ŭs	______________	______________
4. ′shar-luh-tăn	______________	______________
5. kuhn′tĭng-jĕnt	______________	______________
6. fruh′nĕ-tĭk	______________	______________
7. huh′bĭ-luh-tāt	______________	______________
8. muh′bĭl-ĭ-ty	______________	______________
9. puh′rū-zĭl	______________	______________
10. seh′kwĕs-ter	______________	______________

Copyright © 1994 by Harcourt Brace & Company. All rights reserved.

EXERCISE 3: The dictionary shows different syllabifications for some words—one to be used in writing and printing, the other to be used in pronunciation. In the first column below indicate the printing syllabification; in the second, the pronunciation syllabification; and in the third, the meaning of the word.

	Printing	Pronunciation	Meaning
1. alluvial	______	______	______
2. corrugate	______	______	______
3. equilibrium	______	______	______
4. halcyon	______	______	______
5. leguminous	______	______	______
6. ontology	______	______	______
7. pragmatism	______	______	______
8. residuum	______	______	______
9. resplendent	______	______	______
10. surreptitious	______	______	______

EXERCISE 4: According to your dictionary, some of the following words should be capitalized. Correct the words by indicating capitalization. In the second column write the meaning of the word.

	Capitalization	Meaning
1. angst	______	______
2. april fool	______	______
3. british history	______	______
4. indian	______	______
5. levi's	______	______
6. literature	______	______
7. olympic games	______	______
8. penicillin	______	______
9. purple heart	______	______
10. strontium	______	______

Copyright © 1994 by Harcourt Brace & Company. All rights reserved.

NAME ______________________ SECTION ________ DATE ________

EXERCISE 5: In the accompanying blanks write the first meaning given in your dictionary for each of the following *nouns* when capitalized and the first meaning of each noun when not capitalized.

1. Amazon	____________	amazon	____________
2. Catholic	____________	catholic	____________
3. Democrat	____________	democrat	____________
4. Exodus	____________	exodus	____________
5. Frank	____________	frank	____________
6. Hegira	____________	hegira	____________
7. Mandarin	____________	mandarin	____________
8. Messiah	____________	messiah	____________
9. Morocco	____________	morocco	____________
10. Reformation	____________	reformation	____________

EXERCISE 6: If your dictionary provides the information, in the first space write the words or expressions that should be printed or written in italics; in the second space write a brief definition of the term.

	Italics	**Definition**
1. blitzkrieg	____________	____________
2. cum laude	____________	____________
3. gendarme	____________	____________
4. hoi polloi	____________	____________
5. hors d'oeuvre	____________	____________
6. kudos	____________	____________
7. nom de plume	____________	____________
8. ombudsman	____________	____________
9. outré	____________	____________
10. raison d'etre	____________	____________

Copyright © 1994 by Harcourt Brace & Company. All rights reserved.

EXERCISE 7: Consult your dictionary for the printed or written form preferred in American English for each of the following words:

1. aluminium ______________________
2. armour ______________________
3. calibre ______________________
4. cheque ______________________
5. cosy ______________________
6. jewellery ______________________
7. lustre ______________________
8. maihem ______________________
9. pretence ______________________
10. waggon ______________________

EXERCISE 8: Put an X in the space after each of the following sets containing different words; in the second and third spaces write a brief definition of those words. Leave blank the X space after those sets that are merely variants of the same words and then write a definition for the word.

	X	Definition	Definition
1. (1) aegis (2) egis	____________	____________	____________
2. (1) ascent (2) assent	____________	____________	____________
3. (1) consul (2) counsel	____________	____________	____________
4. (1) discreet (2) discrete	____________	____________	____________
5. (1) dispatch (2) despatch	____________	____________	____________
6. (1) missal (2) missile	____________	____________	____________
7. (1) palate (2) palette	____________	____________	____________
8. (1) quean (2) queen	____________	____________	____________
9. (1) visor (2) vizor	____________	____________	____________
10. (1) wander (2) wonder	____________	____________	____________

Copyright © 1994 by Harcourt Brace & Company. All rights reserved.

NAME ______________________________ SECTION ________ DATE __________

EXERCISE 9: In the first blank write the following words, and underline the syllable that receives the heaviest stress according to the first pronunciation given in your dictionary. In the second blank, write a brief definition of each word.

	Syllabification	Definition
1. archipelago	______________	______________
2. charisma	______________	______________
3. coruscate	______________	______________
4. iridescence	______________	______________
5. loquacious	______________	______________
6. lugubrious	______________	______________
7. onerous	______________	______________
8. similitude	______________	______________
9. sycophantic	______________	______________
10. thalassic	______________	______________

EXERCISE 10: Look up the pronunciation of the following words. If your dictionary indicates only one syllable for the main stress, print 1 in the blank following the word; if it gives two different pronunciations permitting main stress on either of two syllables, print 2 in the blank. In the second blank, write a brief definition of the word.

	Stress	Definition
1. abstruse	______________	______________
2. cognizant	______________	______________
3. fillip	______________	______________
4. fluoresce	______________	______________
5. harridan	______________	______________
6. indecorous	______________	______________
7. liaison	______________	______________
8. precursor	______________	______________
9. scurrilous	______________	______________
10. vagaries	______________	______________

Copyright © 1994 by Harcourt Brace & Company. All rights reserved.

EXERCISE 11: Your dictionary probably gives two different pronunciations for the following words. If two pronunciations are given, write both in the following blank; if only one is given, write it in the blank.

1. aficionado ______________________
2. blithe ______________________
3. conch ______________________
4. creek ______________________
5. duke ______________________
6. either ______________________
7. forehead ______________________
8. hegira ______________________
9. junta ______________________
10. kiln ______________________
11. neither ______________________
12. often ______________________
13. quinine ______________________
14. roof ______________________
15. root ______________________
16. schedule ______________________
17. titular ______________________
18. transient ______________________

Copyright © 1994 by Harcourt Brace & Company. All rights reserved.

How long a time lies
in one little word!
William Shakespeare

2 Native and Borrowed Words

The English language now being used is called *Modern English* or *New English.* (Neither designation is ideal, and unfortunately the abbreviations of both MnE and NE cause confusion.) Modern English is viewed as beginning around 1450 or 1500, although some scholars prefer slightly earlier or later dates. This means that we speak of Shakespeare, Spenser, the translators of the King James Bible, Milton, and others as using Modern English. Obviously, however, in works composed around 1600 or 1650, we find many words that we do not know, and, more important to us here, we do not find many words now familiar to us, such as radio, automobile, baseball, airplane, or antibiotic. Thus, new words have been added to the English vocabulary in every year of Modern English, and of necessity will continue to be added.

Sometimes, but by no means always, these new words have been "borrowed" from other languages. After World War II, for instance, we noted that the German language had a word, *schnorchel,* to describe a device for bringing air into a submerged submarine. Rather than make up a totally new word out of English elements to name this device, we simply brought the German word into English, changing its form to *snorkel;* that is, we made an English word out of it by using it in our language. Nineteenth-century English settlers in South Africa observed that their Dutch neighbors used the word *trek* to mean "move or migrate by ox-drawn wagon," and, having no word of their own for this meaning, they borrowed the African Dutch or Afrikaans word and brought *trek* into English. British tourists and businesspeople in China in the eighteenth century liked a thin Chinese silk fabric for which the English language had no word; to name this fabric they borrowed the Chinese word *pongee.* Settlers in North America, observing that Native Americans sometimes lived in a shelter called a *wigwam,* started to use the word themselves and thus borrowed the word into English. Traveling English citizens of Renaissance times came back from Italy with reports of town celebrations and festivities; they used the word *carnival,* borrowed from Italian, to designate them. Borrowing, then, occurs when a word that is originally part of one language comes to be naturally and freely used in another language.

Borrowing into our language from other languages has occurred during every decade, if not during every year, of the Modern English period. And borrowed terms have come from languages all over the world. From Australia comes the word *dingo,* the name for the native wild dog. The word *banana* is of African origin. *Kayak* is from Eskimo. The word *panda* comes from the Nepal region north of India. But ultimately such exotic words, although they are momentarily fascinating, are generally not particularly important. The great majority of the words borrowed into Modern English come from Latin, French, Greek, and other major European languages.

Let us open our dictionaries at random; this writer's at the moment happens to open at compounds involving *field.* Let us check on what we find after that point about words borrowed into Modern English. We see the following: *fiesta* from Spanish, *fife* from German, *filament* from French, *filar* from Latin, *filaria* from Latin, *filature* from French, *filibuster* from Spanish, *filigree* from French, *fimbria* from Latin, *finale* from Italian, *fiscal* from Latin, *fission* from Latin, *fjord* from Norwegian, and *flagellate* from Latin. Another page picked at random begins with phrases starting with *popular.* Following that section are mentioned these words borrowed from other languages into Modern English: *populate* from Latin, *populous* from Latin, *porcelain* from French, *pornography* from Greek, *porrect* from Latin, *portamento* from Italian, *porte-cochere* from French, *portent* from Latin, *portico* from Italian, *portiere* from French, *portmanteau* from French, and *portulaca* from Latin. In these two random lists we find eleven words from Latin and eight from French. Other sections in the dictionary would of course

Copyright © 1994 by Harcourt Brace & Company. All rights reserved.

show somewhat different figures, but any sizable part of the work would be likely to show figures more or less in accord with these.

There are several other things to be said about words borrowed into Modern English, but it will be helpful at this point to have some explanation of dictionary etymologies. In a typical dictionary entry you are likely to find the etymology between the part-of-speech label and the first definition, although in some dictionaries it will be found after the last definition. Most dictionaries give the etymologies in square brackets; some give them in parentheses. In other words, dictionaries vary in etymology procedures. This book cannot hope to explain all procedures in all common dictionaries; we will, however, be able to pay attention to some *WNCD* and *SCD* procedures.

In *WNCD* many etymologies begin with a capitalized language abbreviation printed in Roman. For example, you will find the following: *dissect* ... [L *dissectus* ...]; *disseminate* ... [L *disseminatus* ...]; *dissentient* ... [L *dissentient* ...]; *dissimulate* ... [L *dissimulatus* ...]. It is necessary here to point out first what you do *not* find in these etymologies before pointing out what you do find. You do not find any abbreviation such as *MnE* for *Modern English;* since the entry word is given in the dictionary, that word is obviously in Modern English. You do not find any abbreviation such as *ME* for *Middle English,* the phase of the English language from 1066 or 1100 up to the beginning of Modern English. From this omission you may know that words such as *dissect* and *disseminate* were not present in Middle English but that they entered the English language during the Modern English period, after 1400 or 1450 or 1500. The *L* at the beginning of the etymology indicates that these words were borrowed into Modern English from Latin. Note the following *WNCD* etymologies: *dodo* ... [Pg *doudo* ...]; *dope* [D *doop* ...]; *droshky* [Russ *drozhki* ...]. These etymologies indicate first that the words were borrowed into Modern English (and, of course, that they were not borrowed into Middle English), and second that they came respectively from Portuguese, Dutch, and Russian. Sometimes the etymology starts with the abbreviation of a foreign language and does not include the source word in that language. Thus for *éclat* one finds just [F, splinter, burst ...] and for *epos* just [Gk, word, epic poem]. When the etymology does not give the form of the word in the language of origin but only the abbreviation for that language, the consultant is to understand that there was no change in form in the process of borrowing. Our word *dissect* (for which part of the etymology was given earlier in this paragraph) comes from Latin *dissectus;* we have not retained the final *-us* in English. But the word *éclat* is identical to its own French origin.

Sometimes an etymology does not give the meaning in the language of origin of the word in question. Thus for *gabardine* one finds [MF *gaverdine*] as the whole etymology. The fact that no meaning is given in this etymology for the Middle French word indicates that it meant the same thing as the English word coming from it. If the etymology does not give the meaning of the original form in the source language and there is more than one definition given in the dictionary, one can assume that in the source language the word had the meaning given in the first definition.

Sometimes one finds that an etymology is composed entirely of the abbreviation for the foreign source language. For *gaucho* one finds [AmerSp] as the whole etymology. This means that the word was borrowed into Modern English with no change in form or meaning. An etymologist who cannot know for certain from which of two languages a word came, may so indicate; thus for *garb* one finds an etymology beginning "MF or OIt," which indicates that the word may have come from either Middle French or Old Italian. Often the etymology indicates that a borrowed word has come from a certain source language but also that that word in the direct source language has come originally from another word in an ultimate source language. Thus for *liquefy* one finds the etymology [MF *liquefier,* fr. L *liquefacere*]. This means that the English word *liquefy* has been borrowed from the Middle French word *liquefier,* which in turn developed from the Latin word *liquefacere.* Etymologies of this kind cause a problem for both teacher and student. Would we say that the word *liquefy* is borrowed from French or borrowed from Latin? With complete correctness we could say either; if we called it a borrowing from French we would have in mind the direct and immediate source language, but if we called it a borrowing from Latin we would have in mind the ultimate source language. To give another example, this time from a more-or-less exotic language, the etymology for *nabob* ("a governor or other person of wealth or prominence") is [Hindi *nawwāb,* fr. Ar *nuwwāb* ...]. We could say there was a direct or immediate borrowing from Hindi (one of the common languages of northern India), and an ultimate

Copyright © 1994 by Harcourt Brace & Company. All rights reserved.

borrowing from Arabic. It would be correct to call it a borrowing from either Hindi or Arabic, *provided the speaker or writer makes the meaning clear and the listener or reader is alert enough to perceive that meaning.* This book will attempt in such situations to make clear whether the immediate or the ultimate source language is meant in any comments or questions about borrowing.

Sometimes your dictionary may seem to have neglected an etymology. In *WNCD,* for example, you will not find etymologies for *ejectment* or *ejector,* for *elasticity* and *elasticized,* for *elation,* for *election, elective, elector, electoral,* or *electorate.* Lexicographers must constantly think of saving space in the production of a dictionary—for doing so means saving money for the eventual buyer—and often they presume that you know the simple patterns of English suffixing. Therefore they expect you to be able to go from the entries for *ejectment* and *ejector* to the entry for *eject,* where you will find the etymology for this base word. Etymologies at *elastic, elate,* and *elect* will tell you what you may need to know about the origins for *elasticity, elation, election,* and so on. Usually one does not have much trouble finding the appropriate etymology, but sometimes one has to search around a bit. When an etymology is apparently lacking, you should not conclude that the dictionary is guilty of an omission or that the etymology is unknown. Usually an etymology will tell you if the source for the word in question is uncertain. Thus for the verb *dodge* you will find in the etymology brackets the comment "origin unknown."

But let us at this point leave the matter of dictionary etymologies and return to a few comments about word borrowing into Modern English:

1. As we have noticed, English has borrowed many words from distant, exotic languages. From the Indo-European languages of India *(Indo-European* will be explained later in this chapter) come such words as *chintz, loot, thug, punch* ("mixed drink"), and *nabob.* From non-Indo-European tongues of Asia, English has borrowed, immediately or ultimately, a good many words—*saffron, hazard, camphor, cotton, harem,* and *alkali* from Arabic; *camel, shekel, cherub, hallelujah,* and *messiah* from Hebrew; *horde, tulip,* and *coffee* from Turkish; *tea, tong,* and *kimono* from Chinese and Japanese. North and South American Indian languages are sources for *squaw, hickory, hominy, toboggan, cocoa, canoe, tobacco,* and many other words. *Gingham, bamboo,* and *bantam* come from the languages of the Pacific Islands and Malaysia; *banana* and *gorilla* from those of Africa. One can safely say that there is no language of any international importance that has not made some contributions to Modern English. In addition, the great majority of words borrowed from exotic languages indicate *things* (including animals and plants), in most cases things originally associated with the language areas in question and certainly not the older England of other days and usually not the America that developed from it. You should notice, too, that although we have a few words like *looter, cottony, alkaline,* and *messianic,* the great majority of these words do not lend themselves to use with common English suffixes.

2. Earlier English borrowed many words from the Scandinavian languages. To a limited degree, borrowing from Scandinavian continued in Modern English, particularly in connection with words such as *ski, fjord, geyser,* and *troll,* which can suggest the Scandinavian North. English has borrowed more words from Dutch and Low German than from High German, the standard language of Germany. In the early Modern English period, mercantile and maritime relations with the Dutch led to the borrowing of such words as *ballast, boom* (as on a ship), *boor, boss* ("master"), *cruise, yacht, yawl, switch, wagon,* and *splice.* Borrowings from High German, which began in the eighteenth century, are not numerous, but they include *quartz, plunder,* and *kindergarten.* Recent borrowings from Yiddish, a dialect of High German, include *schmaltz* and *kibitzer.* Modern English borrowings from Scandinavian languages, from Dutch and Low German, from High German and its dialects, often refer to things that were originally less distant, foreign, and romantic than words from exotic languages. Despite words such as *skier, bossy,* and *plunderer,* these words form no great number of derivatives with suffixes.

3. With the Renaissance the English people developed a considerable interest in Italy, Spain, and Portugal. In part this interest depended on cultural matters, in part on trade, commerce, exploration, and even warfare. Words borrowed directly from Italian into Modern English include *ballot, carnival, bandit, umbrella, opera, solo, piano, cameo, studio,* and *balcony;* sometimes, as with *musket,*

Copyright © 1994 by Harcourt Brace & Company. All rights reserved.

citadel, and *cornice,* Italian words were borrowed into Modern English via French. Words from Spanish and Portuguese include *cask, sherry, comrade, tornado, cargo, guitar, caste,* and *tank.* Words from Italian and Spanish and Portuguese generally do not show many derivative forms with suffixes. Many, if not most, Italian, Spanish, and Portuguese words have developed from original forms in Latin.

4. It is hard to summarize the story of the borrowing of French words into Modern English. Many more French words were borrowed into Middle English than into Modern English. But since 1450 no decade has passed without a great deal of borrowing from French into English. The number of words borrowed from French during the modern period is greater than the number borrowed from any other language except possibly Latin. Sometimes words borrowed from French into Modern English suggest fashion, style, luxury, and upper-class avocations and proclivities, but they do not always do so, and they may be encountered in any sphere of activity. Perhaps the best way to acquire a feeling for French borrowings into Modern English is to dip into a dictionary at random and make up lists such as the following: *callous, calorie, camaraderie, camber, camisole, camouflage, camp, campaign, canapé,* and *canard; fabliau, fabric, facade, facet, facile, faience, faille, failure, faineant,* and *farceur; labile, lackey, lamé, lampoon, languid, lassitude, latrine, lavage, layette,* and *legume; ragout, rally, ramify, ramp, rapier, rapport, ratchet, ration,* and *ravage.* A casual scanning of your dictionary will readily supply you with many more words to add to these lists. Some French words are isolated single forms without derivatives and companion forms, but some have accompanying forms *(callosity, calorific, facility, languish, leguminous, ramification,* and so on). The endings *-ette, -eur, -euse, -e* or *-ee* (as in *employe, employee, fiancé, fiancée),* and *-eau* often show French origin. *Ch* is likely to have an *sh* value (as in *chagrin, chaise, chalet, champagne)* in words of French origin. The majority of French words develop from Latin words, and your dictionary is very likely to show many etymologies beginning with "F, fr. L . . . ." Etymologies often indicate specific kinds of French phrases with abbreviations such as *MF, OF, AF, ONF.* An etymologist who cannot be sure whether a word is from French or another language is likely to write "F or L," "F or It," "F or Sp," and so on.

5. From the very beginnings of English cultural development, Latin has supplied the English language with words for borrowing. During the Renaissance many words were borrowed from this source. As with French, borrowing from Latin has continued ever since. Again, a few random lists may give you an idea of the scope of borrowings from Latin: *alleviate, allocate, allude, alluvion, altercate, alternate, aluminum, alumnus, alveolus,* and *alyssum; debilitate, decemvir, decent, deciduous, decile, decimate, declivity, decorate, decorum,* and *decumbent; latent, lateral, latex, laudanum, laureate, lavabo, lector, legislator, lemur,* and *lenis; saturate, scabies, scalpel, scandal, scansion, scapula, scholastic, scintillate, scorbutic,* and *script.* Making a similar list for yourself will give you an even greater awareness. In general, these words borrowed from Latin into Modern English are a bit learned and bookish. Often they represent combinations of prefixes and roots; roots and suffixes; or prefixes, roots, and suffixes. (The terms *prefix, root,* and *suffix* will be explained in detail in subsequent chapters of this book.) Many of the suffixes are quite common and relatively simple: *-ate, -ous, -ity, -ent,* and *-al* for instance. Many nouns borrowed from Latin end in *-us, -um, -o,* or *-a* (although these endings are to be found in words from other languages, too). We can readily find derivatives and companion forms for many or these words: *alleviation, allocation, allusion, alluvial, altercation, alternative,* to consider the first six given in the previous list. Etymologies may sometimes indicate that a word has been borrowed into English from Latin but has been previously borrowed into Latin from Greek. Etymologists often specify different kinds of Latin with abbreviations such as *LL, NL, ML, VL.*

6. Some words of Greek origin came directly or ultimately into the English language before the Modern English period. But Modern English emerged as a phase different from earlier phases of the language at about the beginning of the Renaissance, the period of rediscovery of many of the Greek classics. During the Renaissance, Greek became much better known in England than it had been formerly, and many words of Greek origin found their way into English, often via Latin or via Latin through French. Among such words are *rhythm, theatre, comedy, scene, thesis, period, trophy, athlete, stadium, theme, bulb, physic, category, sphere, scheme, climate,* and *phase.* Words of Greek origin are likely to be accompanied by derivatives and companion forms: *rhythmical, theatrical, comedian, scenic,* and so on. A so-called hard sound—a *k* sound—for *ch,* as in *choir, chemist,* and *architect,* usually shows Greek origin for a word. The combinations *pn, ps,* and *rh,* as in *pneumatic, psychology,* and *rhythm,* usually indicate

Copyright © 1994 by Harcourt Brace & Company. All rights reserved.

eventual Greek origin. A noun having *-on* in the singular and *-a* in the plural, such as *phenomenon-phenomena,* is a borrowing from Greek. Following is a list, picked at random, of Greek words borrowed into Modern English, either directly or via Latin or French or both: *hagiography, halcyon, hamadryad, haploid, harmony, hecatomb, hectic, hedonism, hegemony, heliacal, heliotrope, helix,* and *hellebore.*

Not only has English borrowed whole words from foreign languages, but it has also borrowed word parts, especially from Greek and Latin. In the nineteenth century, for instance, scientists reconstructed various prehistoric animals, among them the dinosaur. The elements of the word *dinosaur* are Greek, although the early Greeks of course did not know the animal. Scientists coined the word *dinosaur* by putting together two Greek forms, *-dino-,* meaning "terrible," and *-saur-,* meaning "lizard." When our electrical engineers wanted to name a device governing or stopping a current, they made up the word *rheostat* from the Greek forms *-rheo-* ("current") and *-stat-* (indicating "device to stop or make stationary"). Persons favoring the policies of a politician named Smith would be called *pro-Smith,* those opposing would be called *anti-Smith. Pro-* and *anti-* are forms borrowed into English, the former from Latin, the latter from Greek. Among the forms beginning with *h-* that English has borrowed from Greek are the form *-hagi-,* meaning "saint," as in *hagiography, hagiolatry;* the form *-halo-,* meaning "salt," as in *halogen, haloid;* the form *-heli-,* meaning "sun," as in *heliocentric, heliostat;* the form *-hemo-,* meaning "blood," as in *hemolysis, hemophilia;* and the form *-hydro-,* meaning "water," as in *hydrolysis, hydrometer.* These word forms will be treated later in this book.

The story of word borrowing into Modern English is of course fascinating. But why is it an essential part of a book devoted to an attempt to increase your vocabulary? The answer is that you must acquire at least an elementary sense of intuition for words coming from different languages. For example, we all know the English word *path* and its simple derivatives such as *footpath* and *pathfinder.* We hardly need to be told what these words mean. But before we can go very far into the English vocabulary we must attain to the intuition or to the knowledge that the *-path-* of *pathology* or *psychopath* or *sympathy* is totally different from that of *footpath* or *pathfinder.* The latter pair show the English word *path,* but in the former three the *-path-* is a Greek form meaning "feeling, suffering," a completely different element. *Sum* is eventually from Latin, as are *summa* and *summit,* the latter two being built on the original base, *sum.* You would, however, be very wrong indeed if you supposed that *summer,* a word not borrowed from Latin, had anything to do with *sum, summa,* and *summit.* The verb *grate* ("to make a rasping sound") is totally different in origin and in meaning from the Latin *-grat-* of *grateful, gratitude,* and *gratis.* You probably already have some feeling for such relationships, and these examples may not surprise you. Some work, however, with borrowed words, especially as they contrast with words not borrowed, will be worthwhile. You may derive either encouragement or discouragement from the fact that nobody has ever been able to learn the entire etymology of all of the words in the English vocabulary.

The extent of word borrowing into English has brought us an embarrassment of richness in synonyms. Choosing among various synonyms can be a problem, one to be treated later in this book. Another problem brought about by word borrowing is that of the pronunciation of words that have been taken into English more or less recently and have retained some or all of the pronunciation features they had in their original language. English has developed standard pronunciations for *police* and *malice,* both borrowed from French, although the former is much closer to French accentuation than the latter. But, faced with a word such as *grimace,* also borrowed from French, one may well wonder which syllable to stress. There is today some fastidiousness about giving the *e* in *rodeo* its Spanish value but rather little about similarly treating the *e* of *adobe.* Just how should one pronounce such words as *collage, pizza, venue, tulle, faille, serape, purée, machete, métier, liqueur, étude,* and *debouch?*

The inflection, especially the manner of forming the plural, may, like the pronunciation of a borrowed word, be carried over into English from the foreign language. Rather than add an *s* to the word *phenomenon* to indicate more than one, we say *phenomena;* rather than *crisises,* we say *crises.* What are the plurals for *adagio, analysis, apparatus, bacillus, census, colossus, decorum, exodus, enigma,* and *rhinoceros?*

Copyright © 1994 by Harcourt Brace & Company. All rights reserved.

But what about the story of the English language in periods before Modern English? Before Modern English there was Middle English (abbreviated ME). The Middle English period lasted from 1066 (the year of the Battle of Hastings) or 1100 down to the beginning of Modern English in 1450 or 1500. The dates are of course approximate; probably your own judgment will suggest to you that things did not work out so that all English people went to bed on December 31, 1449, speaking Middle English and got up the next morning speaking Modern English. The Middle English period is marked first by the subjugation of the English and their language to the Norman French and their language, and second by the gradual resurgence of things English, including the English language. Chaucer, who wrote in the last decades of the fourteenth century, is the best-known author of the Middle English period; *Sir Gawain and the Green Knight* and *Piers Plowman* are two well-known works of other authors. You would find many selections from Middle English difficult or impossible to read without special training or assistance, although you would at once recognize many of the words as familiar.

In *WNCD* the abbreviation ME in an etymology shows that the word in question existed in the English language during the Middle English period. Etymologies of words borrowed into English during that period start with the abbreviation ME, usually continue with *fr.* in small letters (the abbreviation for *from,* not the abbreviation for *French),* then a language abbreviation, and finally the foreign source word and its meaning. One often finds a further source given for the foreign word itself, particularly if it is a French word that derives from Latin. At *solve* one finds the following: [ME *solven* to loosen, fr. L *solvere* to loosen ...]. This means that the word was part of the English language during the Middle English period, that it then had the form *solven,* that this form meant "to loosen," that the word was borrowed from Latin, and that the Latin form was *solvere,* which also meant "to loosen." For the noun *space* there is the following: [ME, fr. OF *espace,* fr. L *spatium* area, room ...]. This means that the word entered Middle English as a borrowing of the Old French word *espace,* which in turn developed from the Latin *spatium,* meaning "area, room ... ." For *odd* the first part of the etymology is [ME *odde,* fr. ON *oddi* point of land, triangle, odd number...], which of course means that the Middle English form *odde,* from which the Modern English word developed, was borrowed from the Old Norse form *oddi,* with meanings as indicated. At this point you should notice that the abbreviation *fr.* may be read as "borrowed from," but you are cautioned very emphatically that it does not always mean that.

At the beginning of an *SCD* etymology (which is placed after the last definition at the end of an entry) one is likely to find a sideways caret mark [<]. This often—but not always—means "borrowed from." Next one will find an abbreviation for the source language, one or two letters in roman with the first one capitalized (L, Sp, Gk, and so on). Then one will find in italics the word in the source language, usually with an indication of its meaning in that language if it differs from the meaning of the resultant English word, and often with an indication of the ultimate origin of that source word. Thus the etymology in *SCD* for *fortune* is as follows: [< OF < L *fortuna* < *fors* chance]. This means that our Modern English word *fortune* is borrowed from the Old French word of the same form and meaning, that this Old French word developed from Latin *fortuna,* and that this ultimate source form evolved in Latin from a root or stem *fors,* meaning "chance." *SCD* uses the terse procedures of *WNCD.* Thus one finds that the complete etymology for *forum* is simply (< L). This means that the word *forum* is borrowed straight from Latin with no change in form or meaning. Unlike *WNCD, SCD* does not distinguish between words borrowed into Modern English and those borrowed into Middle English.

The great majority of words borrowed into Middle English come from three main sources—French, Latin, and Scandinavian. There are occasional borrowings from Greek, from Spanish and Italian, from Dutch and Low German, and even from Arabic (which include some words beginning with *al-*). But at a guess, well over 90 percent of the words borrowed into Middle English are of French, Latin, or Scandinavian origin. Of these three sources French is the most important.

1. In 1066 the victory of the invading Norman French led by William the Conqueror over Anglo-Saxon forces led by King Harold brought the Anglo-Saxon period to an end. England passed under the complete domination of the Normans, whose influence continued to be strong for nearly 300 years. During that time French was the language of the ruling classes in England; English was spoken only by peasants and commoners. French was the language of knights and military affairs, of lawyers and legal matters, of merchants and commercial ventures, of the nobility and fashion, culture, and art.

 Copyright © 1994 by Harcourt Brace & Company. All rights reserved.

Thousands of words were borrowed from French into English, many of them originally suggesting upper-class affairs: *baron, noble, crown, alliance, attorney, decree, ransom, estate, chattels, heritage, battle, banner, garment, satin, ermine, jewel, ruby, venison, grape, spice, cushion, lamp, parlor, dance, carol,* and *pheasant.* Many others, on the other hand, do not have strong upper-class connotations: *age, air, cage, cost, debt, fault, force, grief, hour, noise, order, point,* and others are so familiar and simple that it is a bit surprising to discover they have a French origin. Borrowings from French reached a peak in the fourteenth and fifteenth centuries, but there has been no period since early medieval times in which English has not borrowed liberally from French. In some cases English has borrowed different French dialect forms of the same original word: *castle* and *catch* come from Northern French, *chateau* and *chase* from Central; sometimes it has borrowed an early form and then a later form of the same word, as with *saloon* and *salon.* Most French words come ultimately from Latin, some even from Greek through Latin. Thus the words *air* and *chair* passed originally from Greek through Latin into French, and then from French to English. It is sometimes difficult to tell whether a word has come into English directly from Latin or from Latin through French; the etymologies of many words are given as "Fr or L."

2. During the Middle English period Latin was the usual language of advanced learning, serious writing, religious affairs, and international matters. Under the circumstances a large number of Latin words were borrowed into Middle English, words coming straight from Latin without going through French. Some random sets of such words follow: *cognition, collateral, collation, collision, commend, commit, communion, compact, complement,* and *comprehend; educate, effeminate, effigy, eject, electrum, elevate, elocution, emblem, emend,* and *emergent; perdition, perquisite, personality, perverse, pestiferous, portend, potential, precept,* and *precinct.* Other sets would include *distract, incredible, inferior, infinite, minor, necessary, prevent,* and *solitary.* These more-or-less typical Latin borrowings into Middle English are like Latin borrowings into Modern English in that they often form derivatives and companion forms.

3. The third important source for words borrowed into Middle English is the Scandinavian languages, especially Old Norse, the ancestor language of the modern languages. In the ninth century, England had come under heavy attack by Scandinavian Vikings, many of whom settled in England. In time the English borrowed many words from these settlers. Some words were undoubtedly borrowed before the Middle English period began but exactly when is uncertain, yet many scholars are content to list such words in their treatments of Middle English. Words borrowed from the Scandinavian languages into Middle English are usually short, simple, and familiar: *skill, scrape, get, egg, bank, booth, crook, dirt, rotten, scant, crawl,* and *lift.*

What came before Middle English? The answer is Old English (OE) or Anglo-Saxon (AS). These two terms mean exactly the same thing, although the former is now the more fashionable term. As you know, the Old English period ended around 1050, 1066, or 1100. When it began is difficult to explain. Old English was probably a separate language or at least a quite distinctive dialect by A.D. 400, but we do not have any Old English writing earlier than the seventh and eighth centuries. Interpreting the term widely, the Old English period was marked by the migration, mostly in the fifth century, of the Angles and Saxons from their northern European homeland in the neck of the Danish peninsula and the adjacent sections of what is now northern Germany. These peoples came to Britain and dispossessed the original Celtic inhabitants. When the invading Angles and Saxons brought their own languages into England, the Celtic languages died out. They did not change in some mysterious way into Old English—any more than the North American Indian languages changed in some mysterious way into English when the first colonists came from England in the seventeenth century. The Celtic languages, in fact, had extremely little influence on English. Alfred the Great in the ninth century is the best-known Anglo-Saxon king, and *Beowulf* in the eighth century is the best-known piece of Anglo-Saxon literature. It would be completely impossible, even though you identified a few words here and there, to read Old English without a good deal of special training or assistance. Here, for instance, is the third line of *Beowulf:* "Hū ðā æð elingas elien fremedon" ("How the princes accomplished great deeds").

Now let us consider how a dictionary etymology indicates that a certain word existed in Old English, descended into Middle English, and thence into Modern English. Following are the first parts of three *WNCD* etymologies, those for *deed, deem,* and *deer:* [ME *dede,* fr. OE *dǣd* ...], [ME *demen,* fr.

Copyright © 1994 by Harcourt Brace & Company. All rights reserved.

OE *dēman* ...], [ME, deer, animal, fr. OE *dēor* beast ...]. Each of these etymologies begins with ME, indicating that the Modern English word developed from a Middle English form. Notice the wording "developed from"; one does not speak of borrowing from one phase of a language to another. Next comes the abbreviation *fr.,* which also has been used in connection with borrowing. In these etymologies for *deed, deem,* and *deer, fr.* does not mean "borrowed from" but rather "developing from." As we have said, Middle English words are not borrowed from Old English words. A Middle English form is given only when the Modern English form is different, and a meaning is given for a Middle English form only if in Modern English another meaning has developed for the word in question. The *OE* after the *fr.* is of course the abbreviation for Old English.

Although its forms do seem very strange at first, Old English contains many words similar to Modern English words. Since many Old English words are simply older forms of contemporary English words, this similarity is hardly surprising. These words constitute the so-called native element of the English vocabulary. Native words usually express simple notions that are needed in every language—everyday words such as *father, mother, son, daughter, children, wife, home, land, field, wood, water, sun, moon, star, summer, winter, house, barn, cow, horse, sheep, meat, drink, love,* and *hate.* Most of the irregular verbs in modern English derive from Old English—*ride, choose, sing, swim, bear, drive, bind*—as do most of our pronouns (*I, you, we, who*), shorter numeral words (*two, three, six, ten*), prepositions (*in, to, by, for, at*), and conjunctions (*and, or, but*). The following are some of the words of Anglo-Saxon origin in the *ha* listing of the dictionary: *hack, haft,* and *hail* (noun); *hair* and *hale* (adjective); *half, hallow, hammer, hand, handle, hang, hard, hare, harp, harvest, hate, have, hawk,* and *hawthorn.* One rarely has much trouble about the meanings of Modern English words that have descended from Old English. Native words, referred to in the title of this chapter, are those that have come down from Old English through Middle English into Modern English. Borrowed words have come into English from other languages.

But was there not some borrowing into Old English just as there has been into Middle English and Modern English? Yes, there was some borrowing from Latin. Early in their history, before they left their Continental homeland, the Anglo-Saxons had come into contact with the more advanced civilization of the Romans and had borrowed from them such words as *wall, street, wine,* and *port* (harbor). In 597, through the efforts of Augustine, a missionary sent from Rome to Britain by Gregory the Great, the first of the Anglo-Saxons were Christianized, and so took over many Latin words relating to religion, some of them originally Greek: *abbot, altar, priest, creed,* and *temper.* Throughout the Old English period many other words entered English from Latin, among them: *mat, box, plant, master, fever, verse, cap, sock, purple, chest, beet, cook, pine, lily, anchor,* and *temper.* It is worth noticing that these Latin words are unlike those borrowed from Latin in later periods in that the former have relatively few derivatives or companion forms. How does a dictionary show that a word has been borrowed from Latin into Old English? Let us now consider this. Here is the *WNCD* etymology for *nun:* [ME, fr. OE *nunne,* fr. LL *nonna*]. This entry hardly needs detailed explanation. But were there borrowings into Old English from other languages? There were a few Scandinavian words; in late Old English a few words were borrowed that could have come from either Latin or French. The Celtic contribution to the Old English vocabulary is negligible, however.

But where did the native Old English words come from, and how did the Old English language originate? Perhaps between 750 B.C. and A.D. 250 a common Germanic (*not* German) language was spoken by the ancestors of the later Angles, Saxons, Scandinavians, Germans, Franks, Goths, Vandals, Burgundians, and others. At least theoretically a member of one of these groups could talk intelligibly with a member of one of the others. Regional dialects almost certainly existed, perhaps to a quite noticeable degree, but these dialects had not become so different that they were unintelligible to speakers of other dialects. They were presumably not yet separate languages. English, along with the Scandinavian languages, Dutch and Low German, and High German, developed from that original Germanic language, and for that reason English is called a Germanic language. In their etymologies dictionaries often show that certain words were present in Germanic, Germanic being regarded as a stage in the prehistory of English. Here are the *WNCD* etymologies for *day* and *dead:* [ME, fr. OE *daeg;* akin to OHG *tag* day]; [ME *deed,* fr. OE *dēad;* akin to ON *dauthr* dead ...]. From these one will see that the Modern English words developed (*not* were borrowed) from Middle English, and that the Middle English forms developed (*not* were borrowed) from Old English. After the Old English forms we do not find

Copyright © 1994 by Harcourt Brace & Company. All rights reserved.

fr. but instead *akin to.* These two etymology tags do not mean the same thing. *Akin to* means "developing from the same source as." The Old English and Old High German forms *daeg* and *tag* both developed from the same prehistoric word, a word in Germanic. The Old English forms did not develop from the Old High German forms, nor were they borrowed from them. In connection with *dead,* the Old English word was not borrowed or developed from the Old Norse form, nor vice versa; both forms developed from the earlier Germanic word. Some dictionaries, notably *WNCD,* try in their etymologies to reconstruct the Germanic words, but since we have no extant written materials from Germanic most dictionaries do not try to do so. Other dictionaries, notably *SCD,* are content simply to show the Old English origin. The Modern English words that show an unbroken line of descent from Germanic through Old English and Middle English into Modern English are generally simple and familiar words.

Germanic was spoken in various areas in eastern and northern Europe, north of the Danube and east of the Rhine, and in Scandinavia. Having gone thus far back in the prehistory of the English language, we should go back one stage further into Indo-European. Scholars accept the theory that thousands of years ago, perhaps as far back as 2500 or 2000 B.C., there existed a language that we today call Indo-European. The locale of its use is somewhat uncertain, but probably it was spoken in eastern Europe. As we have seen, a language spoken by a sizable number of people develops dialect forms, that is, forms peculiar to local areas and not used in all places where the language is spoken. (Today, for instance, the English spoken in New York is not exactly that spoken in Boston, Chicago, or San Francisco, to say nothing of London, Cape Town, or Melbourne; each of these places may be said to use its own dialect of English.) In the ancient Indo-European language, various dialects developed. Eventually there developed such wide differences among these dialects that a speaker of one of them was no longer able to understand the others; at this point the dialects became separate, individual languages.

One of these Indo-European dialects or new languages was ancient Greek, which was spoken in the Aegean Sea region in the second millennium before Christ. From it developed later Greek languages and dialects. Another was early Latin, which emerged on the Italian peninsula somewhat later; from it descended later forms of Latin and, in the medieval period, French, Spanish, and Italian. These and other languages stemming directly from Vulgar Latin are known as Romance languages. Another Indo-European dialect gave rise to Sanskrit, the literary language of ancient India, spoken many centuries before Christ; from it have descended many of the languages spoken in India today. There are several other Indo-European divisions; under the entry *Indo-European* a dictionary will probably refer us to a more nearly complete listing. Another Indo-European dialect was Germanic, the common language of the Germanic or Teutonic peoples of Europe circa the beginning of the Christian era, as discussed previously.

Some of our Modern English words show an unbroken line of descent from Indo-European to Germanic, to Old English, to Middle English, to Modern English, and some dictionaries convey this information in their etymologies. For *hail* ("icy rain") *WNCD* has the following: [ME, fr. OE *haegl;* akin to OHG *hagal* hail, Gk *kachlēx* pebble]. We know that this word is traced back to Old English. After we receive this information we find *akin to* (not *fr.*) in the etymology, and we are told that the Old English word and the Old High German word are traced back to a common ancestor source, which can only be a word in Germanic. But following the Old High German word we find a Greek word. Since we know that the ancestor form of *hail* existed in Germanic and since we know that another form existed in Greek, a non-Germanic language, we know that this word is traced all the way back to Indo-European. For *hall* we have this etymology: [ME *halle,* fr. OE *heall;* akin to L *cella* small room ...]. We are told by the *akin to* that the Old English and Latin forms are cognate—that is, they both derive from a common ancestor form. Latin is a non-Germanic language. The common ancestor form for an Old English word and for a Latin form must be Indo-European. Notice that no borrowing is involved in the history of this word. In the etymology, *fr.* refers only to passage from one phase of the English language to another. Neither *fr.* as used here nor *akin to* indicates borrowing from one language to another. Find out for yourself why each of the following *WNCD* etymologies indicates that the Modern English word being treated originates in Indo-European, passes through Germanic, Old English, and Middle English, and emerges in Modern English: *tail* [ME, fr. OE *taegel;* akin to OHG *zagal* tail, OIr *dūal* lock of hair]; *tame* [ME, fr. OE *tam;* akin to OHG *zam* tame, L *domare,* Gk *damnanai*]; *tear* (noun) [ME, fr. OE *taehher, tēar;* akin to OHG *zahar* tear, L *dacruma, lacrima,* Gk *dakry*]; *tear* (verb) [ME *teren,* fr. OE *teran;* akin to OHG *zeran* to destroy, Gk *derein* to skin].

Copyright © 1994 by Harcourt Brace & Company. All rights reserved.

NAME ______________________________ SECTION __________ DATE __________

CHAPTER 2

EXERCISE 1: Indicate the abbreviation your dictionary uses for each of the following languages.

1. Afrikaans ______	7. Danish ______	13. Greek ______	19. Persian ______
2. Armenian ______	8. Dutch ______	14. Italian ______	20. Portuguese ______
3. Avestan ______	9. Frisian ______	15. Low German ______	21. Provençal ______
4. Bengali ______	10. Gaelic ______	16. Norwegian ______	22. Spanish ______
5. Breton ______	11. German ______	17. Old French ______	23. Swedish ______
6. Cornish ______	12. Gothic ______	18. Old Saxon ______	24. Vulgar Latin ______

EXERCISE 2: This exercise contains words borrowed into English; you are to indicate the languages from which these words are borrowed. The answer will never be Middle English or Old English or Anglo-Saxon. As you do this exercise, ask yourself what derivative and companion forms you can easily think of for each of the words.

Give the immediate (not the ultimate) source language for each of the following. In the blank write the abbreviation that your dictionary uses. In the second blank write a brief definition of the word.

Base Word	Immediate Source Language	Definition
1. albino	______________	______________
2. argali	______________	______________
3. begum	______________	______________
4. boomerang	______________	______________
5. dinghy	______________	______________
6. dungaree	______________	______________
7. matzo	______________	______________
8. pogrom	______________	______________
9. taboo	______________	______________
10. totem	______________	______________

EXERCISE 3: In the first blank give the ultimate (not the immediate) source language for each of the following words. In the second blank write a brief definition of the word.

Base Word	Ultimate Source Language	Definition
1. aberration	______________	______________
2. beatitude	______________	______________
3. bursar	______________	______________

Copyright © 1994 by Harcourt Brace & Company. All rights reserved.

Base Word	Ultimate Source Language	Definition
4. chimera		
5. connubial		
6. eschatology		
7. litigate		
8. repertory		
9. sententious		
10. uxorious		

EXERCISE 4: The words in the first list below were borrowed recently into Modern English. The words in the second list are synonyms or brief defining phrases for the borrowed words. Write the number and synonym or defining phrase in the blank after the borrowed word with which it fits. Be able to pronounce the borrowed words in class and to tell from which language each one comes. The words in this exercise have all been taken from contemporary magazines and newspapers. In the second blank, write the source language given by your dictionary.

First List

Base Word	Number/Synonym	Source Language
1. aficionado		
2. avant-garde		
3. batiste		
4. boudoir		
5. bravado		
6. consortium		
7. cortege		
8. crescendo		
9. curé		
10. de jure		
11. detritus		
12. exposé		
13. extravaganza		
14. farceur		
15. fete		
16. fiasco		
17. gourmet		
18. junta		

Copyright © 1994 by Harcourt Brace & Company. All rights reserved.

NAME ______________________ SECTION __________ DATE __________

First List

	Number/Synonym	Source Language
19. maestro		
20. métier		
21. minutiae		
22. moratorium		
23. penchant		
24. peyote		
25. piquant		
26. prognosis		
27. rapport		
28. roué		
29. travail		
30. tyro		

Second List

1. musical conductor
2. leagued association
3. enthusiast
4. mescaline drug
5. modern extremist
6. trivia
7. comedian
8. sheer fabric
9. lavish show
10. food connoisseur
11. delay period
12. funeral procession for a distinguished person
13. one's trade or profession
14. priest
15. painful toil or suffering
16. legal and rightful
17. elaborate party
18. a definite liking
19. novice
20. a woman's private bedroom
21. growing in volume of sound
22. rock fragments
23. scandalous report
24. a ridiculous failure
25. revolutionary council
26. close understanding
27. sexual free-liver
28. engagingly interesting
29. prediction
30. brave display

Copyright © 1994 by Harcourt Brace & Company. All rights reserved.

EXERCISE 5: After each of the following groups of words are two blanks. In the first blank write the number of the word that most closely approximates the meaning of the italicized word. In the second, write the word being defined.

		Number	Word
1.	these elements in the *aggregate:* 1 mass 2 way 3 bases 4 remnant	_______	_______
2.	the *amplitude* of their gestures: 1 abundance 2 worthlessness 3 scarcity 4 commonness	_______	_______
3.	*apex* of a career: 1 zenith 2 nadir 3 genesis 4 trauma	_______	_______
4.	*argot* of criminals: 1 status 2 crimes 3 jargon 4 education	_______	_______
5.	an *assiduous* student: 1 lazy 2 foolish 3 diligent 4 troublesome	_______	_______
6.	regarded as a *bagatelle:* 1 trifle 2 service 3 insult 4 demerit	_______	_______
7.	the *bellicose* nations: 1 adjacent 2 warlike 3 uncivilized 4 inactive	_______	_______
8.	soothing *berceuse:* 1 drink 2 lullabye 3 poem 4 journey	_______	_______
9.	a *bizarre* appearance: 1 attractive 2 outlandish 3 drab 4 repulsive	_______	_______
10.	surprised at his *bounty:* 1 closeness 2 negligence 3 generosity 4 vigilance	_______	_______
11.	an international *cabal:* 1 speech 2 exodus 3 conspiratorial group 4 party	_______	_______
12.	the *catacombs* of the castle: 1 vaults 2 attics 3 storerooms 4 cellars	_______	_______
13.	a taste of *Chartreuse:* 1 candy 2 liqueur 3 cake 4 bread	_______	_______
14.	the lawyer's *chicanery:* 1 testimony 2 bribery 3 trickery 4 persuasiveness	_______	_______
15.	a *clandestine* meeting at night: 1 secret 2 immoral 3 romantic 4 indiscreet	_______	_______
16.	a *connoisseur* of literature: 1 one having astute knowledge 2 illiterate 3 admirer 4 librarian	_______	_______
17.	color as a *criterion:* 1 necessity 2 quality 3 standard 4 adornment	_______	_______
18.	a *delectable* sensation: 1 delightful 2 mistaken 3 moderate 4 unwholesome	_______	_______
19.	unexpected *demise:* 1 promotion 2 acquittal 3 death 4 announcement	_______	_______
20.	the *docile* people of the town: 1 stupid 2 helpless 3 unruly 4 obedient	_______	_______
21.	a *ductile* substance is one readily: 1 stretched 2 broken 3 changed 4 sold	_______	_______
22.	viewing events with *equanimity:* 1 hope 2 calmness 3 despair 4 apathy	_______	_______
23.	to take care of *exigent* matters: 1 dangerous 2 trivial 3 urgent 4 routine	_______	_______
24.	a *fastidious* dresser: 1 meticulous 2 fashionable 3 expensive 4 shabby	_______	_______
25.	*flamboyant* architecture: 1 modern 2 unusual 3 showy 4 ordinary	_______	_______
26.	a *fortuitous* encounter: 1 chance 2 deadly 3 forceful 4 brief	_______	_______
27.	a *genial* greeting: 1 unexpected 2 sudden 3 curt 4 cheery	_______	_______
28.	beginning the *hegira:* 1 flight 2 vacation 3 mission 4 debate	_______	_______
29.	an *imperious* attitude: 1 kind 2 haughty 3 casual 4 popular	_______	_______
30.	an *ingenuous* comment: 1 naive 2 learned 3 wise 4 dishonest	_______	_______
31.	the gift's *intrinsic* value: 1 assumed 2 inherent 3 dear 4 sentimental	_______	_______
32.	to *mollify:* 1 soothe 2 enrage 3 ignore 4 contest	_______	_______
33.	*multifarious* elements: 1 diverse 2 wicked 3 harmonious 4 limited	_______	_______

Copyright © 1994 by Harcourt Brace & Company. All rights reserved.

NAME ______________________ SECTION ________ DATE ________

34. an *opulent* family: 1 foreign 2 wealthy 3 large 4 small ______ ______

35. *pastoral* literature pertains to: 1 ministers 2 kings 3 shepherds 4 landscapes ______ ______

36. a *recalcitrant* person: 1 defiant 2 discouraged 3 rude 4 exultant ______ ______

37. to *reiterate* a reply: 1 misunderstand 2 repeat 3 deny 4 request ______ ______

38. a *reverie* of love: 1 daydream 2 story 3 poem 4 souvenir ______ ______

39. a *sanguine* temperament: 1 gloomy 2 truculent 3 optimistic 4 pessimistic ______ ______

40. *scintillating* conversation: 1 scandalous 2 tiresome 3 learned 4 sparkling ______ ______

41. *succinct* poetry: 1 lengthy 2 clear 3 terse 4 complex ______ ______

42. a *supercilious* attitude: 1 cheerful 2 haughtily scornful 3 threatening 4 dejected ______ ______

43. a *surfeit* of food: 1 excess 2 adequate supply 3 selection 4 paucity ______ ______

44. a *taciturn* mountaineer: 1 daring 2 lonely 3 crude 4 quiet ______ ______

45. a *ubiquitous* problem: 1 serious 2 present everywhere 3 temporary 4 financial ______ ______

EXERCISE 6: Using the pronunciation symbols in your dictionary, show the pronunciation of each of the following words. Give only the first pronunciation. Be prepared to give the meaning of each of these words, and also the language of origin.

1. aegis ______
2. archipelago ______
3. argot ______
4. automaton ______
5. badinage ______
6. berceuse ______
7. cabal* ______
8. chartreuse ______
9. connoisseur ______
10. demise ______
11. denouement ______
12. dossier ______
13. éclat ______
14. ennui ______
15. étude ______
16. fiasco ______
17. fugue ______
18. gauche ______
19. genre ______
20. hauteur ______
21. insouciant ______
22. jejune ______
23. largesse ______
24. libido ______
25. liqueur ______
26. macabre ______
27. malaise ______
28. memoir ______
29. montage ______
30. née ______
31. pelisse ______
32. première ______
33. protégé ______
34. quietus ______
35. rebus ______
36. regime ______
37. risqué ______
38. saga ______
39. salon ______
40. sobriquet ______

* To the student: "Cabal" is an acronym. Be prepared to give its origin.

Copyright © 1994 by Harcourt Brace & Company. All rights reserved.

[T]here are two meanings
packed into one word.
Lewis Carroll

3 Word Analysis: Prefixes

This chapter will explain two main groups of words. The first group of words is composed of those that cannot be split or analyzed into parts: the word *man,* for example. *Man* is not a combination of *m-* and *-an* nor a combination or *ma-* and *-n.* It has no connection with *an* or *ma,* and its meaning is completely independent of theirs. *Feel* is not analyzed into *f-* and *-eel* or into *fee-* and *-l* and means neither a kind of *fee* nor a kind of *eel. Goat* does not split into *goa-* and *-t, go-* and *-at,* or *g-* and *-oat.* Discovering the meanings of such words by any sort of analysis of component parts is impossible; one must treat these words as units and learn their meanings as such:

adz	burl	cote	gaff	lobe	rick
alms	butte	cusp	gawk	marl	scone
auger	cairn	deign	gloss	mulch	shunt
awn	calk	dupe	hart	neb	slough
bask	carat	esker	idem	ogle	squib
bier	caul	flail	jaunt	parse	swale
bilge	chard	flitch	joust	qualm	tout
brunt	chock	frieze	lair	quay	wry

The words in this group could be called *root words.* Linguists call them *morphemes*—or rather one kind of morpheme. A morpheme is a unit, reasonably constant in form, that expresses a meaning and that cannot be divided into smaller meaningful units. Notice how this definition applies to *man, fall, feel, goat, adz, alms, auger, awn,* and so on. These may also be called *single-morpheme words.*

In contrast, many words can be split into two or more morphemes. For example, the word *discovery* breaks into *dis-* and *-cover-* and *-y; unlikely* into *un-* and *-like-* and *-ly; embolden* into *em-* and *-bold-* and *-en.* Although we will discuss the terms *prefix, root,* and *suffix* in detail later, we will use them here and give, first, words composed of prefix and root; second, words composed of root and suffix; and third, words composed of prefix, root, and suffix.

Prefix and Root

aboard	becalm	complete	epigram	inflate	provide
abrade	biped	decide	expel	nonsense	recur
adjoin	catalog	discard	forgive	prepare	subject

Root and Suffix

arctic	copyist	falsity	greasy	lively	pitiful
backward	debtor	fragile	hazardous	massive	rotate
carnage	dormant	grayish	journal	notable	suction

Copyright © 1994 by Harcourt Brace & Company. All rights reserved.

Prefix, Root, and Suffix

acquittal	awaken	committee	effective	immoral	reflection
addiction	bewitchment	definite	enrollment	intravenous	submarine
apology	catastrophic	disgraceful	exporter	proposal	unladylike

One could compile thousands of words illustrating the single-morpheme form and thousands of each of our three groups of words composed of combinations of roots and prefixes or suffixes or both. Except for words from exotic languages, one finds all kinds of words among the borrowed words in English. Latin and Greek words, however, may lend themselves to analysis into different morphemes, and may do so more profitably to the student, than native words and words from the Germanic languages or from Italian and Spanish. In general, words coming in an unbroken line of descent from Indo-European, those coming from Germanic, and those appearing in Old English are likely to be single-morpheme words. Many words illustrating prefix and root and many others illustrating root and suffix were borrowed during the Middle English period. Those showing prefix, root, and suffix are often of Modern English development in one way or another. However, there are many exceptions.

In general, words that show the same morphemic types lend themselves to the same kind of analysis. *Disarm* and *untrue* are easy to interpret. *Abduct* and *detract* can be interpreted by the same process of reading prefix and root. *Kindly* and *service* are easy; *flexion* and *phonic* can also be read by interpreting root and suffix. *Discovery* and *unlikely* are simple when we interpret prefix, root, and suffix; so are *bicameral* and *exculpate* if we use the same procedure.

But there are difficulties. If we look over the previous list of words illustrating prefix-root composition, we find that we readily recognize the *join, calm, card,* and *sense* of *adjoin, becalm, discard,* and *nonsense.* These appear as single-morpheme words, independent of themselves. We call such forms *free forms.* But what about the *rade* of *abrade,* the *ped* of *biped,* the *plete* of *complete,* the *cide* of *decide,* and so on? In these words these elements seem to operate like *join* in *adjoin* and *calm* in *becalm.* Like *join* and *calm,* the elements *rade, ped, plete,* and *cide* are morphemes. They do not, however, make commonly known independent words by themselves. Since for most of us they exist in the English language only in connection with other elements to which they are attached, we call them *bound forms* in contradistinction to free forms.

It would be unfair at this point to imply that division of words of two or more syllables into separate morphemes is always easy and clear. There are many situations in which anybody except the most learned specialist may be doubtful. Is there a relationship between *shove* and *shovel,* and is the latter word therefore composed of two morphemes? Is *corpuscle* connected with *corpus* or *corps?* Is there any connection between *dive* and *diverse?* When can we be reasonably sure that a word is composed of two elements? How do we interpret that word when we can readily attach a meaning to only one of the elements? We realize that *cranberry* is probably composed of *cran* and *berry,* and we know in a general way what a berry is, but how do we interpret *cran?* Are *walnuts* something that grow near walls? *Chestnuts* something that one puts in chests? A *bonfire,* we know, is a fire, but what does *bon* mean? Is this related to *bonny* or to the French word *bon?* We know what spheres are, but what kind of sphere is the *atmosphere?* Does *barber* have anything to do with *barb,* or is it a single, unanalyzable morpheme? Is the *infantry* something composed of infants? Is a *badger* so called because it seems to wear a badge? Is there a connection between *constables* and *stables?* Does an *ambush* occur when opponents emerge from lurking behind bushes? Is there a relationship between *chief* and *mischief?* Questions of this kind could be asked by the thousands.

In one sense the dictionary helps us here. Is there a connection between *cab* and *caboose*—is the second made up from the first plus an added element? We find that etymologically it is not, since *cab* is the shortening of the word *cabriolet,* borrowed from French, and *caboose* is borrowed evidently from the Dutch word *kabuis.* Is *belfry* made up from *bell?* No, their etymologies are different. But often procedures in interpreting words and determining morphemic structures necessarily depend on whether or not the person doing the interpretation is thinking etymologically. Consider these three

Copyright © 1994 by Harcourt Brace & Company. All rights reserved.

sentences: "The state police soon cowed the rioters." "The frightened children were cowering under the bed." "He was too much of a coward to consider attacking rather than retreating." We could say with considerable justification that in these three sentences the form *cow* is the same morpheme and argue that it is a unit reasonably constant in form, expressing a single meaning, and cannot be further subdivided. But our dictionaries will indicate that *cow* as a verb, *cower,* and *coward* all have different etymologies and are unrelated. To the average person the word *nostril* may well be a single morpheme; those who know or look up its etymology discover that it was composed originally of two elements, forms for the words *nose* and *thrill,* the latter meaning "piercing, opening." The general concept of morphemes, then, is not exact for all people; the concept may vary a bit from person to person in practical life. (Such variation is likely to occur with linguistic definitions that depend wholly or partly on meaning; different things have different meanings to different people.)

Fortunately, however, one kind of English morpheme, the prefix used in English words, gives little trouble. A prefix is a short form, usually of one or two syllables, used before another form, sometimes an independent word, to modify the meaning of that second form. Some forms may be both prefixes and independent words, such as *under-* of *underline;* such forms are "free" when used alone. Many prefixes are "bound," such as *un-* in *unhappy,* which is not used as an independent word meaning "not"; no one says, "She thought that she was sick, but the doctor found that she was un." Sometimes some of us amuse ourselves by taking words made up of prefixes and bound forms, detaching the prefixes, and momentarily freeing the bound forms; that is, we may make up the words *ane* and *ert* by dropping the negative prefix *in-* from *inane* and *inert.*

In general, the addition of a prefix does not change the part of speech indicated by the base form: *tell, foretell; do, undo;* and *essential, nonessential.* Sometimes, however, it does make a change: *body, embody; card, discard;* and *able, disable.*

Some prefixes have one more or less constant meaning. Some have various meanings often hard to define. The prefix *un-* in such words as *unable, uneven, unhappy,* and *uncertain* is reasonably fixed in meaning simply "not," in indicating the opposite of whatever is meant by the word to which it is attached. Exceptions occur in a few words like *unloose,* meaning "to loosen, to make loose." On the other hand, a prefix such as *per-* varies widely in its meaning; sometimes, as in *permeate,* it means "through"; sometimes, as in *perfervid,* it means "extremely, very"; sometimes, as in *perjure* or *pervert,* it means loosely something like "down, away, over." The lists that follow in this chapter attempt to call your attention to the fact that some prefixes—such as *circum-, extra-, intro-, and intra-,* for instance—are practically invariable in their meanings, but others are very variable indeed.

Initial combinations such as *un-, ad-, se-,* and *pro-* are not necessarily always prefixes. *Un-* is a prefix in *unconcerned* or *unarmed,* but it is not in *under,* which cannot be analyzed into *un-* and *-der,* nor in *union. Seven* of course does not analyze into *se-* and *-ven,* nor *sequoia* into *se-* and *-quoia.* Consult the dictionary when in doubt. In the etymologies for *seclude* and *seduce,* for instance, you will probably find an indication that in Latin these words were formed by use of the prefix *se-;* you will probably find this element separated in the etymology from the following portions of the original etyma. But for *secular* and *sediment* you will find a different kind of etymology, one in which the *se-* element is not given separately from what follows. This procedure indicates that for practical purposes *se-* is certainly not a prefix in these words.

Sometimes the spelling and pronunciation of the prefix may vary from one word to another. The most frequent cause of variations is *assimilation,* the process by which one of two dissimilar sounds close together changes to make pronunciation easier. Informal English affords many illustrations of assimilation. When we say "give me" quickly and carelessly, we are likely to slur the sound of the *v,* so that we actually say something like "gimme." Similarly, "let me" may be sounded as "lemme." Likewise, the addition of a prefix to a word sometimes brought dissimilar sounds together. Thus prefixing *ad-* to the form *-fect-* in early Latin would have produced the form *adfect.* It was easier to let assimilation take its course and to say *affect* than *adfect,* and the resulting form is of course *affect;* the *af-* is an assimilated form of the prefix *ad-*. This prefix appears also in the assimilated forms *ac-* in *access, ag-* in *aggregate, al-* in *ally, an-* in *announce, ar-* in *arrest, as-* in *assemble,* and *at-* in

Copyright © 1994 by Harcourt Brace & Company. All rights reserved.

attain. The prefixes *com-, dis-, in-, ob-, sub-,* and *syn-* often show assimilation. *Collect* has emerged from the jointure of *com-* and *-lect-, sympathy* from that of *syn-* and *-pathe-.*

Knowledge of prefixes is an aid in coping with the problems of English spelling. We generally suggest the full form of the prefix in our spelling even when by assimilation the last letter of the prefix has become the same as the first letter of the following form. This is one reason for the large number of doubled consonants in English words: *misspeak, overrun, unnatural, abbreviate, addict, affianced, aggrieve, allot, annoyance, approve, commit, corrode, difficult, immoderate,* and *occlude.* Omitting the final letter of the prefix of course causes misspellings. The spelling of the prefixes themselves likewise may give some difficulty: should one write *despatch* or *dispatch, enclosure* or *inclosure?* Is there a difference between *unsanitary* and *insanitary?* Finally, in using recently formed words with prefixes one may wonder whether to hyphenate or not: in writing about removing lice, does one use the form *de-louse* or the form *delouse?* Is a rural newspaper *bi-weekly?* Rules and principles about such questions are hard to formulate, but the form recommended by your dictionary is safe for your use. In learning prefixes, it is advisable to *think* of the prefix as being a part of the whole: that is, *ad* should not be learned as an entity, but rather as a part of *adverse,* for example.

Following is a list of the main prefixes in English, with their most common meanings indicated by examples. They are presented in three groups: those from Old English and hence native in the language, those from Latin (many of which are reinforced by use in French), and those from Greek. The list is by no means exhaustive. Technical and uncommon prefixes such as *endo-* and *meso-* and very obvious prefixes such as *under-* and *up-* have usually been omitted. The meanings given are often merely suggestive and by no means exhaustive. Your dictionary will give you more information about prefix meanings.

PREFIX (AND VARIANTS)	GENERAL MEANING	EXAMPLES

Of Old English Origin

a-	in, on, of, up, to	abed, afoot, astride

Causes few problems. Never followed by a doubled consonant. Does not appear in *acorn, acute, amass, amend, amuse, avoid,* and so on. Do not confuse with Latin *a-* (for *ab-)* in *averse* and Greek *a-,* meaning "without."

be-	around, about, away	beset, besprinkle, behead

Notice range of meanings given in your dictionary. Never followed by doubled consonant. Not the first syllable of *belligerent, benefit, bevel,* and so on. Sometimes with bound forms, as in *bereave* and *betray.*

for-	away, from, off	forswear, forsake, forfend

Do not confuse with *fore-;* see below. Meaning quite variable. Not used in such French and Latin words as *foray, forceps, foreign, forensic, forfeit, fortitude.*

fore-	before, previous	forethought, foreword, forearmed

Do not confuse with *for-;* see above. Not used in *foreign, forensic,* and *forest.* Meaning invariable: always indicates "before."

mis-	badly, poorly, not	misfit, misfire, misbelieve

In some words comes also at least partly from a French prefix *mes-* with the same meaning. Does not appear in *miscellaneous, miscible, misery, missal, missile, mission,* and so on. Often added to words borrowed from French and Latin. Meaning quite constant.

Copyright © 1994 by Harcourt Brace & Company. All rights reserved.

Prefix (and variants)	General Meaning	Examples

Of Old English Origin (Continued)

Prefix (and variants)	General Meaning	Examples
over-	over, excessively	overthrow, overcast, overstate

Often added to words borrowed from French and Latin. Not used in *overture.* Meaning constant. Note spelling of *overreach* and *overrun.*

Prefix (and variants)	General Meaning	Examples
un-	not, opposing	unfold, unknown, ungodly

See dictionary for wide range of use. Does not appear in the following: *unanimous, uncial, unctuous, undulate,* or *unique.* Do not confuse with Latin *uni-,* as in *uniform, unison, unite,* and *universe.* Often added to words borrowed from French and Latin. Meaning constant. Note spelling of *unnatural* and *unnecessary.*

Of Latin Origin

Prefix (and variants)	General Meaning	Examples
ab- (a-, abs-)	from, off, away	abdicate, abjure, averse, abscond, abstain

Not used nearly as frequently as *ad-,* which follows. Assimilates only as indicated above. Meaning fairly constant. Not present in *abandon, abase, abate, abbot, abeyance, abide, abut, abyss,* and so on. Appears as *a-* only before *v.*

Prefix (and variants)	General Meaning	Examples
ad- (ac-, af-, ag-, al-, an-, ap-, ar-, as-, at-)	to, toward, near, very	adverse, advocate, accede, affiliate, aggression, allude, annul, appear, arrogate, assent, attempt

As indicated, very common. Moderately consistent in meaning. Frequently appears as *as-* before *c,* as in *ascend* and *ascertain.* Assimilates widely, as indicated, but may resist assimilation in such relatively new words as *adsorb.* Not present in *adipose* and *adenoid.* To be suspected in any situation in which initial *a* is followed by a double consonant, but not present in *accoutre, ammunition, anniversary,* and so on. Assimilates to *ac-* before *q,* as in *acquire.* Learned words beginning with *all-* or *allo-* may illustrate the Greek form meaning "other" rather than Latin *ad-* assimilated.

Prefix (and variants)	General Meaning	Examples
ante-	before, previous	antedate, ante-meridiem

Constant in meaning. Not present in *antelope* or *antenna.* Appears as *anti-* in *anticipate,* but is otherwise fairly constant in form.

Prefix (and variants)	General Meaning	Examples
bi-	two, twice	biennial, bifocals, bilateral

Constant in meaning and form. Not present in *bias, bilious, bison, bizarre,* and so on. Do not confuse with such initial elements as *bio-* ("life") and *bibli-* ("book") in words of Greek origin such as *biology* and *bibliography.*

Prefix (and variants)	General Meaning	Examples
circum-	around	circumvent, circumspect, circumlocution, circumscribe

Constant in form and meaning. Present with indicated meaning in any word beginning with *circum-.*

Prefix (and variants)	General Meaning	Examples
com- (co-, col-, con-, cor-)	with, together, jointly, very	compare, complicate, coexist, collate, concentrate, corrupt

Copyright © 1994 by Harcourt Brace & Company. All rights reserved.

Of Latin Origin (Continued)

Meaning fairly constant, but often not immediately apparent and more applicable to etymology than to contemporary interpretation. Not present in *comatose, comedy, comet, comic,* and so on, but always probable in words beginning with *comm-*. Assimilates as indicated. Appears as *co-* frequently before vowels, as in *coexist* and *coincide;* before *g,* as in *cognate* and *cognomen;* and h, as in *cohere* and *cohesion.* Frequent in words beginning with *coll-,* although not in *collar, college, collier,* and so on; with *conn-;* and with *corr-,* although not in *corral* or *corridor.* Do not confuse assimilated form *con-,* as in *contact* or *contiguous,* with *contra-,* which follows in this list.

contra-	against, opposing	contradict, contravene

Does not appear in *contract* but otherwise present in all common words beginning with *contra-;* sometimes hard to recognize, as in *contrary* and *contrast.* Form varies occasionally, as in *contretemps* and *controversy.* Do not confuse with *con-,* among the variant forms of *com-* given above. Meaning constant.

de-	away, opposed, off, from, down	demur, demolish, depreciate, desert

Form is constant. Do not confuse with *demi-,* below. Does not appear in words beginning with Greek *deca-,* as in *decathlon;* Latin *deci-,* as in *decibel;* Latin *dei-,* as in *deity;* Greek *dem-,* as in *democracy;* Latin *dent-,* as in *dental;* Greek *derm-,* as in *dermatology;* and so on. There are a considerable number of words from Latin and Greek that begin with *de-* but do not contain this prefix: *decent, decorous, delicate, denim,* and so on.

demi-	half	demigod, demitasse

Meaning and form constant, but this prefix is relatively uncommon.

dis- (di-, dif-)	away, off, down, opposing	dissent, dispel, digress, divert, diffuse, diffident

In many words, such as *disgrace* and *disinfect,* it is readily apparent, but it is not so in such words as *discourse* and *discuss.* Not present in *disciple, distaff, distil.* Do not confuse with Greek *dia-,* as in *diameter,* or Latin and Greek *di-,* as in *diatom.* Assimilates as indicated.

ex- (e-, ef-)	away, from, out, not, missing	excise, exit , expel, eject, eradicate, efface

When used in the sense of "former, previous" in English, usually it is followed by a hyphen, as in *ex-king, ex-wife, ex-convict.* Not used in *ebony, echo, electric, elegy,* and so on, nor in words employing Greek elements *eco- (economics), epi- (epiphany), eu- (euphony),* or Latin elements *ego- (egotism),* and *equi- (equilateral).* Assimilates as indicated. Forms with *e-* common: *eclectic, educate, egregious, ejaculate, elect, emerge, enumerate, evacuate,* and so on. Meaning somewhat variable, as in *ellipse, ecstasy, effigy, elate,* and so on. Do not confuse with *extra-,* below.

extra-, extro-	outside, beyond	extramural, extravagant, extrovert

Does not appear in *extract* or *extradition,* but otherwise appears in every word beginning with *extra-* or *extro-*. Do not confuse with *ex-,* above.

in- (il-, im-, ir-)	not, opposing, un-	incapable, insoluble, illicit, imprudent, irrational

Reasonably constant in form, although liable to confusion with following three prefixes. Assimilates only as indicated.

Copyright © 1994 by Harcourt Brace & Company. All rights reserved.

Prefix (and variants)	General Meaning	Examples

Of Latin Origin (Continued)

in- (il-, im-, ir-)	in, into, within	induct, influx, immigrate, irrigate

Liable to confusion with *in-* ("not") and with two prefixes following. Assimilates only as indicated.

inter-	among, between	intercede, interfere, intersperse, intermittent

See dictionary for fuller statement of meaning. All words beginning with *inter-* employ this prefix although with some, such as *interest* and *internecine,* this information is not very useful.

intro-, intra-	inwardly, to the inside, within	introvert, introduce, intravenous

Does not appear in *intractable* and *intransigent,* but appears in every other word beginning with *intro-* or *intra-*. Meaning constant.

non-	not	nonentity, noncombatant, nonessential

Does not appear in *nonagenarian* and a few other uncommon words, but overwhelmingly great majority of words beginning with *non-* do employ this prefix. Meaning and form are constant. Used with bound forms in *nonchalant* and *nonpareil.*

ob- (oc-, of-, op-)	over, against, toward, very	obtrude, obstruct, occlude, offend, oppose

Does not appear in *obelisk, obey, official, optic,* and some other words. Meaning varies; sometimes useful in word analysis, sometimes not. Form constant. Assimilates as indicated.

per-	through, thoroughly	permeate, perspicuous, pernicious

Not used in *percale, peruke,* and a few other words. Frequently useful in analysis, but not in such words as *perdition, perish,* and a number of others. Do not confuse with Greek prefix *peri-* given later. Constant in form.

post-	after, later, following, behind	postlude, postpone, postscript

Does not appear in *postage, postulate, posture,* but is used in practically every other word beginning with *post-*. Meaning and form are constant.

pre-	before, earlier, in front of	preclude, prelude, event precursor

See dictionary for fuller statement of meaning. Dictionary etymologies often give the earlier Latin form *prae-* for this prefix. Does not appear in *precious, pregnant, pressure, pretzel,* and some other words, but does appear in most words beginning with *pre-*. Usually useful in meaning analysis, although not in such words as *precinct, predicate,* and *premium.*

pro-	earlier, before, in front of; in place of, favoring	protract, proponent, profuse, proceed, pronoun

Copyright © 1994 by Harcourt Brace & Company. All rights reserved.

Prefix (and variants)	**General Meaning**	**Examples**

Of Latin Origin (Continued)

Actually two different Latin prepositions appear as *pro-;* both show a certain spread of meaning. See dictionary for more complete information. Under the circumstances using knowledge of this prefix in the analysis of such words as *prodigal* and *profane* is not very profitable, but for other words it is often very useful. Prefix does not appear in such words as *probate, probity, proctology, proper,* and *prosper.*

re-	back, backward, again	revoke, recede, recur

Constant in form and reasonably constant in meaning in the many words in which it appears. Not useful in such words as *record, recruit, refuge, register, religion,* and *reticent.* Does not appear in such words as *reality, realize, realm, rebus,* and *rendezvous.* Do not confuse with Latin forms *rect-* ("right"), as in *rectitude,* and *reg-* ("king, rule"), as in *regal.*

retro-	back, backward	retrospect, retrograde

Constant in meaning and form. Present in almost every word beginning with *retro-.*

se-	away, aside	secede, seduce, seclude

Constant in form and meaning, but the overwhelming majority of words beginning with *se-* do not contain this prefix: *seance, secant, secret, secretary, section, secular, sedate, sediment, seismograph, semantic, senior, sensitive, sequence, serene,* and many others.

semi-	half, partly	semiannual, semicircular

Reasonably constant in form and meaning and quite useful. Does not appear in *seminal, seminar, seminary, Semitic,* and so on.

sub- (suc-, suf-, sug-, sum-, sup-, sus-)	under, beneath, lower, less	subjugate, subsist, succinct, suffuse, suggest, supplant, sustain

Assimilates as indicated. Usually not hard to identify. Usually useful in word analysis, although not in such words as *sublime, subsidy, subtle, success, suffice,* and *supple.* Does not appear in *succotash, succulent, summit, sumptuary,* and so on.

super-	over, above, extra	superscript, supersede, supervise

See dictionary for further explanation of meaning. Invariable in meaning and form, although analysis of such words as *superstition* may cause problems.

trans-	across, beyond, through	transfuse, transcend, transient

Practically invariable and usually quite helpful in analyzing meaning and form, although appearing as *tra-* in a few words.

ultra-	beyond, excessive	ultramodern, ultraviolet

Invariable in meaning and in form.

Copyright © 1994 by Harcourt Brace & Company. All rights reserved.

PREFIX (AND VARIANTS)	GENERAL MEANING	EXAMPLES

Of Greek Origin

a- (an-)	lacking, without	amorphous, anemic, anorexia, aphagia

The form *a-* usually appears before consonants, the *an-* before vowels. The form *a-* does not appear before doubled consonants, and hence there are few situations in which this prefix can be confused with Latin *ab-* or *ad.* Generally words in which this Greek prefix appears are so learned, and words in which the Old English prefix *a-* appears so simple, that there is little chance of confusing the two. Greek *a-* and *an-* are scattered throughout dictionary sections beginning with *a-*.

ana-	up, against, throughout, back	anagram, analysis, anachronism

Except for *anaconda* and *analgesia,* appears in almost every word beginning with *ana-,* but the variability of meaning makes it not very useful in analytic interpretation of words.

anti-	against, opposing, opposite	antipathy, antitoxin, antithesis

Occasionally appears as *anth-,* but this form is not very useful in word interpretation. Does not appear in *anticipate, antiphony, antiquary,* and so on. Constant in meaning and reasonably constant in form.

apo-	from, off, separate	apogamy, apostate, apostle

Sometimes appears as *ap-* or *aph-*. Appears in the great majority of words beginning with *apo-* but sometimes does not help much with analysis of meaning.

cata- (cat-, cath-)	down, away, thoroughly	catalyst, cataclysm, catastrophe

Does not appear in *catamaran* or *catenate,* but does appear in the great majority of words beginning with *cata-*. Fairly constant in meaning and usually useful in interpretation.

dia-	through, across, apart	diameter, diaphanous, diagnose

Does not appear in *diabolic, diaconal, diamond, diaper,* and so on, but does appear in the majority of words beginning with *dia-*. Constant in form and reasonably so in meaning. Usually useful in analysis.

en- (em-)	in, within, among	endemic, empiric

The great majority of words beginning with *en-* and *em-* do not start with this prefix; it is not very common or very useful. (The verb prefix in *enthrone* and *enslave* is of French origin.) Listed here as useful in a few words.

epi-	on, over, outside	epigram, epidermis, epidemic

See dictionary for more complete account of meaning. Does not appear in *epic, epicure, episcopal,* and so on, but does appear in great majority of words beginning with *epi-*.

eu-	good, pleasant, true	eugenics, eulogy, euphemism

Copyright © 1994 by Harcourt Brace & Company. All rights reserved.

PREFIX (AND VARIANTS)	GENERAL MEANING	EXAMPLES

Of Greek Origin (Continued)

Does not appear in *euchre, eunuch,* and so on, but does appear in the great majority of words beginning with *eu-*. Constant in meaning and form and quite useful in analysis.

hemi-	half	hemisphere, hemiplegic

Constant in form and meaning. Present in every word beginning with *hemi-*.

hyper-	above, excessive	hypercritical, hyperostosis, hyperpyrexia

Constant in form and meaning and quite useful. Always present in a word beginning with *hyper-*.

hypo-	under, down, lower, less	hypodermic, hypochondria, hypoglycemia

Occasionally appears as *hyp-,* but generally as above. Reasonably constant in meaning and usually useful in analysis.

meta-	later, with a change in, over	metabolism, metamorphosis, metastasis

See dictionary for more complete statement of meaning. Sometimes appears just as *met-*. Present in all words beginning with *meta-* except *metal* and *metallic.* Reasonably constant in meaning and useful in analysis.

para-	beside, beyond, related	parallel, paradox, paraphrase

See dictionary for more complete statement of meaning. Sometimes appears just as *par-*. Although not present in *parachute, parade, paradise, paraffin, paramount, parapet,* and so on, is usually present in words beginning with *para-*. Reasonably constant in form and meaning.

peri-	around, near, enclosing	peripatetic, periodontics, periscope, perimeter

Does not appear in *peril, perique, periwinkle,* and so on, but does in most words beginning with *peri-*. Constant in meaning and usually useful.

pro-	earlier, before, in front of	prophesy, prognosis, program

Differs little from Latin prefix *pro-* given earlier; included in this list because it is eventually of Greek origin and is used with many Greek elements in English words.

syn- (sym-, syl-, sys-)	with, together, at same time	synchronize, synthesis, sympathy, syllogism, system

Constant in form and present in every word beginning with any of the forms given. Reasonably constant in meaning and quite useful.

Usually, Old English prefixes are used with other elements of Old English origin, Latin prefixes with other elements of Latin origin, and so on. Later chapters in this book will give information about

Copyright © 1994 by Harcourt Brace & Company. All rights reserved.

which elements are Latin in origin and which elements are Greek. Words with negative prefixes in particular often combine a prefix from one source and the following element from another. Thus the Old English prefix *un-* is quite freely used with words borrowed from French and Latin. A word made up of different elements from different languages is called a *hybrid.* The words *unadorned* and *unaccented* are hybrids. In general, however, the observation given above—that Latin prefixes, for instance, are used with other Latin elements—holds true. In some situations Latin and Greek prefixes are the same in form, as we have seen with *pro-,* but instead of causing troubles this situation may make interpretation a bit easier. Sometimes we have words with two or three prefixes, such as *misapprehension* or *uncomprehending.* In this situation, analysis of the first prefix and momentary separation of it from what follows is usually very easy; it is not very hard to see that *misapprehension* is made up of *mis-* and *apprehension.* Usually there is more of a problem in isolating and interpreting inner prefixes that come as second or third elements in words. Thus one may have problems with both meaning and form in analyzing *apprehension* into *ad-* and *prehension* and then analyzing *prehension* into *pre-* and *hension.* There are admittedly difficulties in those steps. There may be many other difficulties in connection with analysis and interpretation of prefixes. For example, consider the word *hemidemisemiquaver.* Can you isolate the root from the prefixes, or vice versa? Try to do so. The potential rewards will make it worthwhile when you also encounter such a word as *centriculocordectomy.* Using your knowledge of prefixes, define the word by isolating the root from the prefixes or vice versa.

Copyright © 1994 by Harcourt Brace & Company. All rights reserved.

NAME ______________________ SECTION __________ DATE __________

CHAPTER 3

EXERCISE 1: Following are a number of unanalyzable single-morpheme words. In the blank after each word write the number of the word in the *second list* that serves as a synonym for the word in the first list.

First List

1. acme ____________
2. arid ____________
3. bane ____________
4. blithe ____________
5. churl ____________
6. droll ____________
7. gauche ____________
8. grist ____________
9. gusto ____________
10. ilk ____________
11. kelp ____________
12. nadir ____________
13. niche ____________
14. pique ____________
15. rife ____________
16. scion ____________
17. shard ____________
18. sloth ____________
19. waif ____________
20. wraith ____________

Second List

1. comical
2. peak
3. lout
4. zest
5. seaweed
6. dry
7. ground grain
8. ornamental alcove or space
9. low point
10. carefree
11. spur on (v.)
12. inertia
13. ruin
14. kind or type
15. crude
16. fragment
17. heir
18. widespread
19. phantom
20. a stray (n.)

Copyright © 1994 by Harcourt Brace & Company. All rights reserved.

EXERCISE 2: Following are a number of unanalyzable single-morpheme words. In the blank after each word write the number of the word in the *second list* that serves as a synonym for the word in the first list.

First List

1. addle ________	11. dross ________	21. node ________
2. apex ________	12. eschew ________	22. quirk ________
3. bauble ________	13. feint ________	23. sleazy ________
4. brogue ________	14. fiat ________	24. snide ________
5. carp ________	15. frond ________	25. spoor ________
6. chary ________	16. ghoul ________	26. terse ________
7. conch ________	17. gnome ________	27. tome ________
8. cruet ________	18. hale ________	28. twit ________
9. dire ________	19. maim ________	29. wench ________
10. dour ________	20. mien ________	30. whet ________

Second List

1. leaf	11. order (n.)	21. concise
2. grave robber	12. tease (v.)	22. dwarf (n.)
3. cripple (v.)	13. shun	23. eccentricity
4. dialect	14. complain	24. malicious
5. waste (n.)	15. sullen	25. high point (n.)
6. peasant or poor girl	16. sharpen	26. multi-page book
7. shoddy	17. animal track	27. robust
8. demeanor	18. confuse	28. cautious
9. dreadful	19. bottle for condiments	29. swelling
10. trinket	20. pretend	30. seashell

EXERCISE 3: Following are a number of phrases and clauses with italicized unanalyzable morpheme words. In the blank, write the number of the word most closely corresponding in meaning to the italicized word.

1. works of the old *bards:* 1 lawgivers 2 patriarchs 3 alchemists 4 tribal poets — 1. ________
2. a *bland* answer: 1 decisive 2 offensive 3 apologetic 4 smooth and suave — 2. ________
3. to *broach* the subject: 1 avoid 2 dislike 3 introduce 4 exhaust — 3. ________
4. a *buxom* woman: 1 ill-tempered 2 plump 3 busy 4 unhealthy — 4. ________
5. to *cache* the jewels: 1 sell 2 display 3 examine 4 hide — 5. ________
6. to *cant* an instrument: 1 break 2 tilt 3 certify 4 discard — 6. ________
7. to *con* the résumé: 1 disregard 2 disbelieve 3 study 4 approve — 7. ________

Copyright © 1994 by Harcourt Brace & Company. All rights reserved.

NAME ______________________________ SECTION __________ DATE __________

8. a *coy* gesture: 1 brave and defiant 2 stoical 3 ridiculous 4 archly sly 8. ________
9. sitting on the *dais:* 1 lower stair 2 sofa 3 river bank 4 raised platform 9. ________
10. some *deft* touches: 1 showy 2 neatly skillful 3 sarcastic 4 discordant 10. ________
11. to *delve* in the earth: 1 scratch 2 bury 3 dig 4 tunnel 11. ________
12. a *despot* on the throne: 1 fool 2 coward 3 tyrant 4 dreamer 12. ________
13. carrying a *dirk:* 1 pistol 2 flag 3 lantern 4 dagger 13. ________
14. to *doff* one's hat: 1 make 2 inspect 3 repair 4 take off 14. ________
15. a *dun* horse: 1 strong and heavy 2 slow 3 brownish gray 4 old 15. ________
16. to *flout* authority: 1 mock defiantly 2 submit to 3 usurp 4 honor 16. ________
17. to *furl* a flag: 1 fly 2 lower 3 roll up 4 salute 17. ________
18. the street *gamin:* 1 congestion 2 urchin 3 pedestrians 4 hawkers 18. ________
19. a *glib* speaker: 1 persuasive 2 fluent but superficial 3 dishonest and misleading 4 barely audible 19. ________
20. in the *guise* of a hunter: 1 protection 2 company 3 semblance 4 antipathy 20. ________
21. to *hone* a blade: 1 break 2 sharpen 3 cleanse 4 fasten 21. ________
22. a *lithe* dancer: 1 gracefully supple 2 awkward 3 energetic 4 popular 22. ________
23. a *lush* meadow: 1 worthless 2 low-lying 3 green and fertile 4 small 23. ________
24. the noise of the *melee:* 1 cheers 2 confused fight 3 rally 4 ceremony 24. ________
25. the bird's *neb:* 1 nest 2 food 3 flight 4 beak 25. ________
26. the *pelt* of the lion: 1 scent 2 track 3 gait 4 hide 26. ________
27. to *rue* the events: 1 celebrate 2 report 3 atone for 4 regret 27. ________
28. saved by a *ruse:* 1 retreat 2 stratagem 3 compromise 4 charge 28. ________
29. a mountain *tarn:* 1 stone 2 peak 3 snow accumulation 4 pool 29. ________
30. answered in a *trice:* 1 fit of anger 2 instant 3 low voice 4 doubtful mood 30. ________

EXERCISE 4: The following words illustrate less common prefixes. Use your dictionary etymologies to find the meanings of these prefixes. Write the prefix and its meaning in the first blank below. Write the meaning of the complete word in the second blank.

Word	Prefix and Its Meaning	Meaning of Word
1. ambidextrous	________	________
2. amphibious	________	________
3. deuterogamy	________	________
4. dichromatic	________	________
5. dyspepsia	________	________
6. ectoparasite	________	________
7. endocardium	________	________

Copyright © 1994 by Harcourt Brace & Company. All rights reserved.

Word	Prefix and Its Meaning	Meaning of Word
8. exobiology	________________	________________
9. juxtapose	________________	________________
10. preternatural	________________	________________

EXERCISE 5: In the blanks write the correct spelling of the words formed by joining the original or assimilated prefixes and following elements. Notice the frequent doubling of consonants, which is sometimes brought about by assimilation.

1. ad filiate ________________
2. com late ________________
3. dis fident ________________
4. dis similar ________________
5. ex radicate ________________
6. in novate ________________
7. in religious ________________
8. ob casion ________________
9. ob clude ________________
10. sub cinct ________________

Copyright © 1994 by Harcourt Brace & Company. All rights reserved.

NAME ______________________ SECTION ________ DATE ________

CUMULATIVE TEST 1: All the italicized words in the following test appear in the preceding pages of this book. Some appear in the preliminary tests at the beginning, some in the chapters, some in the exercises. In the blank after each question print the number of the word or phrase corresponding most closely in meaning to the italicized word:

1. the master's *adroit* touch: 1 old and fumbling 2 strong and quick 3 dexterous and deft 1. ________
2. by *agamic* reproduction: without 1 sexual mating 2 expected development 3 danger 2. ________
3. *alluvial* soil: 1 very fertile 2 sandy and porous 3 washed down 3. ________
4. *ambidextrous* ability: 1 using both hands equally 2 living equally in water and on land 3 using both feet deftly 4. ________
5. an *amorphous* substance: 1 formless 2 rare and expensive 3 poisonous 5. ________
6. to *ameliorate* conditions: 1 investigate 2 worsen 3 improve 6. ________
7. *animosities* aroused by discussion: 1 enmities 2 answers 3 precautions 7. ________
8. *apothegms* about thrift: 1 problems 2 maxims 3 prejudice 8. ________
9. chief of his *bailiwick:* 1 household 2 dominated area 3 international company 9. ________
10. a *banal* observation: 1 cautious and shrewd 2 cutting and sarcastic 3 trite and trivial 10. ________
11. *benign* appearance: 1 kindly 2 eccentric 3 debilitated 11. ________
12. *bestial* actions: 1 secret 2 beastly 3 foolish 12. ________
13. a *bicameral* legislature: having 1 little power 2 two chambers 3 unruly sessions 13. ________
14. a *bucolic* scene: 1 rural and pleasing 2 dull and boring 3 agitated 14. ________
15. *buxom* woman: 1 beautiful 2 plump 3 well-dressed 15. ________
16. stopping by the *cairn:* 1 mountain spring 2 steep cliff 3 memorial stone pile 16. ________
17. to *cant* the container: 1 rotate and swirl 2 invert 3 tilt 17. ________
18. a new *carafe:* 1 water bottle 2 serving platter 3 knife chest 18. ________
19. fearful of *chimeras:* 1 imaginary monsters 2 poisonous snakes 3 hostile natives 19. ________
20. a *circumspect* attitude: 1 rash and sudden 2 disloyal 3 cautious and watchful 20. ________
21. a *clandestine* meeting: 1 accidental 2 secret and furtive 3 involving relatives 21. ________
22. to *coagulate* and settle: 1 thicken and clot 2 disintegrate 3 warm up 22. ________
23. *contiguous* properties: 1 expensive 2 uncertain as regards ownership 3 adjacent and touching 23. ________
24. an unsatisfactory *criterion:* 1 final decision 2 standard for judging 3 logical procedure 24. ________
25. a *debilitated* patient: 1 discouraged 2 weakened 3 hysterical 25. ________
26. his *decorous* manner: 1 rude and offensive 2 bashful and timid 3 correct and proper 26. ________
27. to *delve* for information: 1 dig 2 scan 3 request urgently 27. ________
28. *discrete* details: 1 private and confidential 2 separate and individual 3 minor but troublesome 28. ________
29. to *disseminate* the news: 1 suppress 2 explain and interpret 3 give out and circulate 29. ________
30. to *dole* out the clothing: 1 repair 2 pack 3 distribute 30. ________
31. a *dour* old man: 1 sick and feeble 2 gray and venerable 3 harsh and sullen 31. ________

Copyright © 1994 by Harcourt Brace & Company. All rights reserved.

32. dispelling her *dubiety:* 1 worry and fear 2 hesitation and doubt 3 tendency to brag 32. ________

33. an *ebullient* person: 1 mournful 2 enthusiastic 3 debilitated 33. ________

34. an *effigy* of the leader: 1 crude image 2 photograph 3 recorded voice 34. ________

35. the player's *elation:* 1 protest 2 joy 3 awkwardness 35. ________

36. an *encomium* for the chairperson: 1 expression of praise 2 disobedient answer 3 indifference 36. ________

37. *endemic* diseases: 1 hard to diagnose 2 peculiar to a region 3 slight but chronic 37. ________

38. to *eschew* liquor: 1 overindulge in 2 be sickened by 3 abstain from 38. ________

39. to *eulogize* the admiral: 1 criticize 2 extol 3 retire 39. ________

40. *euphonious* sound: 1 discordant 2 pleasant 3 inaudible 40. ________

41. a *facsimile:* 1 revision 2 abstract 3 exact copy 41. ________

42. an Indian *fakir:* 1 wandering magician 2 swindler 3 political separatist 42. ________

43. a social *faux pas:* 1 graceful gesture 2 kindly action 3 awkward blunder 43. ________

44. to *felicitate* the groom: 1 assist 2 congratulate and wish happiness to 3 snub and ignore 44. ________

45. to *furl* a flag: 1 display 2 lower 3 roll up 45. ________

46. a street *gamin:* 1 police officer 2 vendor 3 urchin 46. ________

47. a *garbled* story: 1 confused 2 prejudiced 3 terse 47. ________

48. a fearsome *ghoul:* 1 murderer 2 wraith 3 grave robber or molester 48. ________

49. a *glib* speaker: 1 fluent 2 suave or misleading 3 audible 49. ________

50. a *gossamer* cloth: 1 durable 2 light and filmy 3 fashionable and chic 50. ________

51. books on *hagiography:* 1 ancient life 2 religious doctrines 3 saints' lives 51. ________

52. a *hegira* westward: 1 flight or journey 2 direct route 3 severe storm 52. ________

53. a *hiatus* in the diary: 1 break or gap 2 scandalous account 3 contradiction 53. ________

54. an *intractable* minority: 1 powerless 2 foresighted 3 unruly and stubborn 54. ________

55. a *labile* component: 1 unnecessary 2 detrimental 3 constantly changing 55. ________

56. *leery* about newcomers: 1 too enthusiastic 2 cruel and barbarous 3 cautious and suspicious 56. ________

57. a medical *lexicon:* 1 film 2 dictionary 3 program 57. ________

58. to *litigate* the dispute: 1 contest legally 2 ignore 3 intensify and aggravate 58. ________

59. a *macabre* sight: 1 soothing and comforting 2 most unusual 3 frightening and gruesome 59. ________

60. performing *menial* actions: 1 mean and servile 2 treacherous 3 highly commendable 60. ________

61. to *mitigate* the situation: 1 soothe and alleviate 2 postpone action on 3 worry about 61. ________

62. to *mollify* the guard: 1 calm and appease 2 make fun of 3 escape from 62. ________

63. her *monitory* role: 1 warning and advising 2 prying and suspicious 3 lazy and inactive 63. ________

64. to reach a *nadir:* 1 conclusion 2 low point 3 apex 64. ________

65. a *numismatic* specialist: knowledgeable about 1 illnesses 2 coins or money 3 aviation 65. ________

Copyright © 1994 by Harcourt Brace & Company. All rights reserved.

NAME ____________________ SECTION ________ DATE ________

66. showing *obesity:* 1 laziness 2 anemia 3 fatness 66. ________

67. an *obsolescent* word: 1 very learned 2 indecent 3 going out of use 67. ________

68. a *penchant* for music: 1 dislike 2 aptitude and liking 3 critical taste 68. ________

69. consigned to *perdition:* 1 being forgotten 2 permanent exile 3 damnation 69. ________

70. the duke's *perfidy:* 1 dishonesty and treachery 2 hesitation 3 last-ditch defense 70. ________

71. a *penurious* relative: 1 eccentric 2 opulent 3 stingy 71. ________

72. to *presage:* 1 prevent and forestall 2 give out news of 3 foreshadow and warn of 72. ________

73. *primordial* instruments: 1 very early and primitive 2 expensive 3 carefully calibrated 73. ________

74. *reticent* behavior: 1 noisy and demonstrative 2 shy and quiet 3 odd and enigmatic 74. ________

75. a *salubrious* area: 1 impoverished 2 sparsely inhabited 3 healthful and bracing 75. ________

76. a *scintillating* conversation: 1 protracted and dull 2 sparkling and witty 3 serious 76. ________

77. a *scurrilous* story: 1 commonly believed 2 abusive and scandalous 3 mysterious 77. ________

78. a *sequestered* existence: 1 wild and exciting 2 secluded and lonely 3 poor and difficult 78. ________

79. a *snide* remark: 1 widespread 2 malicious 3 lugubrious 79. ________

80. the animal's *spoor:* 1 scent 2 track 3 pelt 80. ________

81. to *stultify* progress: 1 hasten 2 prevent 3 await 81. ________

82. a *succinct* answer: 1 brief and curt 2 evasive 3 lengthy and verbose 82. ________

83. a *surreptitious* approach: 1 secret and stealthy 2 rash and headlong 3 steady 83. ________

84. a *taciturn* person: 1 bold 2 insentient 3 silent and reserved 84. ________

85. a mountain *tarn:* 1 house 2 pool 3 zenith 85. ________

86. an article showing *tautology:* 1 moral conviction 2 needless repetition 3 wide information 86. ________

87. his *temerity* in advancing: 1 showy appearance 2 inspiring example 3 bold daring 87. ________

88. a massive *tome:* 1 file of records 2 recording machine 3 book 88. ________

89. ending her *travail:* 1 rest period 2 term in office 3 painful labor 89. ________

90. legendary *trolls:* 1 sea monsters 2 ghouls 3 cave dwarfs 90. ________

91. a *truculent* answer: 1 apologetic 2 mumbling and indistinct 3 harsh and belligerent 91. ________

92. *ubiquitous* summer visitors: 1 wealthy and prodigal 2 pretentious 3 present everywhere 92. ________

93. the *ultimatum* to Bukovinia: 1 plea for peace 2 diplomatic mission 3 final warning 93. ________

94. an *ungulate* animal: 1 graceful 2 rare 3 hooved 94. ________

95. *unkempt* appearance: 1 fastidious 2 untidy 3 colorful 95. ________

96. a pair of *virgules:* 1 slant bars 2 accent marks 3 superscripts 96. ________

97. to *vitiate* an argument: 1 invalidate 2 reinforce 3 try to answer 97. ________

98. the *wraith* in the castle: 1 old retainer 2 ghost 3 suit or armor 98. ________

99. a *wry* smile: 1 hearty and sincere 2 twisted and ironic 3 half-suppressed 99. ________

100. a *zany's* role: 1 hero's 2 lieutenant's 3 clown's 100. ________

Copyright © 1994 by Harcourt Brace & Company. All rights reserved.

I am biased in favour of boys learning English, and then I would let the clever ones learn Latin as an honour, and Greek as a treat.
Winston Churchill

4 Word Analysis: Greek Roots

In Chapter 3 the unanalyzable words *man, car,* and *goat,* along with many others, were called *root words.* A root—as the term is here used—is an element that cannot be analyzed further, a form from which nothing can be detached or split off. This definition is not complete, but we should discuss it before giving further details. As we said in Chapter 3, *man* is not made up from either *ma* or *an* as a base with something else added; *goat* is not a combination of *go* and *at. Bend* does not represent *b* plus *end,* nor does *cart* represent *c* plus *art;* that is, *man, car, goat, bend,* and *cart* are root words. To continue with our definition, a root is reasonably constant in form, although with some roots there is some variation. This may suggest difficulties. However, you probably have no problem feeling that *stand* has a variant form *stood,* no problem in feeling that these two words are closely related and even the same word underneath. You will have no trouble in feeling that *tooth* and *teeth* are variant forms of a common root. You will readily realize that *applaud* and *applause* are related, and you should be able to detach the assimilated prefix *ad-*. (After doing so you will have the forms *-plaud-* and *-plause-* and will recognize that these are linked together as common forms of the same root.) As this book presents words to you, variations in form should not cause you much trouble.

Words like *man* and *car* are called free roots—*free* because they occur as independent words, *roots* because they defy analysis and show constancy in form and meaning. A root may appear free in some uses, bound in others. *Gram* is an independent root word, but this same root is bound in *grammar, epigram, telegram, monogram, diagram,* and *cardiogram;* associated with it in all these words is the general idea of writing, of some kind or other. The form *micro* is a root in *omicron, microbe, microscope, micrometer,* and *microcosm;* incapable of analysis, it is constant in form and in meaning "small, smallness."

The definition in the preceding paragraph is incomplete, for it may be asked why forms like *com-, de-, anti-,* and *epi-,* called prefixes, are not also called roots, since they fulfill all the requirements of the definition. A root differs from a prefix in that it has a meaning felt to be more important and more specific than that of a prefix and it can stand at the beginning, middle, or end of a word—at least theoretically. However, the dividing line between prefix and root is impossible to draw exactly; the *-auto-* of *automobile, autograph, automaton, autobiography, autonomy,* and *autocrat* might be called either a prefix or a root. Any unanalyzable or indivisible form with a reasonably constant meaning—prefix, root, suffix, or other element—may be called a morpheme.

There is another way to suggest what roots are. Faced with a word beginning with a prefix, we may mentally detach that prefix. We could say that a root is an element that follows a prefix in a typical word. This may seem on the surface a weak or pointless comment, but perhaps it fits in with our mental processes when we encounter a word with a prefix. Occasionally, as the comments in Chapter 3 indicate, our first impressions may mislead us. If our word is like *discuss* or *regime* or *unitary,* we will have to discard our first impression and start again. Sometimes, as with the words *disheveled* or *insipid,* we will find that we cannot attach any particular significance to the latter part of the word, and we simply have to accept the whole expression as essentially a single morpheme. Our intuitions, however, would work very well with *unarmed, disarm,* and *rearm* (or *re-arm).* Most of us, on the other hand, would never dream of trying to analyze *farm* into *f* and *arm, charm* into *ch* and *arm, harm* into *h* and *arm,* or *warm* into *w* and *arm.*

Copyright © 1994 by Harcourt Brace & Company. All rights reserved.

When we analyze and interpret words—either by almost instantaneous intuition or by more deliberate thought—we will often find that knowing meanings associated with bound roots may lead us to good guesses about the meanings of those words. English has many words borrowed from Greek (see Chapter 2) or formed in English from familiar Greek bound roots. Most of these words entered the English language during the Renaissance or later. Many of these words using Greek elements employ the prefix-root pattern—*anagram, epilog* (or *epilogue), diameter, diatom, paradox,* and *syntax,* for instance. Analysis of these words into prefix and root will not always lead to an accurate meaning, but it will often do so. Meanings of common Greek prefixes were given in Chapter 3; meanings of common Greek roots will be given later in this chapter. The thought processes of interpreting words such as *catalog* and *diameter* is often identical to the practically instantaneous process of interpreting such words as *untrue, misspell,* and *overthrow.*

Interestingly, words borrowed from Greek or composed in English of bound Greek roots often illustrate the use of two roots compounded together. English has many words of this kind, such as *microcosm* and *holocaust.* These words may be analyzed and interpreted by the thought processes used in the interpretation of such English compounds as *bearskin* and *gunpowder.* We have little trouble in analyzing *bearskin* into "the skin of a bear." Sometimes words made up of Greek bound forms may be interpreted as quickly and as certainly. *Gunpowder* may well give us more trouble. We may not know at once what the function of the powder may be in connection with guns, or even whether we are to think of a powder formed by or on guns, a kind of rust perhaps. But we can certainly go ahead quickly with our first step in breaking *gunpowder* into *gun* and *powder.* At this point we are not 100 percent ignorant about the meaning of the word, although we have to know something about the operation of guns before we complete our interpretation. Sometimes we need some additional knowledge to see exactly what the existent word specifically means.

In any case, analysis of words composed of Greek bound forms can be both instructive and interesting. Analysis of *microcosm* into *-micro-,* meaning *"small,"* and *-cosm-,* meaning "world," points toward an understanding of the word, although it does not give the exact meaning of a small, restricted sphere, as in "interested only in the concerns of her own little microcosm." *Holocaust* splits into the roots *-holo-,* meaning "all," and *-caust-,* meaning "burn." This analysis leads to the notion that the word indicates a total destruction by fire; the word actually indicates a great fire, as in "more than forty lives were lost in the holocaust." *Knowing the meaning of the parts of this word gives one a more or less useful clue to its actual meaning, although it certainly does not always give the full meaning.*

Analysis of one Greek word may well start one on a whole chain of other Greek words. Colleges and high schools have sophomores. When we analyze the word *sophomore,* we find that the last part is the root *-mor-* or *-more-,* the root of the word *moron,* meaning "dull person, fool, simpleton." The first part is the root *-soph-,* meaning "wise, wisdom." (The *-o-* in the middle is a meaningless connective.) The root meaning of the word is thus "wise fool." The root *-soph-* is also found in the word *philosophy.* The *-phil-* part is a root indicating "friend, love, like, liking," and the roots together mean "love of knowledge." *-Phil-* also appears in *philanthropy,* in which the root *-anthrop-* means "man, mankind," and the roots can be read as "love of man, mankind." In today's English, *philanthropy* suggests benign attitudes and charitable actions toward one's fellow man, not just "love of mankind"; but analysis of the word into its root parts leads one in the right direction in attempting to find the meaning of the word. In *anthropology,* the *-anthrop-* again indicates "man, mankind," the *-o-* is a connective without meaning, and the *-log-* of the ending is a root meaning "writing about, study of." The whole word means "study of mankind." In *astrology* the root *-astr-* means "star," and the word originally meant "a writing about or account of the stars." *Astrology* came to be used to designate such unscientific procedures as reading fortunes by the stars; and today's scientists study *astronomy.* In this word the root *-nom-* means "law," and *astronomy* indicates "the laws of the stars."

This series may be continued: *autonomy* ("self-law, self-rule"); *autograph* ("self-written, one's own signature"); *orthography* ("correct writing, correct spelling"); *orthodox* ("[having] correct opinions"); *heterodox* ("[having] different or unusual opinions"); *heterogeneous* ("[of] different origins

Copyright © 1994 by Harcourt Brace & Company. All rights reserved.

or types"); *oxygen* (literally "acid originating or created"); and *oxymoron* (literally "sharp-dull, acid-dull or flat"), a technical literary term for the joining of opposites, as in "the burning iciness of frostbite." And we are now back to the root *-mor-,* which we had in our first word, *sophomore.*

We have seen that prefixes may vary somewhat in form. Roots may likewise vary; our previous definition mentioned only a "reasonable constancy" in form. Sometimes variation occurs in the vowels at the end of the root. In *sophomore* and *oxymoron* we have two slightly differing forms, *-more-* and *-moron-*. Sometimes the full form of the root appears, such as *-aster-* in *asteroid;* sometimes a shorter form is used, such as *-astr-* in *astronomy.* Such roots, however, can be recognized easily enough to make their study worthwhile.

Sometimes problems of interpretation arise in connection with homographic word parts; same spelling but different meaning, origin, and very often also pronunciation, as the following information illustrates. The Greek root *-more-* or *-mor-* has of course nothing to do with the *more* of such expressions as "more intelligent, more active, more wealthy"; the latter *more* is a totally separate morpheme, from Old English rather than from Greek. Nor does the Greek root *-mor-* figure in the words *morning* (from Old English), *morass* (from French), or *moral* (from Latin). In this connection it is important to notice that roots in the following list express the meanings given for them when they appear as bound forms rather than free forms. To start explaining this matter with an extreme and even ridiculous illustration, you will certainly feel that the root *-the-,* given below as meaning "god, deity," has nothing whatever to do with the common English determiner *the* (as in "the man" or "the car"). Your feeling for eventual origins of words may be weak and undeveloped, but you are unlikely to experience any confusion between *-the-* as a Greek root and *the* as a native English determiner. Often the meanings of free forms and of Greek bound forms differ widely. The form *-pan-,* the element in *panorama* or *Pan-American,* has no connection with the common English word *pan,* meaning "cooking utensil." The *-hem-* of *hemorrhage* has no connection or relationship with the sewing term *hem,* and the *-log-* of *catalog* and *theology* and *logarithm* has nothing to do with *log,* meaning a fallen or cut tree trunk. Sometimes there is some relationship between the meaning of the free form and the bound form. We have a flower called the *aster.* One can be etymological and trace this word back to the Greek word for star and interpret *aster* as "star flower," but the process is a bit cumbersome and for most of us there is no apparent reason why other flowers could not also be so named. Sometimes there is a fairly close connection in meaning between the free form and the bound form. The free form *crypt* and the bound form in the word *cryptic* do not equate exactly in meaning, but with both there is an underlying sense of something concealed or hidden below the surface. Why do situations like the lack of connection between *log* and *-log-* and the not immediately apparent connection between *aster* and *-aster-* take place? Because different languages and their words develop differently. What can be done about this potentially confusing situation? A direct answer is difficult. You can in time do as other persons have done and build a sort of feeling or intuition for such matters. You can start by noting that words employing the Greek bound forms *-pan-, -log-,* and *-the-* are a bit learned and bookish but that such formations of the free forms as *panhandle, frying pan, logger,* and *logging* are rather simple. You may notice that the bound forms *-log-* and *-path-* are likely to be used with Greek prefixes *(apology, epilog, empathy, sympathize)* but that the free forms *log* and *path* do not go with these elements. *Cata-* may mean "down," but we do not have a form *to catalog,* which means "to cut down trees." *A-* may mean "not, without," but *apathy* is not the word that we use to describe an unexplored, pathless area. Very probably nobody ever develops perfect intuition about such matters, but some are able to develop it to a satisfactory or effective point. Meanwhile notice that a feeling for origins of word parts and a feeling for their meanings often go hand in hand.

Following is a list of common roots of Greek origin. Usually the forms are given as simply as possible, without regard to connective letters. Often a word composed of two or even more Greek roots employs such connective symbols as *-o-*. The fact that a noun, for instance, is given as an illustration of a particular Greek word should not be taken as an indication that the root in question can form only nouns. Any sort of root may be found in English in a noun, verb, or adjective. Memorize as many roots in the following list as you can. Simply scanning the list once or twice carelessly will probably just confuse you. Study the illustrations, noting how the root fits into the word, and notice accompanying elements such as prefixes and other roots.

Copyright © 1994 by Harcourt Brace & Company. All rights reserved.

Root	*Meaning*	*Examples*
-agog-	lead, leader	demagogue, pedagog, synagogue

Not related to English *agog* meaning "eager." Occurs more frequently at the ends of English words than at the beginnings. Spelling may be *-agog-* or *-agogue-*. See dictionary for physiological meaning sometimes attached to this form. Sometimes derogatory.

-anthrop-	man, mankind, human being	philanthropy, anthropology, misanthrope

Reasonably constant in form and meaning. The root *-andr-* is usually used rather than *-anthrop-* to indicate "man" in contradistinction to "woman."

-arch-	first, ancient, chief	archaic, monarch, archaelogy

Not used in such words as *arch* and *archery.* Not useful in an analysis of the meaning of *archipelago* or *archive.*

-aster-, -astr-	star	astrobiology, astral, astrology, asterisk, aster

Not used in such words as *astringent* or *astrakhan.*

-auto-	self	automaton, autonomy, autocratic

Usually appears in first part of word rather than second. Not very useful in interpretation of meaning of such words as *autopsy.* Sometimes appears simply as shortening of *automobile* in some twentieth-century words. Reasonably constant in meaning and form.

-bibli-	book	bibliomania, bibliophile, bibliotheca, Bible, bibliophobe, bibliopole

Constant in meaning and form.

-bi-, -bio-	life	amphibious, biology, biography

Usually appears in first part of word. Reasonably constant in meaning and form. Present in most words beginning with *bio-*.

-chrom-	color	chromatic, chromosome, monochrome

Not very useful in interpreting the meaning of *chrome, chromium,* and so on.

-chron-	time	chronometer, synchronize, anachronism

Reasonably constant in meaning and form, although not very useful in interpretation of *chronic.*

-cosm-	order, world	cosmology, cosmic, microcosm

See dictionary for more detailed explanation of meaning. Not very useful in interpreting words such as *cosmetic.*

Copyright © 1994 by Harcourt Brace & Company. All rights reserved.

Root	***Meaning***	***Examples***
-crac-, -crat-	power, rule, govern	democracy, autocracy, democrat

Not present in *crate* or *crater*. Usually used in latter parts of English words rather than in first parts. Meaning and form reasonably constant.

-cryo- -crypt-	freezing, frost secret, hidden	cryogenics, cryometer, cryolite, cryoscope cryptic, cryptogram, cryptogenic

Reasonably constant in meaning and form.

-cycl-	circle, wheel	bicycle, cyclic, cyclone

Reasonably constant in meaning and form, but not very useful in interpreting such words as *cyclopean* and *encyclical.*

-dem-	people	democracy, demotic, epidemic, endemic

Do not confuse with prefixes *demi-,* as in *demigod,* and the quite common *de-,* as in *demand, demarcate, demean, demented, demerit, demesne, demise, demolish,* and *demonstrate.* Not present in *demon.* Otherwise reasonably constant in meaning and form.

-derm-	skin	epidermis, hypodermic, dermatology, dermatitis

Constant in form and meaning.

-dox-	belief, teaching	orthodox, doxology, heterodox

Reasonably constant in form and meaning.

-dyn-	strength, power	heterodyne, dynamic, dynasty

Constant in form and meaning.

-erg-	work, power	erg, energy, energetic

Not present in *ergo, ergot,* and so on. A by-form is used in *metallurgy;* the *-rg-* part appears in *George* or *geo-erge;* "earth worker."

-gam-	marry, mate, sexual union	gamete, monogamous, bigamy

Not present in *gambit, gamble, gambol, gambrel, gamin, gamma, gamut,* and so on. Otherwise reasonably constant in meaning and form.

-gen-	kind, race, source	genetics, genesis, genealogy, eugenics, genes

Identical in form to a Latin root with much the same meaning. It does not make any difference in interpretation here whether you discern between the Latin root and the Greek form. It is impossible to list here those words in which the

Copyright © 1994 by Harcourt Brace & Company. All rights reserved.

Root	*Meaning*	*Examples*

Greek, but not the Latin, root appears. Aside from *genet, geneva,* and *genie,* one or the other appears in practically every word beginning with *gen-*. This information is not very useful in the interpretation of *generous* or *genial* and some others.

-geo-	earth	geography, geodetic, geometry

Constant in meaning and form.

-gon-	corner, angle	trigonometry, polygon, goniometer

More likely to appear in the second part of an English word than the first. May be confused with another Greek root, *-gon-,* which means "sexual, generative," as in *gonorrhea* or *gonad.* Neither root appears in *gondola* or *gonfalon.*

-gram-	write, writing	grammar, telegram, epigram

Likely to appear in second parts of English word. Relatively constant in meaning and form. Not present in *gramercy* or *grampus.*

-graph-	write, writing	graphite, orthography, geography

Likely to appear in second parts of English words. Constant in meaning and form.

-gyn-	woman, female	gynecology, misogynist, androgynous

Constant in meaning and form.

-hem-	blood	hemorrhage, hemoglobin, hemophilia

Has such additional forms as *-haem-, -hemat-,* and *-haemat-.* Meaning constant. Do not confuse with the prefix *hemi-,* as in *hemisphere.* Not present in a few other English words beginning with *hem-,* for instance, *hemlock.* Likely to appear in the first part of an English word.

-hetero-	other, different	heterodox, heterogeneous, heterosexual

Usually found in the first parts of English words. Form and meaning constant.

-homo-	same	homogeneous, homonym, homograph

Usually found in the first parts of English words. Most words beginning with *homo-* contain this root, which is reasonably constant in meaning. There is another Greek root written *-home-, -homeo-,* or *-homoi-,* meaning "similar but not the same," which may easily be confused with this root, but fortunately *-home-* and its variants appear in just a few quite learned words.

-hydr-	water	dehydrate, hydrogen, anhydrous

Everything beginning with *hydr-* contains this root. It is fairly constant in meaning, although in some recent words it indicates "hydrogen" rather than just "water."

Copyright © 1994 by Harcourt Brace & Company. All rights reserved.

Root	*Meaning*	*Examples*
-iatr-	heal, cure	iatric, geriatrics, psychiatry

Usually appears in second parts of English words. Reasonably constant in form and meaning.

-iso-	same, equal	isobar, isotherm, isotope

See dictionary for explanation of additional meanings. Does not appear in *isolate.* Usually constant in meaning. Almost always present in words beginning with *iso-*.

-lith-	rock, stone	monolithic, Neolithic, lithophyte

A variant form, *-lite-,* is sometimes used. Sometimes, as with *lithium* and *lithography,* this is not very useful in interpretation. Not connected with *lithe.*

-log-	speech, word, study, reason	epilogue, logarithm, theology

Quite commonly used; notice the wealth of *-ology* words. Lack of connection between this Greek root and English words such as *logjam* has been explained earlier.

-mega-	large, enlargement	megaphone, megacephalic, megathere

There are variant forms, *-megal-* and *-megalo-.* Otherwise constant in form and meaning.

-metr-, -meter-	measure	diameter, metronome, trigonometry

Greek had another root, *-metr-,* meaning "mother," as in *metropolis* and various medical terms, which may be confused with this. Otherwise constant in meaning.

-micr-	small	microform, microscope, micrometer, microbe

See dictionary for a fuller explanation of meaning. Constant in form and meaning. Present in every word beginning with *micr-*.

-mono-, -mon-	one, single	monogamy, monotonous, monologue

Present in every English word beginning with *mono-*. Constant in form and meaning. More likely to appear in first parts of English words than in second parts. The form *-mon-* is an occasional variant, as in *monarch.* The form *-mon-* does not appear in *monadnock, Monday, money, mongolian, mongrel,* and various other words.

-morph-	form	morphology, amorphous, allomorph, morphic

Reasonably constant in form and meaning.

-necr-	dead, die	necropolis, necrology, necrotic, necromancy

Reasonably constant in form and meaning. More likely to appear in first parts of English words than in later parts.

Copyright © 1994 by Harcourt Brace & Company. All rights reserved.

Root	*Meaning*	*Examples*
-neo-	new, recent	neomorph, neologism, neophyte

See dictionary for fuller explanation of meaning. Reasonably constant in form and meaning. Appears in every English word beginning with *neo-*. A by-form, *ne-*, the original root without the connective *-o-*, does occur but is quite infrequent.

-nom-	law, rule	autonomy, economy, metronome

More likely to occur in second parts of English words than in first. Not in *nomad*. Closely associated with a Latin form, *-nomin-* or *-nomen-*, meaning "name."

-onym-	name, word	anonymous, pseudonym, synonym, homonym

More likely to occur in English words after a prefix or another root than initially. Reasonably constant in form and meaning.

-orth-	straight, correct	orthodox, orthography, orthodontist

Likely to appear initially in English words. Reasonably constant in meaning and form.

-pan-	all, entire	panorama, pandemonium, pantheon, pandemic

See dictionary for fuller statement of meaning. Usually occurs in first rather than later parts of English words. Constant in form and meaning, although not very useful in interpreting such words as *pancreas* and *panegyric*. Does not appear in a number of words beginning with *pan-*, such as *panatela, pander, panel,* and *panic*.

-path-	feeling, disease, sufferer	psychopath, apathy, sympathy, pathology

Reasonably constant in form and meaning.

-ped-	child, boy	orthopedic, pediatrician, pedagogue

May be confused with a Latin root *-ped-*, meaning "foot," as in *pedal* and *pedestrian*, and a second (fortunately uncommon) Latin root beginning with *-pedic-*, meaning "louse." Greek *-ped-* appears in less than half the English words beginning with *ped-*.

-phil-	like, love	philanthropic, bibliophile, philology, philosophy

See dictionary for fuller statement of meaning. Does not appear in *philately, philippic, Philistine,* and so on. Reasonably constant in meaning and form.

-phon-	sound	phonics, phonetics, telephone, euphony

Appears in every English word beginning with *phon-* (except *phoney*). Constant in meaning and form.

Copyright © 1994 by Harcourt Brace & Company. All rights reserved.

Root	*Meaning*	*Examples*
-phor-	bearing, carrying, having	semaphore, phosphorus, gonophore

Appears in English words in later rather than initial positions. Reasonably constant in meaning and form.

-phos-, -phot-	light	phosphorescent, photograph, photostat

Appears in every English word beginning *phos-* or *phot-*. Not very useful in interpreting words such as *phosphate.* Constant in meaning and form.

-pod-	foot	tripod, podiatrics, podium

The equivalent Latin root with the same meaning is *-ped-*. Reasonably constant in meaning and form.

-poly-	many	polygon, polygamy, polytheistic

See dictionary for fuller statement of meaning. Constant in meaning and form, although not very useful in interpreting such words as *polyp.* Much more likely to stand initially in an English word than elsewhere. Every English word starting with *poly-* contains this root.

-psych-	mind	psychiatry, psychology, psychic

See dictionary for fuller statement of meaning. More likely to occur initially than elsewhere. Constant in form and meaning.

-pyr-	fire	pyrophobia, pyrotechnic, pyre, pyromania

Present in every English word beginning with *pyro-*. Not present in a number of words beginning with *pyr-,* such as *pyramid* and *pyrrhic.*

-scop-	watch, look at	microscope, telescope, horoscope

Usually found in later rather than initial positions in English words. Reasonably constant in meaning and form.

-soph-	wise, wisdom	sophomore, philosopher, theosophy

Reasonably constant in form and meaning. Usually found in later rather than initial positions in English words.

-tax-, -tact-	arrange, arrangement	taxidermy, tactics, syntax

The identical Latin root *-tact-,* meaning "touch," appears in such words as *contact* and *tactile.*

-techn-	art, craft, technique	polytechnical, technical, technician

Reasonably constant in form and meaning.

Copyright © 1994 by Harcourt Brace & Company. All rights reserved.

Root	*Meaning*	*Examples*
-tele-	far, distant	television, telegram, telephone, telepathy

There is a less common Greek root, *-tel-* or *-telo-,* but confusion of this with *-tele-* is unlikely. Usually found in initial rather than later positions in English words. Constant in form and meaning.

-theo-	god	theist, thearchy, atheist, theology

Occurs in almost every English word beginning with *theo-* and in some others such as *theist.* Reasonably constant in meaning and form.

-therm-	heat	thermophilic, thermal, thermometer, isothermal, thermograph

Constant in form and meaning.

-tom-	cut, split	atom, appendectomy, computed tomography (CT scan)

Does not appear in the words *tomahawk, tomato, tom-tom,* and so on. Common in many words indicating surgical operations.

-zo-	life, animal	zoography, zoology, zoophile, zoomorphism

Present in every word spelled with *zoo-* and in most with *zo-,* although not very useful in interpreting such words as *zodiac.*

Some Greek roots, or combining forms, are important in English because they appear in common English words. The root *-auto-* is important because it figures in such common words as *automobile, automatic,* and *autograph,* as well as in more learned terms such as *autogenesis, autolysis,* and *autoplasty.* But sometimes a root acquires importance as a combining form because it is used in a great many words, although few of them are in the common vocabulary. Thus, the root *-heli-,* meaning "sun," appears in few common words, but it is used in many scientific coinages: *heliacal, heliocentric, heliochrome, heliograph, heliogram, helioscope, heliotaxis,* and *heliotropic.* The root *-pter-,* meaning "wing," likewise appears in no very common English word, but it is used throughout the biologist's classification of insects: *hemiptera, diptera, orthoptera,* and so on, as well as in *pterodactyl,* the batlike reptile of prehistoric times. Learning the meanings of frequently used combining forms is an invaluable preliminary step in the study of any science. Dictionaries commonly have entries for important combining forms; note entries in your dictionary for *micro-, megalo-,* and *masto-*. As etymologies will indicate, a Greek root or combining form often passes through Latin into English rather than being borrowed directly from Greek into English. This situation rarely causes any difficulty.

To what extent will your dictionary give you information about Greek roots, and what do you need to be told at this point in order to acquire that information? Your dictionary will give you rather full information, but its procedures in giving it may vary from word to word. Sometimes the etymology of the word will give you all the information. But sometimes there may be a separate entry for one of the roots. If you look up *orthodox* in your dictionary, you may find an indication that *-dox-* means "teaching, opinion, belief," but you may find no explanation for *-orth-*. You may instead simply find a cross-reference to a separate entry for *-orth-* or *-ortho-*. In that separate entry you may be told that *-orth-*

Copyright © 1994 by Harcourt Brace & Company. All rights reserved.

means "straight, correct," among other things. Sometimes you may find that the etymology for a word is very brief—that, for instance, it simply says *NL* or *ISV* (meaning New Latin or International Science Vocabulary). Thus for *otitis* you may simply find "NL" as the complete etymology. This means that you are expected to divide the word *otitis* into *-ot-* and *-itis* and look up entries for these two elements. Sometimes, perhaps at *pneumotropic,* you will find no etymology at all—not even "NL" or "ISV." This means that the etymologist expects you to be able to find the entries for the two parts of the word by yourself. Procedures for individual entries may vary widely within any given dictionary, and procedures used in different dictionaries are almost certain to vary. Many dictionaries do not use the word *root* in labeling such elements as *-dino-* or *-deino-*, *-saur-*, *-orth-*, and *-dox-*. (Actually *root* as used in this book is not an exact term; it is used here rather than any other term because many teachers and students are familiar with it.) Instead of *root* your dictionary may use the term *combining form,* which has the advantage of suggesting that the elements being discussed are often combined or compounded with others. It is probable that the introduction to your dictionary will give you a good definition of *combining form.*

You need to know another detail about the dictionary treatment of Greek roots (and of Latin roots too). This concerns a difference between English words and Greek and Latin words as they were actually used. Much of the time in English we use only the simplest, or base, form of a word, and it is easy for us to feel that this *is* the word. Faced with the word *dog,* we feel that this *is* the word and that *dog's, dogs, and dogs'* are just grammatical forms of the base word. Perhaps we use *dog* more frequently than all the other forms put together. And *turn,* we feel, is the base word, and *turns, turning,* and *turned* are just grammatical forms of this base word. Perhaps we use the base form *turn* more frequently than we do *turns, turning,* and *turned.* In English it is usually easy for us to isolate the simple base form. But in Greek and Latin the base or root form was much less commonly used than forms with something added to that base; some bases were never used by themselves. The equivalents for such forms as *dog's, dogs, dogs'* and *turns, turning, turned* were much more common than simple bases or their equivalents. Faced with this situation, the dictionary etymologist is likely to give a nominative singular form for a noun or adjective and a present infinitive or past participle form for a verb, but any of these forms would be likely to have an additional grammatical syllable at the end. The etymologist does this because the bare root might well be either uncommon or even nonexistent in itself in Latin or Greek. In the etymology of *demagogue,* then, you may find your dictionary mentioning *dēmos* ("people"), and *agōgos* ("leading") from *agein* ("to lead"). At this point the etymologist is not telling you that the *roots* are *dēmos* and *agōgos,* but is simply giving the Greek grammatical forms that employ as bases the shorter roots. If *dēmos* and *agōgos* were the roots, the English word would be *demosagogos.* In the etymology for *crypt* you may find the Greek words *kryptē, kryptos,* and *kryptein.* It is up to you to abstract from these words the base or root *krypt* or *crypt* (the change from *k* to *c* means nothing). *Dēmos, agōgos, agein* and *kryptē, kryptos, kryptein* are related to the bases or roots *-dem-*, *-agog-*, and *-crypt-* as *dog's, dogs, dogs'* and *turns, turning, turned* are to *dog* and *turn.* In studying this book, doing the exercises in it, and considering and interpreting English words in the future, be sure to find the root.

Copyright © 1994 by Harcourt Brace & Company. All rights reserved.

NAME ______________________________ SECTION ________ DATE ________

CHAPTER 4

EXERCISE 1: Write in each blank the number of the word or phrase closest in meaning to the italicized word. If you simply look up the meanings of the words in your dictionary, you will probably be able to give the right answers. You will learn and retain more, however, if you use the list of roots in this chapter and try to analyze the present English words into their parts. The objective of the exercise is not to introduce you to these words in themselves but to give you practice in using the roots.

1. *agamic* reproduction: 1 rapid 2 without mating 3 prolific 4 occasional — 1. ________
2. an *amorphous* mass: 1 disgusting 2 shapeless 3 heavy 4 congealed — 2. ________
3. *anthropomorphic* gods: 1 unusual 2 romantic 3 false 4 human-shaped — 3. ________
4. *antipathy* for the group: 1 dislike 2 loyalty 3 fondness 4 regret — 4. ________
5. *archetype* of modern rifle: 1 early model 2 invention 3 necessity 4 ammunition — 5. ________
6. *archon* of Athens: 1 building 2 history 3 soldier 4 ruler — 6. ________
7. *asteroids:* 1 plants 2 starlike bodies 3 high altitudes 4 wind currents — 7. ________
8. *autonomy* in the country: 1 self-rule 2 no law 3 aid 4 peace — 8. ________
9. a *cryptographer:* 1 mapmaker 2 code analyst 3 strategist 4 clerk — 9. ________
10. mild *dermatitis:* 1 allergy 2 insomnia 3 cramp 4 skin ailment — 10. ________
11. *euphony* of the poem: 1 theme 2 style 3 setting 4 pleasing sound — 11. ________
12. *genealogy* of the family: 1 religion 2 family history 3 economics 4 loyalty — 12. ________
13. *heterodox* ideas: 1 earnest 2 pious 3 unorthodox 4 conventional — 13. ________
14. these words are *homophones:* having 1 same use 2 same meaning 3 same sound 4 same origin — 14. ________
15. a *monochromatic* effect: 1 single color 2 dull 3 clear 4 cloudy — 15. ________
16. *Neolithic* Age: 1 medieval 2 ancient 3 new stone 4 modern — 16. ________
17. a *polyphonic* effect: an effect of 1 strength 2 many colors 3 many sounds 4 a montage — 17. ________
18. *psychopaths:* 1 madmen 2 wanderers 3 exiles 4 criminals — 18. ________
19. a victim of *pyromania:* mania of 1 hunger 2 love 3 money 4 fire — 19. ________
20. *sophisticates*: 1 urbanites 2 actors 3 travelers 4 worldly wise people — 20. ________

EXERCISE 2: Each italicized word in the following phrases contains a Greek root explained in this chapter and a Greek root that may be new to you. Find the meaning of the new root and write it in the space provided. Sometimes you will find this new root explained in the etymology of the word, sometimes in a nearby related word, and sometimes in its own entry as a combining form. Be sure to find the meaning of the new root, not the word containing it.

1. *acronymic* words	acr: ____________	onym: name
2. an *androgynous* plant	andr: ____________	gyn: female
3. *autochthonous* plants	auto: self	chthon: ____________
4. intolerable *cacophony*	caco: ____________	phon: sound
5. a *cytology* text	cyt: ____________	log: study
6. medieval *hagiographers*	hagi: ____________	graphy: write

Copyright © 1994 by Harcourt Brace & Company. All rights reserved.

7. *heliotropic* flowers	heli: sun	trop: ____________
8. a church *hierarchy*	hier: ____________	arch: rule
9. *megatheres*	mega: large	there: ____________
10. a serious *neoplasia*	neo: new	plasi: ____________
11. a *nephritis* case	nephr: ____________	itis: disease
12. *odometer* on a car	odo: ____________	meter: measure
13. *pentameter* verse	penta: ____________	meter: measure
14. *phyllopod* order	phyll: ____________	pod: foot
15. a *polydactylous* animal	poly: many	dactyl: ____________
16. *polyglot* section	poly: many	glot: ____________
17. *seismographic* measure	seism: ____________	graph: write
18. a *tautological* style	taut: ____________	log: write
19. ancient *thaumaturgy*	thaum: ____________	urg: work
20. *theophany*	the: god	phan: ____________

EXERCISE 3: The following pairs of words contain the same Greek root. Isolate the root and write its general meaning in the blank provided. You may find the meaning for the root in the etymology of one or both words; you may find it in the etymology of nearby words, or you may find that it is entered as a combining form by itself.

Remember, you are to write the roots as they appear in the words below; you are not to write the full grammatical forms of Greek words, but you are to *omit grammatical endings.* Remember also to give the meaning of the root, not of the whole word.

	Root	Meaning
1. agnosticism–gnostic	____________	____________
2. aphagia–esophagus	____________	____________
3. carcinogen–carcinoma	____________	____________
4. claustrophobia–agoraphobia	____________	____________
5. epigastrium–gastritis	____________	____________
6. epiphany–diaphanous	____________	____________
7. epode–prosody	____________	____________
8. gonad–archegonium	____________	____________
9. mastoid–mastectomy	____________	____________
10. megathere–theriomorphic	____________	____________
11. narcotism–narcosis	____________	____________
12. necromancy–chiromancy	____________	____________
13. neuralgia–neurology	____________	____________

Copyright © 1994 by Harcourt Brace & Company. All rights reserved.

	Root	Meaning
14. neuritis–otitis	________	________
15. osteotomy–tomography	________	________
16. otitis–otoscope	________	________
17. pyorrhea–empyema	________	________
18. rhododendron–dendrology	________	________
19. sarcasm–sarcoma	________	________
20. toxicology–toxicosis	________	________

EXERCISE 4: The following pairs of words contain the same Greek root. Isolate the root and write its general meaning in the blank provided. You may find the meaning for the root in the etymology of one or both words; you may find it in the etymology of nearby words. Or you may find that it is entered as a combining form by itself. Remember that you are to write the roots as they appear in the words below; you are not to write the full grammatical forms of Greek words, but you are to omit grammatical endings. Remember also to give the meaning of the root, not of the whole word.

	Root	Meaning
1. androgenous–androgynous	________	________
2. anthrax–anthracite	________	________
3. autopsy–optical	________	________
4. bathyal–bathysphere	________	________
5. bibliopole–bibliotheca	________	________
6. cardiac–cardiomyopathy	________	________
7. catalepsy–epilepsy	________	________
8. chiropractor–chiropodist	________	________
9. chrysanthemum–anthology	________	________
10. cosmos–cosmonaut	________	________
11. cryogenics–cryometer	________	________
12. ethnic–ethnographer	________	________
13. euthanasia–thanatos	________	________
14. exophthalmic–ophthalmic	________	________
15. gynarchy–gynecology	________	________

Copyright © 1994 by Harcourt Brace & Company. All rights reserved.

	Root	Meaning
16. hemiplegia–paraplegia		
17. hemodialysis–hemotoma		
18. hieroglyph–hierophant		
19. hydrocephalous–hydrophobia		
20. hydrotherapy–chemotherapy		
21. iconography–iconoclast		
22. idiomorphic–idiosyncrasy		
23. mesentery–enteron		
24. neologism–neonate		
25. nephroscope–stethoscope		
26. neuroblast–neurocyte		
27. octopus–platypus		
28. pandemic–panorama		
29. pathos–pathology		
30. pepsin–dyspeptic		
31. phagocyte–leukocyte		
32. philander–philanthropist		
33. pterodactyl–dipterous		
34. pyrogen–pyrophobia		
35. rheumatology–rheumatism		
36. rhinitis–rhinoceros		
37. strophe–apostrophe		
38. thermostable–thermotherapy		
39. thyroid–thyroidectomy		
40. xylography–xylophone		

Copyright © 1994 by Harcourt Brace & Company. All rights reserved.

NAME ______________________ SECTION ________ DATE ________

EXERCISE 5: SUPPLEMENTAL EXERCISE The following words have been selected from Exercises 3 and 4. This exercise gives you an opportunity to define the complete word, not merely the root and its meaning, as was done in those exercises. In the blank provided write a brief definition of the word in correct sentence form.

1. (a) androgenous: ______________________

   (b) androgynous: ______________________

2. (a) anthrax: ______________________

   (b) anthracite: ______________________

3. (a) aphagia: ______________________

   (b) esophagus: ______________________

4. (a) bibliopole: ______________________

   (b) bibliotheca: ______________________

5. (a) carcinogen: ______________________

   (b) carcinoma: ______________________

6. (a) cardiac: ______________________

   (b) cardiomyopathy: ______________________

7. (a) chrysanthemum: ______________________

   (b) anthology: ______________________

8. (a) claustrophobia: ______________________

   (b) agoraphobia: ______________________

9. (a) hemodialysis: ______________________

Copyright © 1994 by Harcourt Brace & Company. All rights reserved.

(b) hemotoma: ____________________

10. (a) hydrotherapy: ____________________

(b) chemotherapy: ____________________

11. (a) mastoid: ____________________

(b) mastectomy: ____________________

12. (a) megathere: ____________________

(b) theriomorphic: ____________________

13. (a) neologism: ____________________

(b) neonate: ____________________

14. (a) neuralgia: ____________________

(b) neurology: ____________________

15. (a) osteotomy: ____________________

(b) tomography: ____________________

16. (a) otitis: ____________________

(b) otoscope: ____________________

17. (a) pathos: ____________________

(b) pathology: ____________________

18. (a) pyorrhea: ____________________

Copyright © 1994 by Harcourt Brace & Company. All rights reserved.

NAME ______________________ SECTION ________ DATE ________

(b) empyema: ______________________

____

19. (a) thyroid: ______________________

____

(b) thyroidectomy: ______________________

____

20. (a) xylography: ______________________

____

(b) xylophone: ______________________

____

Copyright © 1994 by Harcourt Brace & Company. All rights reserved.

The truth is that most words are more than the sum of their parts.
Lee C. Deighton

5 Word Analysis: Latin Roots I

Although it is impossible to make statistically accurate statements about the etymologies of various groups of English words, we can say that about three-fifths or two-thirds of our words come directly or indirectly and ultimately from Latin. It naturally follows that English contains a great many words showing Latin roots. Some Latin roots appear in large numbers of English words. The root *-ced-,* with its by-forms *-ceed-* and *-cess-,* meaning "to give, give way, let go, go," appears in more than seventy common English words—*cede, accede, concede, exceed, secede, proceed, succeed, access, accession, process, procession, success,* and *succession,* for instance. Other roots occur in only one or two words in English. Thus *-truc-,* meaning "fierce," occurs only in *truculent* and *truculence* and their derivatives; *-ruct-,* meaning "belch," occurs only in *eruct* and *eructation;* and *-met-,* meaning "fear," only in *meticulous* and *meticulosity* and their derivatives. This chapter is concerned only with common Latin roots. The following chapter treats roots that are also important but appear less frequently. It is always difficult to be precise about arranging word elements in order of frequency or importance; the division in these two chapters cannot pretend to scientific statistical accuracy.

Latin roots lend themselves to the same sort of word analysis as Greek roots. We saw that the Greek word *holocaust* broke into the elements *-holo-* and *-caust-* and that the word meant "a great fire, a major conflagration." The Latin word *genuflect* similarly breaks into the elements *-genu-,* meaning "knee," and *-flect-,* meaning "to bend"; the whole word means "to bend the knee, to kneel."

The Greek word *sophomore* breaks into *-soph-,* meaning "wise" and *-more-,* meaning "fool." The Latin word *aqueduct* similarly analyzes into the roots *-aque-,* meaning "water," and *-duct-,* meaning "to lead, a leading," and the word means "that which conducts or leads water; a conduit, channel, or similar structure." The Latin word *crucifer* breaks into *cruci-,* meaning "cross," and *-fer-,* meaning "to bear, a bearer": the whole word means "cross bearer," as in various religious processions and ceremonies.

Sometimes Latin and Greek roots show similarities. Thus from Greek comes the combining form *-odont-,* meaning "tooth," as in our word *orthodontist.* And from Latin comes the combining form *-dent-,* likewise meaning "tooth," as in our word *dentistry.* Greek *-pod-,* illustrated in the English word *podiatrist,* and Latin *-ped-,* illustrated in the English words *pedal, velocipede,* and *quadruped,* both mean "foot." Sometimes roots from both languages are identical, and for practical purposes little differentiation between such roots is needed. For instance, in *petrography,* "the study of rocks and stones, a form of geology," the root *-petr-* is used with the Greek combining form *-graph-;* in *petrify,* "to turn to stone," it appears with the Latin element *-fy.* Occasionally such situations may cause trouble. Greek *-dendr-,* as in *dendrology,* may remind you of the Latin root *-dent-,* and you might guess that dendrology has something to do with teeth. But the Greek root *-dendr-* means "tree," and dendrology is the study of trees. Perhaps the most noticeable of these possible confusions comes about through the fact that although Greek *-pod-* and Latin *-ped-* mean "foot," Greek *-ped-* means "child," and a *pediatrician* is a doctor taking care of children rather than feet. Most of the time, however, there are few situations involving possible confusions about Greek and Latin elements in words of any frequency in our language.

As Chapter 2 has indicated, we started to borrow Latin elements early in the cultural history of our language. Many of the Latin words that came into English before the Norman Conquest, such as *wall* and *street* in very early times and *fever* and *monk* during the Anglo-Saxon period, have been so

Copyright © 1994 by Harcourt Brace & Company. All rights reserved.

thoroughly assimilated into English that we go back to original Latin forms in our later, more bookish vocabulary. Most of us do not bother to perceive the etymological relationship between *wall* and *circumvallation, street* and *stratification, fever* and *febrile,* and *monk* and *monastic.* To an astonishing degree Latin words have been added to English in all periods, and later periods all show addition of both Latin words and Latin bound roots to the English word stock. Later Middle English and the early New or Modern English of the Renaissance seem especially rich in the number of such additions. In general, the processes used in the formation of English words with Latin elements and those used in formations with Greek elements do not differ greatly, although perhaps Greek gives us more illustrations of words made up of two bound roots compounded, such as *pachyderm* or *thermometer* or *acronymic.*

Latin roots show various changes in form. One kind of variation came about in early Latin through the operation of assimilation of the past-participle forms of verbs. In many verbs a *d* or *t* in the present tense was changed to *s* or *ss* because of other dental sounds in the past participle. The present-tense form *-vert-* changed to *-vers-* in the past participle *versus.* In English the verb *revert* shows the original Latin present-tense form, the noun *reversion* the Latin past-participle form. This same variation between present-tense form and past-participle form is illustrated by *corrode* and *corrosion, pendant* and *suspense, conclude* and *conclusive,* and *sentiment* and *sense.* Similarly a *g* in a present-tense form was often changed to *ct* in a past-participle form. The English word *agent* is from a present-tense form, *actor* from a past-participle form; *regent* is from a present-tense form, *rector* from a past-participle form. Sometimes, as with *-clud-* and *-clus-,* both forms are important in English; sometimes only the past-participle form is used in English words. We have several words using the past-participle form *-rupt-,* meaning "breaking, to break," as *erupt, disrupt,* and *rupture,* but none in the common vocabulary using the corresponding present-tense form *-rump-.*

Latin roots used in English words also show variation in stem vowels. The Latin root for "to do, make" appears with *a* in *factory* and *manufacture, e* in *effect* and *defective, i* in *efficient* and *deficient,* and even *y* in *terrify* and *mollify.* One finds the root for "to see" appearing as *-spec-* or *-spect-* (in *spectacle* and *spectrum)* and as *-spic-* (in *conspicuous* and *suspicion);* the root meaning "to put, place" as *-sta-, -stal-* (in *stable, status,* and *stationary)* and as *-stit-* (in *substitute* and *constitution).* Many of these changes in the stem vowels occurred in early Latin centuries before the Christian era—the time also of changes in the consonant structure. Changes in root vowels often occurred because of an early Latin tendency to stress words on their initial syllables rather than their root syllables.

Latin roots often come into English directly, with little or no change in form. When they come into English indirectly—that is, through French, Spanish, or Italian—they often undergo major changes in form, changes that only an etymologist can trace. From the Latin root *-capit-,* meaning "head," come English *capital* and *decapitate.* In French this root underwent changes so drastic that one can hardly recognize it in *chief* and *chef.* From the Latin root *-curr-,* meaning "to run, a running," come the English words *current, discursive,* and *curriculum.* This form has been changed to *-cour-* in many words that we have received from French, such as *courier* and *courant,* and to *-corr-* in words from Spanish, such as *corral.*

The list of Latin roots in this chapter suggests the effect of changes in forms of roots in earlier Latin but does not attempt to list French and other Romance forms that show such startling developments as *chief* and *chef* from Latin *-capit-.* Despite this simplification, however, there remain difficulties in both writing and studying a text such as this. What can be done with such situations as that of *-frag-* and *-fract-,* as in such pairs as *fragment* and *fraction?* These forms are obviously related by the common meaning of "break, to break" and by similarity, although not identity, in form. But which is the root, which is the morpheme? Linguistic science has worked out a fairly satisfactory terminology and, more important, a way of thinking for such situations. Forms or morphemes are, as we have seen, not always constant. Let us evolve another word on the basis of the root *-morph-,* one that will suggest a variation in form. From Greek we have the element *allo-,* meaning "other, different, change, variety." The made-up word, *allomorph,* can indicate a different or varied form. We could say that the final *-t* in *dreamt* was an allomorph of the *-ed* in *dreamed.* We can think of *-frag-* and *-fract-* as allomorphs. But what are they allomorphs of, and what is the morpheme? We cannot write or even say the morpheme in this case; we could cumbersomely say that the morpheme or root was the element *-fra-* plus a voiced

Copyright © 1994 by Harcourt Brace & Company. All rights reserved.

velar stop [g] or a voiceless velar stop [k] and a following dental or alveolar. But such a description would depend for its meaning on a familiarity with phonetic description, and that is outside the sphere of this book. Perhaps you can see the ease of the following explanation: a morpheme is the total of its allomorphs, although it may be difficult or impossible to express the morpheme by a single form in either writing or speaking.

In giving lists of prefixes and of Greek roots, we have carefully called to your attention situations in which the syllable in question in a particular word should not be interpreted as a given prefix or root—that the *mis-* of *misery* was *not* to be interpreted as the prefix *mis-*, as in *misdeal* or *misfeasance,* for instance, and that the *-pan-* of *pantry* or *pantywaist* had no connection with the Greek root *-pan-,* meaning "all." There are some situations in which a similar caution might be needed in connection with roots in the following list. The forms *-cur-* and *-curs-,* given as Latin roots meaning "run, course," should not be interpreted as having anything to do with either *cur* (as in "a mangy cur") or *curse.* Your dictionary will tell you that the first of these words is of unexplained Middle English origin and that the second is an Old English word; both, then, are unrelated to the Latin root. The Latin root *-clus-* and the originally Old English word *cluster* are completely unrelated, as are the Latin root *-fin-* and the originally Old English word *finger.* It would be cumbersome to annotate roots in the following list with such comments. But if you do not feel at once that it would be ridiculous to connect *cur* with *currency* and *curriculum,* for instance, you must develop such a feeling in order to understand and appreciate the English vocabulary. The following list contains most of the frequently used Latin roots. To learn as many roots as possible will greatly enhance the augmentation of your vocabulary.

Root	***Meaning***	***Examples***
-ag-, -act-	do, drive, impel	agent, agenda, agitate, active, reaction, transact
-cap-, -capt-, -cept-, -cip-	take, seize	capture, captivate, capacious, reception, intercept, anticipate
-ced-, -ceed-, -cess-	go, yield	secede, intercede, precede, proceed, recession, concession
-clud-, -clus-	close, shut	conclude, preclude, occlude, recluse, seclusion, exclusion
-cur-, -curr-, -curs-	run, course	concur, recurrent, currency, curriculum, cursory, precursor
-dic-, -dict-	say, speak, word	indicate, abdicate, diction, dictionary, contradict, predict
-duc-, -duct-	lead	adduce, reduce, educate, conductor, abduction, seduction
-fac-, -fact-, -fect-, -fic-	do, make	facile, facsimile, calefacient, defect, proficient, efficacious
-fer-	bear, yield	conifer, fertile, transfer

Copyright © 1994 by Harcourt Brace & Company. All rights reserved.

Root	*Meaning*	*Examples*
-fid-	belief, faith	fidelity, perfidious, infidel
-fin-	end, limit	final, infinite, definitive
-flect-, -flex-	bend, twist	flexible, flexure, circumflex, deflector, genuflect, reflection
-form-	form, shape	formative, transform, reformation
-frag-, -fract-	break	fragile, fragment, fraction, infraction, refract, fractionation
-fus-	pour	transfuse, suffuse, effusive
-gen-	birth, origin, kind	generate, progeny, generic
-grad-, -gress-	step, go	gradient, gradual, degrade, digress, egress, aggression
-jac-, -ject-	throw, hurl, cast	ejaculate, eject, projectile
-junct-	join	juncture, adjunct, disjunctive
-leg-, -lig-, -lect-	choose, read	legible, eligible, negligent, election, select, lectern
-mit-, -miss-	send	remit, admittance, submit, missile, emissary, transmission
-pend-,-pens-	hang, weigh	suspend, pendant, appendix, suspense, pensive, dispense
-plic-, -pli- (-ply-)	fold	duplicate, implicate, duplicity, pliant, accomplice, imply
-pon-, -pos-	place, put	postpone, component, proponent, interpose, composure, indisposed
-port-	carry	transport, portage, importation
-reg-, -rig-, -rect-	rule, straight, right	regent, regimen, incorrigible, rectitude, directive, rectangular
-scrib-, -script-	write	inscribe, transcribe, subscribe, scriptures, manuscript, prescription

Copyright © 1994 by Harcourt Brace & Company. All rights reserved.

Root	*Meaning*	*Examples*
-sed-, -sid-, -sess-	sit, seat	sedentary, supersede, assiduous, residual, session, sessile
-sent-, -sens-	feel	sensory, sensuous, insensate, sentient, presentiment, sentimental
-sequ-, -secut-	follow	sequel, consequence, subsequent, consecutive, persecute, prosecute
-solv-, -solu-, -solut-	loosen, free	solvent, dissolve, soluble, solution, absolute, dissolute
-spec-, -spic-, -spect-	look, see	specimen, despicable, perspicacity, aspect, circumspect, suspect
-spir-	breathe	aspire, perspiration, inspiration
-string-, -strict-	bind tight	stringent, restrict, stricture
-ten- ,-tin-, -tent-	hold	tenure, untenable, continence, content, detention, retentive
-tend-, -tens-, -tent-	stretch	distend, tendency, pretense, tension, extensive, contentious
-tract-	draw, pull	traction, distract, extraction
-ven-, -vent-	come, go	intervene, convene, event, prevent
-vert-, -vers-	turn	convert, divert, inadvertent, aversion
-vid-, -vis-	see	provident, evident, visualize, vision, television, supervisory
-voc- (-vok-)	call	vocal, vociferous, advocate, evoke, provoke, revoke
-volv-, -volu-, -volut-	roll, turn	evolve, devolve, involvement, evolution, revolution, convolution

(The forms *-ply-* and *-vok-* are placed in parentheses to call attention to the fact that their spelling does not exist in the original Latin.)

Copyright © 1994 by Harcourt Brace & Company. All rights reserved.

How does your dictionary inform you about Latin roots? It is not the function of the dictionary to give information about the roots themselves, unless those roots also commonly serve in Modern English as combining forms, bound roots from which many new words may still be built up today. Under the circumstances it will seem that dictionaries are more likely to give entries to Greek roots than to Latin roots. As we saw in Chapter 4, many of the Greek roots have entries of their own in dictionaries, but we look in vain for separate entries for some of the most common Latin roots, for instance *-clud-* and *-clus-*, *-fin-*, and *-frag-* and *-fract-*. The etymologies, however, will mention the common Latin roots very frequently. The etymologist is likely to give a complete Latin grammatical form, with a grammatical ending, rather than simply an isolated root. In the etymology for *capture,* for instance, you may be told that this word goes back to *captura,* which is made up from *captus,* but it is up to you to abstract from this the bare root *-capt-*. The Latin grammatical forms *factus* and *factio* may appear in etymologies for words such as *fact, faction, factious, factitious, factor,* and *facture,* but you may not find in the etymologies the bare root form *-fact-*. Similarly, the etymologies for *pendant, pendentive, pendulous,* and *pendulum,* along with those for *depend, compendium, perpend,* and so on, will give full Latin grammatical forms but not *-pend-* by itself. In doing the exercises in this book and in studying and considering English words of Latin origin, split the root and the grammatical suffix that may appear in an etymology, and concentrate on the former. The grammatical suffixes that you will often have to split off will include such endings as *-us, -a, -um, -are, -ere,* and *-ire,* endings frequently used in Latin with noun and verb forms.

It is hard to overstate the importance of the Latin roots in the previous list. From this short list of Latin roots come thousands of English words, an astonishingly large portion of the English vocabulary. Many of these words are made up by the combination of the Latin prefixes mentioned in Chapter 3 and the roots in the list, with or without additional elements. With the prefix *com-,* for instance, the roots listed yield the following: *co-act, coagulate, conception, concede, concession, conclude, conclusion, concur, conduce, conduct, confection, confer, conference, confide, confine, conform, confuse, congenital, conjecture, conjunction, collect, commit, commission, compendium, comply, complicate, component, compose, comport, correct, conscribe, conscript, consent, consequence, conspectus, conspicuous, conspire, constrict, constringe, contend, content, continent, contract, convene, convent, convert, conversion, convoke,* and *convolution.* The following table contains a select list of words derived from common Latin roots.

A Select List of Words Derived from Common Latin Roots

abject	assent	conifer	diction	enact	genesis
absolve	astringent	consecutvie	differ	evident	genitive
access	auspicious	conspiracy	diffuse	evoke	genuine
accomplish	avert	contradict	digress	evolve	illegible
actual	benediction	controvert	dirigible	exceed	impend
adduce	benefactor	convention	discursive	except	import
adjacent	capacious	crucifer	dismiss	exclude	impost
admit	capture	currency	disport	expect	include
advent	cede	curriculum	dissolve	expire	incur
adversary	circumference	cursory	distend	export	induct
advice	circumscribe	deception	divert	expose	infect
advocate	circumspect	deduce	ductile	extent	infer
afferent	circumvent	defect	duplicate	facile	infuse
affinity	college	defer	edifice	fertile	injunction
aggression	comfit	define	effect	fiction	inscribe
agile	commissary	deflect	efferent	finite	insensate
allege	compliant	degrade	effusion	formula	inspire
anticipate	composite	deject	egress	fragile	intense
appliance	concept	deport	eject	fragment	intercede
apposite	congenial	depose	elect	fusion	intercept
ascribe	congress	detract	emit	gender	interject

Copyright © 1994 by Harcourt Brace & Company. All rights reserved.

intermit
intervene
introduce
introvert
invent
invoke
juncture
juxtapose
lecture
legacy
legend
legible
manufacture
missile
multiply
neglect
nitrogen
nonsense
object
obsess
occur
offer
omit
opponent
opportune
pendant
pensive
perceive
perfect
perpend
persecute
perspire
pliable
portable
position
possess
postpone
precept
preclude
predict
prefect
preside
president
prevent
principle
proceed
process
product
profuse
progeny
progress
project
propose
prosecute
protract
provide
purpose
reagent
recede
recompense
rectify
recur
refection
refer
reform
refract
refuse
regent
regress
reject
remiss
repository
resent
reside
resolve
respect
restrict
retract
retrograde
reverse
revoke
sacrifice
satisfy
scribe
secede
sedulous
select
sensuous
sentient
sequence
session
solvent
specimen
spirit
strict
stringent
subjunctive
submit
subsequent
subvert
success
suffice
supersede
supervene
suspect
tendon
tract
traduce
transcribe
transfuse
transgress
transpose
traverse
uniform
universal
venture
version
visible
vision
vociferous

Copyright © 1994 by Harcourt Brace & Company. All rights reserved.

NAME ______________________________ SECTION __________ DATE __________

CHAPTER 5

EXERCISE 1: In the blank provided, print the number of the word closest in meaning to the word italicized in the preceding phrase. Use the list of prefixes in Chapter 3 and the list of Latin roots in this chapter to work out your answers. Be prepared to explain roots and their meanings. The objective of this exercise is not to have you concentrate on the meanings of the words themselves but to practice recognition of roots within large words.

1. an *abject* expression: 1 downcast 2 happy 3 ugly — 1. ________
2. to *abjure* old habits: 1 retain 2 regret 3 forswear — 2. ________
3. an *abscess* of the mouth: 1 tumor 2 collection of pus 3 fracture — 3. ________
4. to *abscond:* 1 sing 2 write 3 flee secretly — 4. ________
5. *abstinence:* 1 worry 2 indulgence 3 self-denial — 5. ________
6. *agamic* reproduction: without 1 danger 2 development 3 sexual mating — 6. ________
7. *alluvial* soil: 1 washed down 2 fertile 3 sandy — 7. ________
8. an *amorphous* substance: 1 rare 2 formless 3 poisonous — 8. ________
9. *avert* the danger: 1 ignore 2 enhance 3 prevent — 9. ________
10. a *bicameral* legislature: having 1 two cameras 2 two chambers 3 two lights — 10. ________
11. a *biennial* plant: blooming 1 every year 2 in the second year 3 never — 11. ________
12. a *bilateral* treaty: affecting 1 two sides or parties 2 one party 3 nobody — 12. ________
13. employing *circumlocution:* 1 simple language 2 a round-about means of travel 3 prolix language — 13. ________
14. a *circumspect* attitude: 1 disloyal 2 unreasonable 3 chary — 14. ________
15. causing to *coagulate:* 1 warm 2 thicken and clot 3 disintegrate — 15. ________
16. to *collate* research: 1 eradicate 2 begin 3 examine and assemble — 16. ________
17. to show *commiseration:* express 1 greed 2 joy 3 sorrow — 17. ________
18. *contiguous* properties: 1 of uncertain ownership 2 adjacent and touching 3 inexpensive — 18. ________
19. to *contravene:* 1 respect 2 go against 3 test — 19. ________
20. a *cursory* reading: 1 slow 2 thorough 3 hasty — 20. ________
21. a *demagogue:* 1 half a group of people 2 an elected leader 3 a leader of the common people — 21. ________
22. *demigod:* 1 having godlike attributes 2 an abnormally short god 3 a half statue — 22. ________
23. to *demur:* 1 agree 2 argue 3 reject — 23. ________
24. *discrete:* 1 minor 2 private 3 separate and individual — 24. ________
25. to *dispel* shyness: 1 increase 2 admire 3 drive away — 25. ________
26. to *disseminate* the news: 1 interpret 2 scatter or circulate 3 suppress — 26. ________
27. a *distended* pod: 1 stretched 2 small 3 blighted — 27. ________
28. in *diverse* ways: 1 unlucky 2 illegal 3 distinctly different — 28. ________
29. *divert* criticism: 1 provoke 2 prevent 3 cause — 29. ________
30. aware of his *dubiosity:* 1 fear 2 uncertainty 3 honesty — 30. ________

Copyright © 1994 by Harcourt Brace & Company. All rights reserved.

31. the mayor's *edict:* 1 annual address 2 farewell address 3 official proclamation 31. ________

32. *efferent* blood vessel: one that 1 is weakened 2 bears outward 3 is congested 32. ________

33. an *effigy* of the athlete: 1 recording 2 photograph 3 a crude image 33. ________

34. the *effusion* of sorrow was evident: 1 lack of 2 pretense 3 outpouring 34. ________

35. an *encomium* for the teacher: 1 indifference 2 praise 3 regret 35. ________

36. *endemic* diseases: 1 chronic 2 peculiar to a region 3 unknown 36. ________

37. disapproving of *euthanasia:* 1 pleasant sounds 2 cacophony 3 painless death 37. ________

38. *exculpate* a person: 1 blame 2 free from blame 3 provide for 38. ________

39. objecting to *exogamy:* 1 marriage within the tribe or clan 2 divorce
3 marriage outside the tribe or family 39. ________

40. fearful of not being *exonerated:* 1 believed 2 selected 3 exculpated 40. ________

41. *factitious* sorrow: 1 sincere 2 deep 3 contrived 41. ________

42. having *finite* authority: 1 limitless 2 limited 3 none whatsoever 42. ________

43. a *geomorphic* study: relating to the configuration of the 1 sun 2 earth 3 moon 43. ________

44. *infinite* hope: 1 trivial 2 dramatic 3 endless 44. ________

45. to *infuse:* 1 detect 2 omit 3 pour in 45. ________

46. an *intractable* minority: 1 angry 2 powerless 3 stubborn 46. ________

47. the *juxtaposition* of good and evil: 1 diversity 2 similarity 3 placing side by side 47. ________

48. using a *lectern:* 1 a yardstick 2 a reading stand 3 a lantern 48. ________

49. an abnormal *libido:* 1 sexual drive 2 physique 3 glandular functioning 49. ________

50. to *litigate* the dispute: 1 ignore 2 aggravate 3 contest legally 50. ________

51. consumed with *misogamy:* hatred of 1 women 2 men 3 marriage 51. ________

52. known for *misogyny:* hatred of 1 marriage 2 women 3 sports 52. ________

53. a *numismatic* expert: knowledgeable about 1 medicine 2 coins 3 stocks and bonds 53. ________

54. an *obsolescent* word: 1 scholarly 2 going out of use 3 nonstandard 54. ________

55. teeth do not *occlude:* 1 match 2 close together 3 show decay 55. ________

56. the duke's *perfidy:* 1 honesty 2 dishonesty 3 defense 56. ________

57. *precursors:* 1 teachers 2 observers 3 forerunners 57. ________

58. to *presage* disaster: 1 recall 2 prevent 3 foreshadow 58. ________

59. *primordial* religions: 1 very devout 2 austere 3 early and primitive 59. ________

60. *progeny* of a clan: 1 ethnicity 2 descendants 3 weaknesses 60. ________

61. *rectitude:* 1 force 2 promptness 3 rightness 61. ________

62. a strict *regimen:* 1 ruler 2 diet 3 schedule 62. ________

63. *respiratory* organs: of 1 digestion 2 sight 3 breathing 63. ________

64. to *retract:* 1 respect 2 affirm 3 withdraw 64. ________

65. to *retrogress:* 1 surprise 2 consider 3 go backward 65. ________

66. *retrospective:* 1 determining 2 looking back 3 doubting 66. ________

Copyright © 1994 by Harcourt Brace & Company. All rights reserved.

NAME ______________________ SECTION ________ DATE ________

67. *rupture* of friendship: 1 beginning 2 ending 3 breaking 67. ________

68. a *salubrious* climate: 1 melancholy 2 humid 3 healthful 68. ________

69. a *sedentary* job: requiring 1 much talking 2 much sitting 3 much reading 69. ________

70. *sequestered* existence: 1 poor 2 exciting 3 secluded 70. ________

71. to *subvert* liberties: 1 analyze 2 propose 3 destroy 71. ________

72. *succinct* poetry: 1 lengthy 2 complex 3 brief and curt 72. ________

73. to *supersede:* 1 to go before 2 to replace 3 to reject 73. ________

74. a *surreptitious* approach: 1 noisy 2 secret and stealthy 3 unsteady 74. ________

75. a *suspensory* bandage: 1 loose 2 supporting 3 antiseptic 75. ________

76. a *symphony* orchestra: blending of 1 wind instruments 2 string instruments 3 harmonious sound of all instruments 76. ________

77. *synchronous* events: occurring 1 at different times 2 at the same time 3 infrequently 77. ________

78. *tenable* beliefs: 1 proven 2 held 3 changed 78. ________

79. a *tenacious* person: 1 intractable 2 affable 3 sadistic 79. ________

80. *tenets* of an organization: 1 renters 2 opinions or principles 3 schedules 80. ________

81. *thanatopsis:* meditation upon 1 life 2 death 3 love 81. ________

82. *thanatos:* a wish for 1 wealth 2 health 3 death 82. ________

83. being *theriomorphic:* having the shape or form of 1 a man 2 a woman 3 a beast 83. ________

84. being *thermophilic* indicates a need of: 1 water 2 heat 3 food 84. ________

85. a *timorous* person is: 1 angry 2 bold 3 apprehensive and fearful 85. ________

86. a massive *tome:* 1 filing cabinet 2 library 3 book of many pages or volumes 86. ________

87. an interest in *tomography:* techniques for making 1 maps 2 X-ray pictures 3 atomic bombs 87. ________

88. *transient* laborers: 1 needy 2 remaining only briefly 3 permanent 88. ________

89. a *truculent* person: 1 timid 2 esoteric 3 belligerent 89. ________

90. to *validate* the tickets: 1 vitiate 2 make official 3 reject 90. ________

91. to *vitiate* his argument: 1 defend 2 reinforce 3 invalidate 91. ________

92. a *vivacious* person: 1 debilitated 2 lethargic 3 animated 92. ________

93. to *vivify* literature: 1 simplify 2 make realistic 3 make more intense 93. ________

94. to study *vivisection:* 1 dissecting the body of a dead animal for experimentation 2 X-raying an animal 3 dissecting the body of a living animal for experimentation 94. ________

95. to pursue one's *vocation:* 1 hobby 2 talent 3 career or profession 95. ________

96. a *vociferous* speech: characterized by 1 softness 2 well-chosen vocabulary 3 loudness 96. ________

97. an act of *volition:* 1 indecision 2 conscious choice 3 intimidation 97. ________

98. a *voluble* person: 1 quiet 2 loquacious 3 vulnerable 98. ________

99. a *vulgar* statement: 1 affable 2 common 3 minor 99. ________

100. studying the *vulgate:* 1 common usage or vernacular 2 learned 3 prattle of children 100. ________

Copyright © 1994 by Harcourt Brace & Company. All rights reserved.

EXERCISE 2: Following are a number of words employing the Latin roots given in this chapter. Underline the root in each word, being careful to indicate where your underlining begins and stops. Write the meaning of that root in the blank after the word.

1. abstract ______________
2. accidental ______________
3. anticipate ______________
4. append ______________
5. attraction ______________
6. complex ______________
7. component ______________
8. concept ______________
9. conclusion ______________
10. conducive ______________
11. confine ______________
12. correct ______________
13. definition ______________
14. deformity ______________
15. different ______________
16. difficult ______________
17. efficient ______________
18. ejaculate ______________
19. expect ______________
20. extent ______________
21. extract ______________
22. factor ______________
23. imply ______________
24. important ______________
25. impose ______________
26. include ______________
27. induction ______________
28. infinite ______________
29. inscription ______________
30. introduce ______________
31. occurrence ______________
32. opponent ______________
33. oppose ______________
34. perception ______________
35. perfection ______________
36. permissible ______________
37. perverted ______________
38. produce ______________
39. proposal ______________
40. reduce ______________
41. resent ______________
42. residence ______________
43. respect ______________
44. restrict ______________
45. retention ______________
46. solution ______________
47. subject ______________
48. subscribe ______________
49. transmit ______________
50. visible ______________

EXERCISE 3: Following is a list of words with portions italicized. After each word is a Latin root accompanied by a very brief indication of the meaning of that root. Place an *X* in the blank after each item in which the italicized portion of the word does *not* illustrate the given Latin root. Check the dictionary etymology of each word before answering.

1. ad*jac*ent -*jac*- “cast” ______________
2. *ag*ony -*ag*- “do, drive” ______________
3. *cap*illary -*cap*- “take” ______________
4. *cap*on -*cap*- “take” ______________
5. *cip*her -*cip*- “take” ______________
6. con*gress* -*gress*- “go” ______________
7. *duc*al -*duc*- “lead” ______________
8. *fac*ade -*fac*- “do, make” ______________
9. *fer*ocious -*fer*- “bear” ______________
10. *fin*agle -*fin*- “end” ______________
11. *fus*tian -*fus*- “pour” ______________
12. *gene* -*gen*- “birth, kind” ______________
13. *gen*eric -*gen*- “kind” ______________
14. in*junct*ion -*junct*- “join” ______________
15. *jac*kal -*jac*- “cast” ______________
16. *leg*horn -*leg*- “choose, read” ______________
17. *lig*nite -*lig*- “choose, read” ______________
18. *mit*osis -*mit*- “send” ______________
19. *mit*ten -*mit*- “send” ______________
20. *pend*ulous -*pend*- “hang” ______________
21. *pon*iard -*pon*- “place” ______________
22. *port*ray -*port*- “carry” ______________
23. *reg*ard -*reg*- “rule” ______________
24. *rig*marole -*rig*- “right” ______________
25. *sess*ion -*sess*- “sit” ______________
26. *spir*al -*spir*- “breath” ______________
27. *spir*it -*spir*- “breath” ______________
28. *tin*sel -*tin*- “hold” ______________
29. *vert*ex -*vert*- “turn” ______________
30. *vis*cous -*vis*- “see” ______________

Copyright © 1994 by Harcourt Brace & Company. All rights reserved.

NAME ______________________________ SECTION ________ DATE __________

CUMULATIVE TEST 2: The following words occur in the preceding sections of this book. In the blank provided, write the number of the word closest in meaning to the italicized word.

1. *adduce:* 1 refute 2 bring out 3 ignore 4 study 1. ________
2. *altercation:* 1 dispute 2 injury 3 metamorphosis 4 message 2. ________
3. *apathy:* 1 revulsion 2 indifference 3 ecstasy 4 admiration 3. ________
4. *apostasy:* 1 backsliding 2 indolence 3 disease 4 fear 4. ________
5. *astral:* 1 starry 2 fiery 3 risqué 4 technical 5. ________
6. *bizarre:* 1 commercial 2 strange and unusual 3 warlike 4 alcoholic 6. ________
7. *blithe:* 1 happy and carefree 2 earnest and studious 3 eccentric 4 acrobatic 7. ________
8. *bucolic:* 1 industrial 2 mysterious 3 dangerous 4 rural 8. ________
9. *carcinoma:* cancer in 1 tissue 2 bones 3 blood 4 tongue 9. ________
10. *celibate:* without 1 plan and order 2 sexual relations 3 anxiety 4 activity 10. ________
11. *charlatan:* 1 researcher 2 expert 3 publicity agent 4 fraud 11. ________
12. *clandestine:* 1 accidental 2 memorable 3 familial 4 secret 12. ________
13. *cliché:* 1 trite comment 2 political slogan 3 chemical formula 4 ditty 13. ________
14. *cognizance:* 1 locality 2 knowledge and responsibility 3 mechanical ability 4 range of hearing 14. ________
15. *comatose:* 1 laughable 2 unconscious 3 well-groomed 4 in pain 15. ________
16. *congenital:* 1 ocular 2 psychological 3 trivial 4 present at birth 16. ________
17. *contiguous:* 1 swampy 2 segregated 3 expensive 4 adjacent and touching 17. ________
18. *cornice:* 1 foundation 2 angle 3 wall topping 4 main hall 18. ________
19. *culpable:* 1 humorous 2 blameworthy 3 irrelevant 4 reliable 19. ________
20. *decorous:* 1 nautical 2 surgical 3 popular 4 proper 20. ________
21. *deprecate:* 1 praise 2 evaluate 3 disparage 4 notice 21. ________
22. *desiccated:* 1 learned 2 humorous 3 weak 4 dried out 22. ________
23. *disheveled:* 1 attractive 2 startling 3 shadowy 4 untidy 23. ________
24. *disseminate:* 1 spread widely 2 suppress 3 comment on 4 slant 24. ________
25. *dynamic:* 1 destructive 2 popular 3 forceful and energetic 4 foolish 25. ________
26. *éclat:* 1 contempt 2 silence and neglect 3 publicity and acclaim 4 insincere praise 26. ________
27. *effulgent:* 1 bright and radiant 2 stimulating 3 expensive 4 remote 27. ________
28. *egress:* 1 exit 2 danger zone 3 concentration point 4 safety escape 28. ________
29. *emulous:* 1 timid 2 hoping to imitate 3 weak 4 assertive 29. ________
30. *epigram:* 1 inscription 2 prescription 3 brief witticism 4 analysis 30. ________
31. *epitome:* 1 introduction 2 typification 3 acceptance 4 evaluation 31. ________
32. *eructation:* 1 coloring 2 belching 3 stammering 4 crying out 32. ________
33. *evoke:* 1 call forth 2 loan 3 repeat 4 deny 33. ________
34. *exculpate:* 1 imprison 2 free from blame 3 sacrifice 4 charge 34. ________

Copyright © 1994 by Harcourt Brace & Company. All rights reserved.

35. *expedite:* 1 confuse 2 dismiss 3 facilitate and speed up 4 approve 35. ________
36. *facet:* 1 side or phase 2 drawback 3 covering 4 improvement 36. ________
37. *facetious:* 1 flippant and joking 2 improper 3 sorrowful 4 adolescent 37. ________
38. *febrile:* 1 powerful 2 poisonous 3 feverish 4 rich 38. ________
39. *felicitous:* 1 tragic 2 customary 3 religious 4 happy 39. ________
40. *filch:* 1 nail down 2 conceal 3 steal 4 yield 40. ________
41. *finagle:* 1 work with 2 ridicule 3 defraud and trick 4 complete 41. ________
42. *flout:* 1 reverse 2 usurp 3 scorn 4 submit to 42. ________
43. *frenetic:* 1 easy 2 ill-done 3 musical 4 frenzied 43. ________
44. *fresco:* 1 water color 2 painting on plaster 3 etching 4 cameo 44. ________
45. *geomorphic:* shape of 1 sun 2 earth 3 moon 4 trees 45. ________
46. *geriatric:* concerning 1 diets 2 occupational therapy 3 care of the aged 4 criminal activity 46. ________
47. *hegemony:* 1 censorship 2 democracy 3 conspiracy 4 political domination 47. ________
48. *hemostat:* device for 1 helping breathing 2 pulling teeth 3 setting broken bones 4 stopping bleeding 48. ________
49. *heterodox:* 1 orthodox 2 blessed 3 democratic 4 unorthodox 49. ________
50. *homonyms:* having 1 like meaning 2 like form, unlike meaning 3 unlike form, like meaning 4 like form 50. ________
51. *indigent:* 1 needy 2 busy 3 angry 4 native to 51. ________
52. *interdict:* 1 prohibit 2 interfere 3 confuse 4 overlook 52. ________
53. *intractable:* 1 powerless 2 reverent 3 cooperative 4 stubborn 53. ________
54. *kudos:* 1 praise 2 promotion 3 blame 4 penalty 54. ________
55. *lapidary:* pertaining to 1 public speaking 2 gem cutting 3 cloth making 4 glass making 55. ________
56. *liaison:* 1 enmity 2 isolation 3 communication 4 proximity 56. ________
57. *lucrative:* 1 useless 2 burdensome 3 uncertain 4 profitable 57. ________
58. *mayhem:* action of 1 trespassing 2 crippling 3 fleeing 4 arresting 58. ________
59. *mollify*: 1 make effeminate 2 enlarge 3 calm and soothe 4 liquefy 59. ________
60. *moratorium:* 1 postponement 2 convalescence 3 extinction 4 enforcement 60. ________
61. *narcosis:* 1 stupor 2 death 3 liveliness 4 immorality 61. ________
62. *necrotic:* 1 sweet 2 nervous 3 dead 4 calm 62. ________
63. *nonchalant:* 1 cool and carefree 2 out of breath 3 undemonstrative 4 odorous 63. ________
64. *onerous:* 1 proper 2 timely 3 burdensome 4 complicated 64. ________
65. *outré:* 1 original 2 frightening 3 dishonest 4 strikingly unusual 65. ________
66. *panorama:* 1 pictorial overview 2 momentary flash 3 travelogue 4 collage 66. ________
67. *patent:* 1 clear, apparent 2 legal 3 falsely based 4 new and shining 67. ________
68. *pathology:* study of 1 geography 2 disease 3 nervous system 4 mineral ore 68. ________

Copyright © 1994 by Harcourt Brace & Company. All rights reserved.

NAME ______________________ SECTION ________ DATE ________

69. *perfidious:* 1 stingy 2 treacherous 3 dangerous 4 friendly 69. ________

70. *piquant:* 1 sharp and cutting 2 fussy 3 provocative 4 self-centered 70. ________

71. *podiatry:* study of 1 bad diets 2 foot care 3 tree growth 4 children 71. ________

72. *polychromatic:* 1 very ill 2 wealthy 3 many-colored 4 complaining 72. ________

73. *portend:* 1 presage 2 forbid 3 reject 4 consider 73. ________

74. *portico:* 1 harbor 2 covered entrance 3 small port 4 freight depot 74. ________

75. *psychopath:* a person who is 1 gravely dyssocial 2 always walking 3 overeating 4 always seeking 75. ________

76. *ragout:* 1 thick stew 2 clothing sale 3 ointment 4 scraps of cloth 76. ________

77. *rectitude:* 1 regular habits 2 severity 3 accuracy 4 moral uprightness 77. ________

78. *refract:* 1 deflect 2 agitate 3 repeat 4 obey 78. ________

79. *residuum:* 1 effect 2 location 3 significance 4 remainder 79. ________

80. *restive:* 1 dormant 2 surly 3 indolent 4 uneasy 80. ________

81. *reticent:* 1 neat 2 effective 3 shy and restrained 4 thrifty 81. ________

82. *rheostat:* device for 1 charting rivers 2 regulating currents 3 drying hair 4 scraping paint 82. ________

83. *schizophrenia:* psychosis marked by 1 overeating 2 anorexia 3 pyrophobia 4 ego withdrawal 83. ________

84. *scintillate:* 1 laugh 2 pilfer 3 cut 4 sparkle 84. ________

85. *scion:* 1 angel 2 heir 3 ancestor 4 ruler 85. ________

86. *secular:* 1 accommodative 2 separatist 3 not pertaining to a religious community 4 subdivided 86. ________

87. *shard:* 1 a trace 2 blade 3 fragment 4 outer layer 87. ________

88. *taciturn:* 1 reciprocal 2 courteous 3 uncommunicative 4 stingy 88. ________

89. *temerity:* 1 shyness 2 boldness 3 determination 4 good humor 89. ________

90. *theism:* belief in 1 taxes 2 existence of God 3 outer space 4 war 90. ________

91. *therapeutic:* 1 destructive 2 fantastic 3 curative 4 primitive 91. ________

92. *tout:* 1 complain 2 advertise urgently 3 deprecate 4 criticize 92. ________

93. *turbid:* 1 frightening 2 rapid 3 attractive 4 soiled and muddy 93. ________

94. *turpitude:* 1 moral depravity 2 skill 3 inactivity 4 sarcasm 94. ________

95. *undulant:* 1 worthless 2 wavy 3 indolent 4 inconsiderate 95. ________

96. *ungulate:* having 1 thick skin 2 hooves 3 bulging eyes 4 protruding teeth 96. ________

97. *vacillate:* 1 ridicule 2 persuade 3 hesitate 4 argue 97. ________

98. *vitiate:* 1 invalidate 2 corrupt 3 inspire 4 consider 98. ________

99. *voracious:* 1 kindly 2 friendly 3 ravenous, zealous 4 aggressive 99. ________

100. *whimsy:* 1 fever 2 hair piece 3 a pet 4 capricious fancy 100. ________

Copyright © 1994 by Harcourt Brace & Company. All rights reserved.

NAME ______________________________ SECTION __________ DATE __________

CUMULATIVE TEST 3: The first part of this exercise lists fifty words, each followed by a blank. In that blank write the number of the synonym appearing in the second list.

List 1

1. accoutrement __________
2. allomorph __________
3. amnesty __________
4. autonomy __________
5. bevel __________
6. camisole __________
7. catenation __________
8. charisma __________
9. dendroid __________
10. denigrate __________
11. dermal __________
12. dilation __________
13. dirk __________
14. egregious __________
15. epos __________
16. euphoria __________
17. flexure __________
18. genuflection __________
19. gonfalon __________
20. guise __________
21. hieroglyph __________
22. holocaust __________
23. impecunious __________
24. innocuous __________
25. intrepid __________
26. louver __________
27. mestizo __________
28. meticulous __________
29. miscible __________
30. monochromatic __________
31. morocco __________
32. nemesis __________
33. neoplasia __________
34. occlusion __________
35. ornithology __________
36. otitis __________
37. pandemic __________
38. pediatrician __________
39. pendant __________
40. pepsin __________
41. precept __________
42. quorum __________
43. regimen __________
44. sarcoma __________
45. scone __________
46. spleen __________
47. succinct __________
48. traumatic __________
49. truculent __________
50. viscous __________

List 2

1. brave
2. thick and sticky
3. fierce and belligerent
4. slatted door
5. distension
6. single color
7. pertaining to wounds
8. brief
9. schedule
10. order or principle
11. happy feeling
12. earache
13. almost universal
14. personal magnetism
15. semblance
16. cutaneous
17. flag or banner
18. fearfully careful
19. a digestive enzyme
20. anger
21. conspicuous
22. equipment
23. admitting mixing
24. tumor
25. tea-cake biscuit
26. bird study
27. slanting cut
28. sleeveless undershirt for women
29. suspended ornament
30. penniless
31. emblematic writing
32. epic
33. dagger
34. kneeling
35. variant form
36. avenging agent
37. goatskin leather
38. of mixed blood
39. group pardon
40. self-rule
41. shutting together
42. cancer
43. adequate number
44. harmless
45. interlinkage
46. children's doctor
47. fatal fire
48. tree-like
49. belittle
50. bending

Copyright © 1994 by Harcourt Brace & Company. All rights reserved.

NAME ______________________ SECTION __________ DATE __________

CUMULATIVE TEST 4: In the preceding chapters your attention has often been called to the fact that the same or similar combinations of syllables may be etymologically unrelated and may express totally different meanings. The *path* of *pathfinder,* for instance, has no connection with the *-path-* of *pathology,* nor is there any connection between the *-cur-* of *concurrent* and *cur,* "a mean sort of dog." Following are sixty sets of words. Place an *X* in the blank after each set containing unrelated words.

1. amenable–preamble ______
2. anthropology–anthem ______
3. atom–tomato ______
4. autograph–monograph ______
5. bailiwick–wicked ______
6. banal–banner ______
7. barometer–barter ______
8. bigamy–gambler ______
9. bole–hyperbole ______
10. canton–canter ______
11. chimaera–chimney ______
12. consequence–sequel ______
13. contiguous–tiger ______
14. cursive–curse ______
15. debilitate–billion ______
16. decorum–declamation ______
17. democrat–crater ______
18. dinosaur–diner ______
19. diverse–versify ______
20. dour–doughty ______
21. effigy–fig ______
22. elated–belated ______
23. empathy–pathfinder ______
24. encomium–empathy ______
25. epilog–depilatory ______
26. eschew–chew ______
27. expedite–peddler ______
28. facsimile–similar ______
29. felicitate–fellow ______
30. filibuster–filial ______
31. forensic–forestry ______
32. gallant–gall bladder ______
33. grammar–grampus ______
34. hagiology–hagridden ______
35. hegira–hegemony ______
36. hemorrhage–hemstitch ______
37. labile–labial ______
38. litigate–literate ______
39. macabre–macaroon ______
40. mastoid–mastic ______
41. missile–mistress ______
42. mitigate–emit ______
43. mollify–molecule ______
44. obese–obey ______
45. pantomime–pansy ______
46. pentameter–penthouse ______
47. polygon–gondola ______
48. postpone–postage ______
49. primordial–orderly ______
50. pyre–pyrrhic ______
51. scurrilous–scurry ______
52. specimen–speckle ______
53. stricture–constrict ______
54. subsidiary–assiduous ______
55. suggest–sugar ______
56. taboo–tabular ______
57. theology–theory ______
58. travail–travesty ______
59. unction–uncle ______
60. vitiate–vitamin ______

Copyright © 1994 by Harcourt Brace & Company. All rights reserved.

The more words we know, the
closer we can come to expressing
precisely what we want....
It is hard to stretch a small
vocabulary to make it do all
the things that intelligent
people require of words.
Bergen Evans

6 Word Analysis: Latin Roots II

Like Greek roots, Latin roots are often used as combining forms in English to make up new words needed in science. Sometimes these combining forms do not appear in any relatively common words but are used in many technical terms. The Latin root *-ovi-,* meaning "egg," has been used in the composition of many words such as *oviduct, oviferous, oviparous,* and *ovipositor,* and is likely to be used again to form new compounds. Even though these roots do not appear in common words, their scientific use makes it important to know them.

It would be possible to draw up a list of hundreds of Latin roots appearing in English words, but such a list would not be very profitable. Many of these roots appear in too few English words to make their study worthwhile. Many others appear in many English words but their root meanings have been obscured, and knowing them therefore does not contribute much to an understanding of the current English vocabulary. The Latin root *-clay-,* meaning "key," appears in such English words as *autoclave, conclave, clavichord,* and *clavicle,* but knowledge of the meaning of the root does not lead to the present meaning of these words. Our knowledge of prefixes will suggest to us that *assist, consist, desist, persist,* and *resist* probably begin with assimilated *ad-, com-, de-, per-,* and *re-,* and that *-sist-* is probably a root. Attaching the etymological meaning of "stand" to *-sist-* does not really help us very much in interpreting the words. Roots such as *-clay-* and *-sist-,* whose derivatives in English present an unusual number of problems of semantics (meaning and interpretation), have been omitted from the following list. Remember that the following should be regarded as Latin roots but never as word parts that will always have the indicated meanings. For example, the word *artichoke,* coming through Italian from Arabic, does not illustrate the root *-art-,* as in *artisan* or *artifice.* Remember, too, that dictionary etymologies are likely to show full Latin grammatical forms and that to obtain the root you will frequently have to detach an *-are, -ere, -ire, -us, -a,* or *-um* from the full grammatical form. Learn the following:

Root	***Meaning***	***Examples***
-ac-, -acr-	sharp	acute, acrid, acumen
-agr-	field	agriculture, agronomy, agrarian
-ali-	other	alien, alibi, alias
-alter-, -altr-	other, change	alter, alternate, alterant
-am-, -amic-	love, friend	amity, amatory, amicable
-anim-	mind, soul, spirit	animate, magnanimity, animosity

Copyright © 1994 by Harcourt Brace & Company. All rights reserved.

Root	*Meaning*	*Examples*
-ann-, -enni-	year	annals, anniversary, perennial
-apt-, -ept-	adjust, fit	adapt, aptitude, inept
-aqu-	water	aquatic, aqueduct, aquarium
-arm-	arm, weapon	army, armory, disarmament
-art-	skill, craft, art	artisan, artificial, artifice
-aud-, -audit-	hear	audible, audience, auditorium
-aur-	gold	aureate, aureole, auriferous
-bel-, -bell-	war	bellicose, belligerent, rebel
-ben-, -bene-	well, good	benefit, benediction, benefactor
-brev-	short, brief	brevity, abbreviate, breviary
-cand-	white, glowing	incandescent, candent, candle
-capit-	head	capital, per capita, decapitate
-carn-	flesh	incarnate, carnivorous, carnal
-cent-	hundred	century, centennial, centipede
-cern-, -cert-	perceive, decide	discern, certify, ascertain
-cid-, -cis-	cut, kill	incision, homicide, fratricide
-cit-	summon, impel	excite, citation, incite
-civ-	citizen	civilian, civilize, civility
-clam- (-claim-)	shout, cry out	clamor, exclamation, proclaim
-clar-	clear	clarify, clarity, declare
-clin-	bend	decline, inclination, recline
-cogn-	know, be acquainted	recognize, cognizant, incognito

Copyright © 1994 by Harcourt Brace & Company. All rights reserved.

Root	*Meaning*	*Examples*
-corp-	body	corpuscle, corpulent, corpse
-cred-	belief, trust	credible, credulous, credit
-cruc-	cross	cruciform, crucify, crucifer
-culp-	fault, blame	culpable, culprit, exculpate
-cur-	care, care for	accurate, security, curator
-dec-	ten	decimal, decimate, decennial
-dent-	tooth	dentist, denture, indent
-dign-	worth, worthy	dignify, indignity, condign
-doc-, -doct-	teach, prove	docile, doctrine, indoctrinate
-du-	two	duet, duel, duplicate
-dur-	hard, lasting	durable, obdurate, duration
-ego-	I, self	egotist, egoist, egocentric
-equ-	equal	equity, equinox, equilibrium
-err-	wander	errata, erratic, aberration
-ev-	time, age	medieval, longevity, primeval
-ferv-	boil, bubble	fervor, perfervid, effervescent
-firm-	strong	confirm, infirmary, affirm
-flor-	flower	floral, florid, floriculture
-flu-, -fluct-	flow	influence, flux, superfluous
-fort-	strong	fortify, fortitude, effort
-grat-	please, favor	gratitude, gratify, gratuity
-grav-	weigh, heavy	gravity, gravitation, aggravate
-greg-	flock	congregate, aggregate, segregate
-her-, -hes-	cling, stick	adhere, coherence, adhesion

Copyright © 1994 by Harcourt Brace & Company. All rights reserved.

Root	Meaning	Examples
-it-	go, travel	exit, transit, circuit
-jud-	judge	judicious, adjudicate, prejudice
-jur-	swear	conjure, adjure, perjury
-labor-	work	laboratory, elaborate, laborious
-leg-	law	legislate, legitimate, illegal
-lev-	light, rise	levitation, elevate, levity
-liter-	letter	literal, alliterate, illiterate
-loc-	place	locus, locality, locale
-loqu-, -locut-	talk, speech	colloquial, colloquy, locution
-luc-	light	translucent, lucid, elucidate
-magn-	large	magnitude, magnanimous, magnify
-mal-	bad	malady, malevolent, malediction
-man-, -manu-	hand	manacle, manicure, manual
-mar-	sea	marine, maritime, submarine
-mater-, -matr-	mother	maternity, matricide, matriarchy
-medi-	middle	mediocre, mediate, medieval
-merg-, -mers-	dip, plunge	submerge, emergent, immersion
-min-	less, little	minus, minimize, minority
-mob-, -mot-	move	mobile, automobile, remote
-mon-, -monit-	warn	admonish, monitor, admonition
-mor-, -mort-	die, death	moribund, mortuary, immortal
-mor-	custom	morality, amoral, mores

Copyright © 1994 by Harcourt Brace & Company. All rights reserved.

Root	*Meaning*	*Examples*
-multi-	many	multitude, multiple, multifarious
-mut-	change	immutable, transmute, commute
-nav-	ship, sail	naval, navigate, circumnavigate
-neg-	deny	negate, renege, negative
-nomen-, -nomin-	name	nomenclature, nominee, nominate
-nov-	new	novelty, innovate, renovate
-ocul-	eye	ocular, oculist, binocular
-omni-	all	omnipotent, omnivorous, omniscient
-ora-	speak, pray	orate, oratorio, oracular
-orn-	decorate	ornate, adorn, ornament
-par-	equal	par, disparity, disparate
-pater-, -patr-	father	paternal, patrimony, patristic
-ped-	foot	pedal, centipede, quadruped
-pel-, -puls-	drive	repel, compulsion, impulsion
-pet-	seek	petition, competitor, petulant
-pot-	power	impotent, omnipotent, potentiality
-press-	press	compress, expression, repressive
-prim-	first	primer, primitive, primeval
-quir-, -quis-	ask, seek	inquire, inquisition, requisition
-reg-	rule	regal, regicide, interregnum
-rid-, -ris-	laugh	ridiculous, deride, derision
-rog-	ask	interrogate, rogation, interrogative

Copyright © 1994 by Harcourt Brace & Company. All rights reserved.

Root	*Meaning*	*Examples*
-rupt-	break	rupture, abrupt, interrupt
-sanct-	holy	sanction, sanctuary, sanctimonious
-seg-, -sect-	cut	segment, sector, dissect
-simil-	like	similar, similitude, assimilate
-sol-	alone	solitude, solitaire, desolate
-son-	sound	unison, resonant, dissonance
-struct-	build	structure, construct, destruction
-suad-, -suas-	advise	persuade, dissuade, suasion
-sum-, -sumpt-	take	resume, assumption, presumption
-tang-, -ting-, -tact-, -tig-	touch	tangible, contingent, contiguous
-tempor-	time	contemporary, temporal, temporary
-tenu-	thin	tenuous, attenuate, extenuate
-terr-, -ter-	land	terrestrial, subterranean, disinter
-test-	witness	testify, testimony, testament
-tort-, -tors-	twist	distort, contortion, torsion
-trib-	assign	attribute, distribute, contribution
-trud-, -trus-	thrust	obtrude, protrusion, abstruse
-turb-	agitate	turbid, turbulence, disturbance
-umbr-	shade	umbrella, adumbrate, penumbra
-und-	wave	undulant, inundate, abundant
-uni-	one	unity, uniform, unison

Copyright © 1994 by Harcourt Brace & Company. All rights reserved.

Root	*Meaning*	*Examples*
-urb-	city	urban, suburban, urbanity
-vac-	empty	vacant, vacuous, evacuate
-vad-, -vas-	go	pervade, evasion, pervasive
-verb-	word	verbal, verbose, verbiage
-ver-	true	verily, veracity, verisimilitude
-vest-	dress	vesture, divest, vestment
-vinc-, -vict-	conquer	convince, victor, victorious
-vit-	life	vitality, revitalize, vitamin
-viv-	life, lively	vivid, vivacious, survivor
-vol-	wish	volition, volunteer, malevolent
-vulg-	common	vulgar, vulgate, divulge

Copyright © 1994 by Harcourt Brace & Company. All rights reserved.

NAME ______________________________ SECTION __________ DATE __________

CHAPTER 6

EXERCISE 1: Split each word in the following list into prefix and root. In the first column write the prefix (in its original, unassimilated form), and in the second column write its meaning. In the third column write the root (remembering that you may have to detach the Latin grammatical ending from the form given in the dictionary etymology), and in the fourth column write the meaning of the root.

	Prefix	Meaning	Root	Meaning
1. abrade	________	________	________	________
2. abscond	________	________	________	________
3. arrive	________	________	________	________
4. collude	________	________	________	________
5. commute	________	________	________	________
6. confute	________	________	________	________
7. conjure	________	________	________	________
8. deflate	________	________	________	________
9. exhale	________	________	________	________
10. expunge	________	________	________	________
11. imbibe	________	________	________	________
12. immure	________	________	________	________
13. indent	________	________	________	________
14. obstruct	________	________	________	________
15. perfume	________	________	________	________
16. preside	________	________	________	________
17. promote	________	________	________	________
18. relapse	________	________	________	________
19. secure	________	________	________	________
20. submerge	________	________	________	________

EXERCISE 2: Find the word or phrase closest in meaning to the italicized word and write its number in the blank provided. Use the list of roots in this chapter. Viewing this as an exercise simply in finding the meanings of the italicized words will defeat its purpose. Analyze the words, find the roots, and determine their meanings.

1. to *abjure* old habits: 1 forswear 2 retain 3 recall 4 regret — 1. ________
2. the crowd's *acclamations:* 1 threats 2 weapons 3 cheers 4 signs — 2. ________
3. said with *acerbity:* 1 softness 2 good humor 3 reverence 4 sharpness — 3. ________
4. acting with much *acumen:* 1 knowledge 2 keenness 3 vision 4 mercy — 4. ________
5. to *adjudicate* the claim: 1 refuse 2 repeat 3 plead 4 judge — 5. ________

Copyright © 1994 by Harcourt Brace & Company. All rights reserved.

6. to *alleviate* distress: 1 ignore 2 intensify 3 explain 4 lighten and soothe 6. ________
7. his *amatory* attentions: 1 medical 2 financial 3 love-making 4 tutorial 7. ________
8. living in *amity:* 1 hardship 2 friendship 3 danger 4 ease 8. ________
9. an *attenuated* liquid: 1 tested 2 thinned 3 colored 4 poisonous 9. ________
10. other *auriferous* ores: 1 gold-bearing 2 auspicious 3 worthless 4 heavy 10. ________
11. *bellicose* tribesmen: 1 diseased 2 exiled 3 warlike 4 primitive 11. ________
12. a *benevolent* man: 1 embittered 2 lonesome 3 rich 4 kindly and well-meaning 12. ________
13. *carnivorous* animals: 1 red-colored 2 swift 3 fur-bearing 4 flesh-eating 13. ________
14. to *commutate* a current: 1 check 2 detect 3 change 4 increase 14. ________
15. the *confluence* of the streams: 1 source 2 mouth 3 flowing together 4 silt load 15. ________
16. man's *corporeal* existence: 1 spiritual 2 military 3 bodily 4 unhappy 16. ________
17. acting under *duress:* 1 order 2 hardship 3 impulse 4 misunderstanding 17. ________
18. the plants' *efflorescence:* 1 decay 2 care 3 blooming 4 growth 18. ________
19. a list of *errata:* 1 indices 2 acknowledgments 3 mistakes 4 charts 19. ________
20. *excision* of dead tissue: 1 cutting out 2 cleansing 3 marking 4 healing 20. ________
21. *exculpated* by the evidence: freed from 1 hope 2 doubt 3 guilt 4 danger 21. ________
22. a *fervid* appeal: 1 intensely zealous 2 dishonest 3 religious 4 foolish 22. ________
23. *gregarious* animals: tending to 1 fight 2 migrate 3 sleep by day 4 flock together 23. ________
24. glowing *incandescently:* with 1 redness 2 heat 3 clarity 4 whiteness 24. ________
25. *indurated* tissue: 1 diseased 2 hardened 3 purified 4 amputated 25. ________
26. the *infirmities* of age: 1 pleasures 2 whims 3 wisdom 4 weaknesses 26. ________
27. *itinerant* printers of old: 1 unlearned 2 clever 3 busy 4 traveling 27. ________
28. *juridical* studies: 1 abstruse 2 legal 3 historical 4 economic 28. ________
29. a *loquacious* old man: 1 weak 2 kindly 3 talkative 4 forgetful 29. ________
30. severe with *malefactors:* 1 disloyal persons 2 slackers 3 evildoers 4 prisoners 30. ________
31. *maritime* commerce: 1 local 2 oceanic 3 airborne 4 dangerous 31. ________
32. a *moribund* movement: 1 unpopular 2 approaching an end 3 fanatic 4 patriotic 32. ________
33. a *pellucid* stream: 1 deep 2 icy 3 muddy 4 very clear 33. ________
34. *piscine* specimens: those showing 1 cattle 2 insects 3 snakes 4 fish 34. ________
35. *sonorous* wording: 1 careful 2 offensive 3 scientific 4 high-sounding 35. ________
36. the *undulation* of the brush strokes: 1 carelessness 2 beauty 3 color 4 waviness 36. ________
37. the *vacuity* of his arguments: 1 passion 2 emptiness 3 force 4 influence 37. ________
38. the *verbiage* of the talk: 1 wordiness 2 sincerity 3 terseness 4 emotion 38. ________
39. a *veridical* statement: 1 hesitant 2 ambiguous 3 true 4 brief 39. ________
40. *vulgate* dialects: used by 1 scholars 2 commoners 3 armies 4 shepherds 40. ________

 Copyright © 1994 by Harcourt Brace & Company. All rights reserved.

NAME ______________________ SECTION ________ DATE __________

EXERCISE 3: Fill in the blanks as indicated.

1. *Bovine* and *ursine* mean "pertaining to __________" and "pertaining to __________" respectively.
2. The word *scriptures* etymologically means __________.
3. The word *transfusion* as in "blood transfusion" etymologically means a __________.
4. The words *adjourn* and *journey* are linked by a common root, meaning __________.
5. From its two roots, *medieval* literally means "pertaining to the __________."
6. The word *unicorn* splits into two roots, meaning __________.
7. According to the roots, the *Mediterranean* literally is the ocean "between or in the middle of the __________."
8. The root *-fer-* means "to bear, a bearing"; the root *-ferr-,* as in *ferric* or *ferrocyanide,* means __________.
9. In an *aviary* one would expect to find __________, in an *apiary* to find __________.
10. A *regicide* is one who kills a __________; a *fratricide* is one who kills a __________.
11. According to the meaning of the roots, the word *genuflect* means __________.
12. The human appendix is called *vermiform,* meaning "shaped like a __________."
13. The meaning of the root of *vaccinate* indicates that vaccines first came from __________.
14. The word *inoculate* suggests by its form that it was first used in connection with treatments of the __________.
15. The common root of the words *insinuate* and *sinuous* means __________.
16. *Dilapidate* and *lapidary* are linked by a common root, meaning __________.
17. The *leopard* actually bears the names of two animals, the __________ and the __________.
18. *Lucifer* is another name for Satan; it means literally __________.
19. An *immaculate* thing is without a *macula,* that is, without a __________.
20. The word *mellifluous* etymologically means "flowing with __________."
21. *Commensurate* and *mensuration* are linked by a root meaning __________.
22. A musical *nocturne* is a composition suitable for singing or playing during the __________.
23. The common root of *sylvan* and *Pennsylvania* means __________.
24. From the root of the word, an *optimist* is one who always expects the __________.
25. *Percussion* and *concussion* are linked by a common root meaning __________.
26. *Defunct* and *function* both contain the Latin root -__________-, which means __________.
27. The Latin root of *bursar* and *bursitis* means __________.
28. In *aberration* and in the *errant* of "knight errant" is the root -__________- which means __________.
29. *Bulletin* is related to the *bull* of "papal bull"; the root means __________.
30. *Rubric,* originally meaning __________ is related to *ruby;* the root means __________.
31. The word *equinox* is composed of two roots, -__________-, meaning __________, and -__________-, meaning __________.
32. *Belligerent* contains two Latin roots, -__________-, meaning __________, and -__________-, meaning __________.

Copyright © 1994 by Harcourt Brace & Company. All rights reserved.

33. Etymologically the word *circumlocution* means a ____________ (as the root indicates) and ____________ (as the prefix indicates).
34. *Exhume* and *humus* both contain the root -____________- which means ______________________________.
35. In *dorsal* and *endorse* the Latin root -____________- means ______________________________.
36. *Equilibrium* contains two roots, -____________- meaning ____________ and -____________-, meaning ____________.
37. *Patrician, patricide, patriotic, patron,* and *patroon* are all linked together by a Latin and Greek root -_________-, meaning ____________.
38. As you probably know, *Vermont* is made up of two eventually Latin roots, -____________-, meaning ____________ and -____________-, meaning ____________.
39. The root in the word *Florida* is -____________-, and its meaning is ____________.
40. An *alma mater* is rather a different thing from a *dura mater; alma* means ____________ and *dura* means ____________.

EXERCISE 4: Look up the following words in your dictionary. In the first column write the root present in each of the two words given. In the second column write the meaning of the root.

	Root	Meaning
1. abrasion–erasure	____________	____________
2. cadence–cadaver	____________	____________
3. condole–dolorous	____________	____________
4. conflagration–flagrant	____________	____________
5. conjugate–conjugal	____________	____________
6. denigrate–nigrescent	____________	____________
7. depilatory–capillary	____________	____________
8. dormant–dormitory	____________	____________
9. dorsal–endorse	____________	____________
10. exhume–inhume	____________	____________
11. expedite–biped	____________	____________
12. expurgate–purgatory	____________	____________
13. frigid–refrigerator	____________	____________
14. incinerate–cinerous	____________	____________
15. incision–excision	____________	____________
16. jocose–jocular	____________	____________
17. lactation–lacteal	____________	____________
18. miscreant–recreant	____________	____________
19. nocent–innocuous	____________	____________

Copyright © 1994 by Harcourt Brace & Company. All rights reserved.

NAME ______________________ SECTION ________ DATE ________

	Root	Meaning
20. novice–innovation	________	________
21. resurgent–insurgent	________	________
22. salad–saline	________	________
23. sanguinary–consanguineous	________	________
24. senescent–senility	________	________
25. sublunar–lunatic	________	________

Copyright © 1994 by Harcourt Brace & Company. All rights reserved.

Clutter is the disease
of American writing.
William Zinsser

7 Word Analysis: Suffixes

A suffix is a short form added after a word or root to modify its meaning or function. The word *government,* for instance, is made up of *govern* and the form *-ment,* here a suffix, as in *abasement, complement, enjoyment, fragment, filament,* and *experiment.* Many suffixes are bound: *-ness* in *coldness, -ize* in *regularize,* and *-hood* in *neighborhood.* Some usually bound may appear as free forms: *-teen,* bound in *thirteen,* is free in "teenagers" and "entering his teens." Other suffixes often appear as free forms, such as *-less* in *hopeless* and *-some* in *frolicsome.* As English words have developed over the centuries, we find suffixes used after free forms, as in *boyhood* from *boy,* and after bound forms, as in *adolescent* (we have a suffix *-escent* but we do not have a free form *adol).*

It is impossible to demarcate exactly between suffix and root, particularly a root often used terminally. *Milkman* is likely to be analyzed as a compound of two independent roots, but *man* may be called a suffix in such expressions as "his sister is a good fisherman" and "this boy is the third baseman." In general, suffixes, like prefixes, have less specific meanings than roots.

It is often impossible to assign one single specific meaning to a common suffix. The suffix *-er* often indicates the doer of an indicated action; a *dancer* dances, a *swimmer* swims. But *diner* may indicate a dining establishment, *officer* an office holder, *hatter* a hat dealer or maker, *broiler* a fowl for broiling. In the list following, general meanings are assigned to suffixes, but they are merely indicative and not definitive. Observation of suffixes in use is much more informative than study of definitions of their meaning.

A given suffix may form only one part of speech. *Freedom, largeness, baggage, safety,* and *educator* are nouns, and *-dom, -ness, -age, -ty, -or* are called *noun suffixes. Effervesce, terrify,* and *criticize* are verbs, and *-esce, -fy, -ize* are called *verb suffixes.* Other suffixes form two or more parts of speech. The suffixes *-ant, -al, -an, -ary, -ese, -ian,* and *-ine* form adjectives and nouns. Comments about parts of speech formed by suffixes are not absolute; for instance, *-ship* and *-age* are listed below as noun suffixes, but they appear in the verbs *worship* and *rummage.*

Theoretically, any short form added to the end of a word may be called a suffix. But suffixes such as the *-ed* of *walked* and *turned,* the *-ing* of *talking* and *going,* the *-s* of *makes* and *drowns,* the *-s* of *dogs* and *hats,* and the *-est* of *highest* and *hottest* are usually regarded as part of our grammar and omitted from treatments of word analysis. These grammatical suffixes are unlike derivational suffixes in that they are not felt to create new words. Grammarians sometimes disagree on exact demarcation between morphological and derivational suffixes, some treating the feminine *-ess* of *countess* with the first group, some with the second. There are, however, few such situations. Suffixes in the English language present an odd picture. Naturally, the language started with Anglo-Saxon suffixes. These suffixes were added to some early Latin borrowings to form such hybrids as *martyrdom* and *planter.* But as Latin borrowings became more common, Latin suffixes became more common, more familiar, and more readily added to other words. Some of these Latin suffixes, however, went through changes in form as Old French developed from Latin. The Latin suffix *-atus* developed in Old French to *-e* or to *-ee,* which in some words eventually appeared as *-y.* Latin *armatus* eventually yields *army* in English. With the Spanish form of the Latin *-atus,* we also have in English the word *armada.* Since English utilizes a good many different patterns of suffixing and other methods of showing relationships between related words, but since it rarely employs any one procedure consistently (the adverbial ending *-ly* is an exception), there are many problems connected with suffixing. If the verb *obey* is accompanied by

Copyright © 1994 by Harcourt Brace & Company. All rights reserved.

the noun *obedience,* is the verb *convey* accompanied by the noun *convenience?* If we have *destroy–destruction,* may we also have *constroy–construction?* Since *construction* is the noun for two different verbs, *construct* and *construe,* do we perhaps have a verb *destrue?* With the noun *heresy* we may have either *heretic* or *heretical,* yet with the noun *lunacy* we have *lunatic* but not *lunatical.*

The bewildering variety of English in this respect may be illustrated by considering interrelationships between noun, verb, and adjective in synonyms. We have the verb *rob;* with it is the actor noun *robber* and acting noun *robbery.* We do not have an adjective like *robberious* or *robberine.* We have the verb *steal,* with *stealer* as an accompanying noun. But *stealth,* with its own derivative *stealthy,* does not mean either the actor or the action of stealing. With *burglar* we have *burglary* and *burglarious,* but the verb *burgle,* as we will see, is humorous and marginal. With *purloin* we occasionally find the noun *purloiner,* but not *purloinance* or *purloinarious.* The actor noun *thief* is accompanied by the action noun *theft* and also by *thievery.* It also gives us the verb *thieve* and the adjective *thievish. Larceny* is accompanied by the nouns *larcener* and *larcenist,* neither of them very common, and the adjective *larcenous,* but we have no verb such as *larcenate, larcenize,* or *larcenify.* Any other series of synonymous words is likely to show a similarly baffling variety in suffixing patterns involving companion words.

English seems to show many irregularities in suffixing. Sometimes connective letters seem to have been added: *habit + ate, habituate; grace + ous, gracious; arbor + al, arboreal; censor + ous, censorious; contempt + ous, contemptuous;* and *college + ate, collegiate.* Sometimes it appears that letters have been omitted; we have *administrate,* not *administerate.* Sometimes one part of speech—the verb, for instance—employs one form of a root; the companion noun made up with a suffix employs another: *assume, assumption.* Difficulties arise in the choice of nearly identical suffixes or variant forms of the same suffix: *portable* and *considerable* with *-able,* but *credible* and *visible* with *-ible; vigilant* and *repugnant* with *-ant,* but *confident* and *existent* with *-ent.* Often only the early history of the words involved can explain these apparently capricious choices. The root *-port-* takes *-able* and the root *-vis-* takes *-ible* because the Latin verb *portare* came in the first conjugation, the verb *videre* in the second.

Many words end in combinations identical in form with suffixes but actually are parts of the roots. *Mother* is not made up of a root *-moth-* and the suffix *-er.* A *heifer* is not something that does the action of heifing. Final syllables such as *-er, -or, -ure, -age, -ant,* and *-al* are often not suffixes. Because of this situation an amusing development sometimes takes place, called *back formation.* When it appears that a word is composed of root or base and suffix, people will sometimes detach the part that looks like a suffix and thus create a new, shorter word. From the word *burglar* the *-ar* is sometimes detached, under the impression that it is a suffix, and the word *burgle* emerges. The words *butcher* and *usher* have been so treated, giving such sentences as "He butches at the supermarket," and "She ushes at the theatre downtown." As these sentences indicate, back formation often operates to create a new verb from an old noun. As they also indicate, back formations may seem humorous, especially if they are new. On the other hand a good many respectable words have been formed by this process. *Donate* and *edit,* for instance, are back formations from longer words.

The suffixes *-ic, -ize, -ism,* and *-ist* are originally Greek, but have passed through Latin in their transmission to English. Many Latin suffixes are reinforced by free use in French before passing into English.

The suffixes listed below show varying degrees of activity in today's English. Some, such as *-ard* and *-ose,* are used in relatively few new word formations. Some, such as *-ize,* are quite active. It is always hard to predict the reaction to a new formation with a suffix. We have, for instance, accepted *formalize* and *commonize* without much hesitation, but some people still object to *finalize.* The suffix *-wise* is commonly added to nouns to make up new adverbs (as in "sentence-wise his writing leaves much to be desired," "sales-wise the company's position is not very good"). Some instructors and critics dislike these common formations. Some suffixes, such as *-ish* and *-less,* give the impression of perpetual re-creation rather than establishment of the words in which they appear. Two noun suffixes used with unfortunate results are *-ness* and *-ment.* Although they are quite well established and utterly unobjectionable in hundreds of words, their use elsewhere may indicate that the user is either too ignorant or too lazy to employ an established form ending in another suffix. *Adornment* is the established form, but *adorement* instead of *adoration* would be unfortunate. *Abjectness* is quite satisfactory,

Copyright © 1994 by Harcourt Brace & Company. All rights reserved.

but *dejectness,* instead of *dejection* or *dejectedness,* would raise doubts about a speaker's competence in English. As *dejectedness* indicates, words can show the use of two or three or perhaps even more suffixes: *hopelessness, accommodative, democratization, discouragement, elasticity,* and *existentialism.* These situations usually cause little difficulty, particularly in interpretation of meaning. But considerations of suffixing patterns and procedures in English could be endless. Study the following list, noticing that the statements about meanings are intended to be only suggestive:

Adjective and Noun Suffixes

Suffix	***Illustrations***	***Speech Part***	***Meaning***
Old English Origin			
-dom	thralldom, serfdom, wisdom	n.	state, condition, rank
-en	ashen, wooden, golden	adj.	made of, showing, like
-er	hunter, writer, softener	n.	actor, doer, maker, dweller, dealer
-ful	thankful, zestful, masterful	adj.	full of, marked by
-hood	manhood, likelihood, statehood	n.	state, condition
-ish	warmish, girlish, devilish	adj.	rather, suggesting, like
-less	hopeless, helpless, countless	adj.	without, lacking
-like	childlike, beastlike, dreamlike	adj.	like, similar
-ly	kindly, friendly, softly	adj., adv.	like, of the nature of, in the manner of
-ness	greatness, tallness, incisiveness	n.	quality, state
-ship	friendship, workmanship, clerkship	n.	condition, office, skill
-some	tiresome, meddlesome, lonesome	adj.	tending to, apt to, showing
-t	flight, weight, drift	n.	act, state, quality
-th	growth, warmth, width	n.	act, state, quality
-ward(s)	backward, upward, forward	adj., adv.	in the direction of
-y	hilly, wavy, sticky	adj.	showing, suggesting, apt to
Foreign Origin			
-able	capable, tolerable, affable	adj.	able, fit, likely
-age	passage, bondage, baronage	n.	process, state, rank, place, collection
-al	animal, rival, capital	n.; adj.	act, process, doer; pertaining to, doing

Copyright © 1994 by Harcourt Brace & Company. All rights reserved.

Suffix	*Illustrations*	*Speech Part*	*Meaning*
-an	human, Cretan, European	adj.; n.	pertaining to; one belonging to
-ance -ancy	acceptance, vigilance, hesitancy	n.	act, state, condition, fact
-ant	pendant, servant, ascendant	adj.; n.	doing, showing; actor, agent
-ar	regular, velar, capitular	adj.; n.	pertaining to; one marked by
-ard -art	braggart, drunkard, wizard	n.	one doing, especially excessively
-ary	auxiliary, primary, adversary	adj.; n.	belonging to, showing; one connected with
-ate	sublimate, senate, delegate	n.	product, rank, office
-ate	separate, animate, desolate	adj.	having, having received, showing
-ation	occupation, visitation, starvation	n.	action, state, result
-cy	celibacy, accuracy, captaincy	n.	state, office, rank
-ee	employee, refugee, mortgagee	n.	one receiving action, one showing
-eer	auctioneer, engineer, racketeer	n.	doer, maker, worker at
-ence -ency	evidence, diligence, emergency	n.	act, state, condition, fact
-ent	adherent, confident, solvent	adj.; n.	doing, showing; actor, agent
-er	diner, fencer, rejoinder	n.	doer, dealer in; action, result of action
-ery	robbery, surgery, slavery	n.	action, skill, state, place, collection
-escent	obsolescent, quiescent, maturescent	adj.	beginning, becoming, growing
-ese	Chinese, Portuguese, Johnsonese	adj.; n.	of a place, tongue, style; place, language, style
-esque	picturesque, statuesque, grotesque	adj.	in the style of, like
-ess	governess, patroness, lioness	n.	feminine
-et -ette	islet, midget, suffragette	n.	diminutive, feminine
-fic	terrific, beatific, soporific	adj.	making, causing
-ian	barbarian, Christian, reptilian	adj.; n.	pertaining to; one belonging to, marked by

Copyright © 1994 by Harcourt Brace & Company. All rights reserved.

Suffix	*Illustrations*	*Speech Part*	*Meaning*
-ible	edible, possible, divisible	adj.	able, fit, likely
-ic	alcoholic, classic, cosmetic	adj.; n.	dealing with, like, caused by; person or thing showing
-ice	service, justice, malice	n.	act, state, quality
-id	acid, fluid, solid	n.; adj.	one marked by; marked by, showing
-ile -il	juvenile, missile, fossil	adj.; n.	marked by, showing; one marked by
-ine	marine, canine, divine	adj.; n.	marked by, dealing with; one marked by or treating
-ion	fusion, union, opinion	n.	action, state, result
-ism	barbarism, socialism, baptism	n.	act, manner, state, doctrine
-ist	monopolist, atheist, anarchist	n.; adj.	doer, practicer, believer; doing, practicing, believing
-ite	favorite, composite, anthracite	adj.; n.	formed, showing, treated with; one marked by
-ition	volition, expedition, nutrition	n.	action, state, result
-ity	acidity, virginity, civility	n.	state, quality, condition
-ive	corrective, detective, native	adj.; n.	belonging to, tending to; one belonging or tending to
-ment	refreshment, embodiment, adornment	n.	result, means, action, state
-mony	matrimony, ceremony, sanctimony	n.	resulting state, condition
-or	elevator, juror, honor	n.	doer, office, action, state
-ory	contributory, accessory, offertory	adj.; n.	doing, pertaining to; place or thing for
-ose	bellicose, comatose, morose	adj.	marked by, given to, like
-ous	religious, furious, riotous	adj.	marked by, given to
-ry	heraldry, dentistry, jewelry	n.	condition, practice, collection
-tion	creation, contrition, relation	n.	action, state, condition
-tude	fortitude, certitude, multitude	n.	quality, state, result
-ty	paucity, enmity, activity	n.	quality, state
-ure	exposure, culture, signature	n.	act, result, state, means
-y	jealousy, inquiry, entreaty	n.	result, action, quality

Copyright © 1994 by Harcourt Brace & Company. All rights reserved.

VERB SUFFIXES

Suffix	*Illustrations*	*Meaning*
Old English Origin		
-en	deepen, darken, strengthen	become, cause to be or have
Foreign Origin		
-ate	separate, animate, sublimate	become, form, treat
-esce	convalesce, coalesce, acquiesce	become, grow, continue
-fy	deify, fortify, glorify	make, cause, cause to have
-ish	punish, astonish, embellish	do, make, perform
-ize	sterilize, motorize, criticize	make, cause to be, treat with

Suffixing causes spelling problems. With words and roots ending in consonants *(swim, plan, rest, -fer-, -graph-),* if the suffix begins with a vowel (such as *-ing, -able)* the final consonant of the word or root is doubled if it is immediately preceded by a single vowel that will be accented in the new form: *swimming, planned, rested, inferred, conferred* (but *conference),* and *graphic.* A suffix beginning with a consonant is simply added with no change: *priesthood, weakling, artless,* and *inward.*

If a word ends in a final silent *-e-* (such as *ride, interfere),* the *-e-* is dropped before a suffix beginning with a vowel: *riding* or *interference.* Exceptions occur mostly with words ending in *-ce* and *-ge. C* indicates both the so-called soft *c* (the *s* sound) as in *city* and *nice,* and the so-called hard *c* (the *k* sound) of *county* and *picnic. C* is usually hard before *a, o,* and *u,* and soft before *e* and *i.* To retain indication of the soft sound, the *e* is retained after *c* before suffixes beginning with *a* and *o: service–serviceable* and *notice–noticeable. G* is sometimes soft *(gem, gymnasium, singe)* and sometimes hard *(gamble, gum, finger).* To retain indication of the soft sound common before *e* and *i,* rare before *a* and *o,* the *-e-* of *change* and *courage* is retained in *changeable* and *courageous. Singeing, shoeing,* and *mileage* also retain the *-e-*. A suffix beginning with a consonant is simply added to a word ending in silent *-e-* without addition or subtraction *(careful, whiteness, lovely, safety),* although *argument, truly, awful,* and *ninth* are exceptions.

If a word ends in *-y-* preceded by a vowel, a suffix, regardless of how it begins, is usually added without other change: *joy–joyous, employ–employer, way–wayward,* and *coy–coyly.* If a word ends in *-y-* preceded by a consonant, the *-y-* is generally changed to *-i-* before a suffix not beginning with *-i-: busy–business, beauty–beautiful, deny–denial,* but *hurry–hurrying.*

Copyright © 1994 by Harcourt Brace & Company. All rights reserved.

NAME ______________________ SECTION ________ DATE ________

CHAPTER 7

EXERCISE 1: At first glance the following sets of words will seem to have nothing in common. The words in each set, however, are linked through the fact that they all on occasion take the same suffix. Aside from being one-syllable verbs there does not seem at first to be anything in particular linking *cure, talk,* and *fix,* but consideration indicates that they can all take the suffix *-ative* to make *curative, talkative,* and *fixative. Pastor, person,* and *music* are linked in that they all can take the suffix *-al* to make *pastoral, personal, musical. Serpent, elephant,* and *crystal* can use *-ine* to form *serpentine, elephantine,* and *crystaline.*

In the blank after each set write the suffix that all of the words in the set can take. Do not use any grammatical or morphological suffixes such as *-s* or *-ed.*

1.	beast, comrade, prince, scoundrel, wife	adjective suffix ________
2.	carry, cover, haul, pack, pass	noun suffix ________
3.	cavern, clamor, danger, peril, poison	adjective suffix ________
4.	close, depart, expose, fail, proceed	noun suffix ________
5.	secure, senile, similar, singular, superior	noun suffix ________
6.	awe, burden, meddle, quarrel, tire	adjective suffix ________
7.	critic, fossil, public, satire, signal	verb suffix ________
8.	assist, assure, clear, perform, sever	noun suffix ________
9.	baron, brigand, orphan, peer, peon	noun suffix ________
10.	budget, custom, element, honor, parliament	adjective suffix ________
11.	blazon, herald, jewel, mimic, revel	noun suffix ________
12.	auction, ballad, engine, private, profit	noun suffix ________
13.	claim, expect, inform, inhale, serve	noun suffix ________
14.	betray, deny, refuse, rehearse, renew	noun suffix ________
15.	athlete, period, prophet, scene, stanza	adjective suffix ________
16.	coarse, length, sharp, soft, white	verb suffix ________
17.	decorate, possess, prohibit, relate, secrete	adjective suffix ________
18.	antique, benign, bestial, brutal, catholic	noun suffix ________
19.	brazen, drunken, shrewd, stubborn, sudden	noun suffix ________
20.	appoint, assign, divorce, employ, grant	noun suffix ________
21.	clerk, friend, lord, manager, professor	noun suffix ________
22.	ascertain, assess, assort, comport, deface	noun suffix ________
23.	anecdote, arithmetic, artery, brute, fiction	adjective suffix ________
24.	earth, gold, oak, wood, wool	adjective suffix ________
25.	bankrupt, decent, infant, secret, vacant	noun suffix ________

Copyright © 1994 by Harcourt Brace & Company. All rights reserved.

EXERCISE 2: Form verbs from the adjectives and nouns below by adding appropriate suffixes. In each case your answer must be a verb ending in a suffix. Use your dictionary and check your answers; there are some spelling problems in this assignment.

1. acid ______
2. alien ______
3. American ______
4. ample ______
5. beauty ______
6. brutal ______
7. caliber ______
8. canon ______
9. capital ______
10. central ______
11. civil ______
12. crystal ______
13. diverse ______
14. fossil ______
15. general ______
16. granule ______
17. human ______
18. ideal ______
19. immortal ______
20. italic ______
21. local ______
22. particular ______
23. popular ______
24. pure ______
25. tranquil ______

EXERCISE 3: By adding appropriate suffixes to the following base words, form adjectives indicating possession of the quality indicated, given to the action indicated, or pertaining to the thing indicated. Your answer must always be an adjective ending in a suffix. In some situations you may have a choice between two or more answers; always select the word that seems most common. If you have a choice between a run-on and a main-entry word, always select the latter.

1. acronym ______
2. algebra ______
3. amateur ______
4. arithmetic ______
5. autumn ______
6. bacteria ______
7. beast ______
8. bulb ______
9. caprice ______
10. carbon ______
11. circuit ______
12. demon ______
13. elephant ______
14. enigma ______
15. euphemism ______
16. family ______
17. fancy ______
18. harmony ______
19. knave ______
20. mountain ______
21. ocean ______
22. prince ______
23. residue ______
24. rogue ______
25. sloth ______
26. sophomore ______
27. stanza ______
28. suffice ______
29. suicide ______
30. synonym ______
31. territory ______
32. thief ______
33. thunder ______
34. tone ______
35. torrent ______
36. ulcer ______
37. unit ______
38. vigil ______
39. whimsy ______
40. zeal ______

Copyright © 1994 by Harcourt Brace & Company. All rights reserved.

NAME ______________________ SECTION __________ DATE __________

EXERCISE 4: The following words have relatively uncommon suffixes. Write the suffixes in the first blank, a brief statement of their meaning in the second, and a brief meaning of the complete word in the third.

Words	Suffix	Meaning of Suffix	Meaning of Word
1. acidulous	____________	____________	____________
2. Americana	____________	____________	____________
3. asterisk	____________	____________	____________
4. brooklet	____________	____________	____________
5. darkling	____________	____________	____________
6. equestrienne	____________	____________	____________
7. foliaceous	____________	____________	____________
8. fraudulent	____________	____________	____________
9. fusillade	____________	____________	____________
10. halogen	____________	____________	____________
11. hillock	____________	____________	____________
12. Pleistocene	____________	____________	____________
13. reticule	____________	____________	____________
14. spheroid	____________	____________	____________
15. tonsillitis	____________	____________	____________

EXERCISE 5: Spell correctly the derivative words formed by adding suffixes to the words below.

1. abhor ence ______________
2. advise able ______________
3. argue able ______________
4. appear ance ______________
5. charge able ______________
6. concur ent ______________
7. hardy hood ______________
8. issue ance ______________
9. juice y ______________
10. like able ______________
11. manly ness ______________
12. notice able ______________
13. perverse ity ______________
14. prefer ed ______________
15. prod ing ______________

EXERCISE 6: One of the words in each of the following sets has been misspelled. Spell it correctly in the blank following.

1. acquaintance, appearances definate, equipped 1. ______________
2. adversary, accessory, grievance, responsable 2. ______________
3. anchorage, antecedant, argument, incorrigible 3. ______________
4. attendence, susceptible, received, repentance 4. ______________

Copyright © 1994 by Harcourt Brace & Company. All rights reserved.

5. audible, advantagous, adjacent, acquiescence 5. ______________
6. coalescence, coherent, insistance, debatable 6. ______________
7. committed, competant, conceivable, changeable 7. ______________
8. conveniant, confidence, eligible, invincible 8. ______________
9. intelligance, irresistible, guidance, hindrance 9. ______________
10. ninety, noticeable, incidentally, indispensible 10. ______________
11. obediance, occasional, occurrence, outrageous 11. ______________
12. resistence, referred, professor, pleasant 12. ______________
13. severely, sincerely, tendancy, scarcely 13. ______________
14. usuage, vigilance, transferred, seizure 14. ______________
15. visible, accessible, inflexable, endurance 15. ______________

EXERCISE 7: In the blank after each of the following nouns and adjectives, write the verb implied or indicated by the base of the noun or adjective—that is, write the companion verb. This list has been chosen to involve atypical and difficult situations. Use your dictionary etymologies, noticing how groups of words are treated. Prefer the simplest form if you find two possible answers. Do not, for instance, use *unionize* as an answer to number 30. Use no dictionary run-ons. Remember that each answer must be a verb.

Example: conclusion *conclude*

1. abstention ______________
2. adhesion ______________
3. antagonism ______________
4. appellate ______________
5. clarity ______________
6. cohesive ______________
7. consumption ______________
8. criticism ______________
9. declension ______________
10. demolition ______________
11. diminution ______________
12. dirigible ______________
13. dissolution ______________
14. emission ______________
15. erosion ______________
16. evolution ______________
17. induction ______________
18. inquisitive ______________
19. negligent ______________
20. obligatory ______________
21. obtrusive ______________
22. occupation ______________
23. prophecy ______________
24. redemption ______________
25. secession ______________
26. suspension ______________
27. transcript ______________
28. transmission ______________
29. tremulous ______________
30. union ______________

EXERCISE 8: For each of the suffixes given below find four illustrative words—words not given in this chapter. Check your answers in your dictionary and be sure that you are giving existent words, and that the syllables in question actually serve as suffixes in your words; check the dictionary etymologies.

1. -age ______________ ______________ ______________ ______________
2. -an ______________ ______________ ______________ ______________
3. -ance ______________ ______________ ______________ ______________
4. -ant ______________ ______________ ______________ ______________
5. -ary ______________ ______________ ______________ ______________
6. -ence ______________ ______________ ______________ ______________

Copyright © 1994 by Harcourt Brace & Company. All rights reserved.

NAME ______________________ SECTION __________ DATE __________

7. -ent ________ ________ ________ ________

8. -ery ________ ________ ________ ________

9. -fic ________ ________ ________ ________

10. -ic ________ ________ ________ ________

11. -ile ________ ________ ________ ________

12. -ine ________ ________ ________ ________

13. -ity ________ ________ ________ ________

14. -ive ________ ________ ________ ________

15. -ment ________ ________ ________ ________

16. -mony ________ ________ ________ ________

17. -ory ________ ________ ________ ________

18. -ous ________ ________ ________ ________

19. -ty ________ ________ ________ ________

20. -ure ________ ________ ________ ________

EXERCISE 9: Many modern grammarians feel that it is quite important to distinguish always between a grammatical or morphological suffix and a derivational suffix. A grammatical or morphological suffix is one that simply makes up a certain grammatical form of a base word rather than a new and separate word. The *-s* of *bridges,* the *-ed* of *employed,* and the *-est* of *sweetest* are grammatical or morphological suffixes. Derivational suffixes, on the other hand, make up new and different words when added to bases. The *-ful* of *spiteful,* the *-less* of *fearless,* and the *-some* of *quarrelsome,* for instance, are derivational suffixes. Place a *1* in the blank after each word containing a grammatical or morphological suffix, a *2* after each containing a derivational suffix.

1. actor's ________
2. admittance ________
3. chieftain ________
4. churches ________
5. committed ________
6. cowardice ________
7. deducted ________
8. deeper ________
9. delightful ________
10. determination ________
11. deviation ________
12. empowered ________
13. happier ________
14. injuring ________
15. lovable ________
16. malicious ________
17. muddy ________
18. oxen ________
19. papers ________
20. parentage ________
21. payment ________
22. poisonous ________
23. referral ________
24. refusal ________
25. reliable ________
26. retaining ________
27. soonest ________
28. twisted ________
29. withdrawal ________
30. withering ________

Copyright © 1994 by Harcourt Brace & Company. All rights reserved.

What's in a name?
William Shakespeare

8 Word Analysis:
A. Reservations
B. Semantic Change

As we have seen, analyzing words into prefixes, roots, and suffixes often leads to good guesses about their meanings. Knowing that *-lun-* is a root meaning "moon" can lead to the correct notion that *sublunar* means "being under the moon, pertaining to things under the moon." It would, however, be misleading not to indicate that this procedure has certain limitations, that its application is not always as simple as the bald presentation of lists of prefixes, common roots, and suffixes might lead us to believe. In a language with a copious vocabulary there will always be problems in determining word meanings.

Naturally, the uncommon word causes difficulties. In Chapter 3 uncommon morpheme words were mentioned; words such as *bask, bland,* and *brunt* have to be learned by themselves. In Chapter 6 words containing uncommon roots were mentioned. Words such as *truculence, bucolic, abscond, augury, hedonism, malleable,* and *nepotist* illustrate uncommon roots.

A second situation causing difficulty in determining or guessing at meaning occurs when words are falsely analyzed. The observation that both *collapse and capsize* have the common element *-aps-* may lead to the notion that somehow these two words are or should be related. More thoughtful analysis will make clear that in *collapse* the first element is the prefix *com-* assimilated to *col-,* and that the root is *-laps-* or *-lapse-,* a form not present in *capsize.* At first glance the pair *fragile* and *fragrant* may appear to have some possible connection, but closer analysis will lead to the conclusion that the first is built on the root *-frag-,* which means "break," the second on the root *-fragr-,* which means "odor." *Use* and *contuse* no longer seem connected when one realizes that the root of the second must be *-tus-,* meaning "to beat."

A third sort of difficulty arises when one is confronted with pairs of words having the same root form but coming into English from completely different language groups that are not closely related. Rarely do identical root forms from completely different language groups have the same meaning. Thus the Anglo-Saxon word *stride,* "to walk with long steps in a purposive or pompous manner," is in no way connected with the Latin word *strident,* "harsh-sounding, shrilly raucous." The Scandinavian word *cog* has no connection with the Latin word *cogent,* meaning "forcefully persuasive." Anglo-Saxon *sallow,* "marked by sickly pallor," is not related to Latin *saline,* "briny, salty." Although it may be difficult at first to determine languages of origin for words, affixes used with roots are often indicative. The fact that *sallow* forms *sallowness* with an Anglo-Saxon suffix and that *saline* forms *salinity* with a foreign suffix might lead one to guess that the first word was native, the second borrowed. Note the following pairs in which the first word, completely unrelated to the second, is of Germanic origin, the second eventually from Latin or Greek: *ache–Achaean, ail–aileron, say–assay, crane–cranial, sister–consist,* and *iron–irony. Cherish,* which we have from Latin via French, does not have the same root as *cherub,* which comes ultimately from Hebrew. There is no connection between the word *bible,* which illustrates the Greek root for "book," and *bibulous,* "given to heavy drinking," formed on a Latin root. The word *tobacco* is of South American or West Indian origin; it has no connection with *baccate,* "berry-like," and *bacciform,* "berry-shaped," which employ Latin elements.

Sometimes unrelated words from the same language have the same root forms, and a fourth sort of difficulty occurs. English, for example, has the adjective low, as in "low water, low lands," and the verb low, as in "cows lowing in the meadow," a word unrelated to the adjective in origin or meaning but

Copyright © 1994 by Harcourt Brace & Company. All rights reserved.

now the same in form. Similarly we have the verb *to brook* and the completely unrelated noun *brook,* meaning "stream." Languages such as Latin that have made large-scale contributions to English have likewise given us roots or root forms that are homographic, that is, spelled the same way, but unrelated and different in meaning. *Edible* and *edify* both show the form *-ed-* with common suffix elements, but the first is built on a root meaning "to eat," the second on one meaning "to build." *Serene, serine, serous,* and *serried* are all built on different *-ser-* roots, all unrelated. *Cereal* and *ceremony* appear to show the same root, with the suffixes *-al* and *-mony.* The words, however, are unrelated; *cereal* is connected with the name of the Latin grain-goddess *Ceres,* but *ceremony,* from the Latin *caerimonia,* has a different root. Similarly, there is no connection between *accelerate* and *celery, homage* and *homily,* and *impotent* and *potable.* Sometimes one finds that forms now dissimilar in meaning came eventually from the same original root but that one has to go back into ancient history to discover the connection. The word *admonish* illustrates the Latin root *-mon-,* "to warn," apparently unrelated to the word *monetary,* "pertaining to money," despite the presence in both of the element *-mon-*. The latter word comes from the Latin *monetarius,* a derivative of *moneta,* "a mint." *Moneta* is the shortened form of *Juno Moneta,* the goddess in whose temple money was coined; in this name *Moneta* meant "the warner." Thus, although the two words are eventually related, one may as well ignore that relationship for practical purposes in the analysis of modern English.

Another factor complicating the interpretation of affixes and roots in words is the tendency of words and word parts to undergo sound change (changes in pronunciation, which are likely to produce changes in spelling) in certain situations while remaining constant in others. It was noted in the discussion of Latin roots that the form *-stat-,* "stand, standing, situation," sometimes appeared as *-stit-,* as in modern English *institution* and *constituent.* Similarly, the root *-al-* or *ali-,* meaning "food, nourishment," as in *alimentary* and in *alimony,* "food money for a divorced woman," appears with an *o* instead of an *a* in *adolescent,* etymologically "one being nourished, one growing," and with a *u* in *adult,* "one nourished, one grown and matured." Many sound changes took place as French was emerging from Vulgar Latin. The English words *rational* and *ratiocination* show the *a* of the original root, but *reason* shows one of the forms resulting from such sound changes. Our English word *acerbity* shows the root *-ac-,* "sharp," of the original Latin, while *eager* comes from this same root affected by sound changes.

The first word of each of the following pairs shows the form of the original root, the second the form affected by sound changes: *pulverize–powder, audience–obedience, cordial–courage, crescent–increase, factory–feat, fidelity–faith, conjunction–enjoin, location–lieutenant,* and *aquiline–eagle.* Phonological changes likewise have affected numbers of native words as they have passed from Old English through Middle English into New English. As the sense may indicate, *fox* and *vixen* show the same root, the latter being influenced by sound changes. Similar pairs are *blood* and *bleed, full* and *fill, doom* and *deem, heal* and *health, goose* and *gosling,* and *clean* and *cleanse.*

Another factor—perhaps the most important—making for difficulties in trying to find meanings of words by analysis into affixes and roots is semantic change, the tendency of words to change their meanings over the course of centuries. This phenomenon will be dealt with in this chapter.

According to the meaning of its prefix and root, the word *atom* indicates that which may not be cut or split: *a-* is a Greek prefix meaning "no, not, un-," as in *anarchy,* literally "un-rule, un-government"; the root *-tom-* means "cut, split," as in *dichotomy,* "a splitting in two." A person fearful of the awesome consequences of modern warfare may or may not derive consolation from knowing that according to the etymology of the word *atom,* the explosive fission of atoms is a fantastic impossibility. According to the meaning of its root, the word *vaccine* indicates a substance, specifically a serum, that comes from cows; the root *-vacc-* means "cow." By the same kind of analysis, *inoculate* means "to put something in one's eye"; the *-ocul-* of this word is the same as that of *oculist.* If one analyzed the meanings of the roots, a sentence such as "He was inoculated in the arm with a vaccine made by exposing horses to the disease" would seem impossible. The three words, *atom, vaccine,* and *inoculate,* have changed from their original meanings—they have undergone semantic change. The process whereby a word comes to indicate something different from its original meaning is called semantic change. Over the centuries a great many English words have changed their meanings—sometimes in

Copyright © 1994 by Harcourt Brace & Company. All rights reserved.

English, sometimes in other languages before being borrowed into English. It should be remembered that the majority of our roots are thousands of years old and that their long histories have provided abundant opportunity for changes in both form and meaning.

There are many fascinating instances of semantic change. From Latin we have a root *-ambul-*, as in *perambulate,* meaning "to stroll about, to walk over or through." This root figures in the word *ambulance,* which came into English from the French phrase *hôpital ambulant,* "a moving field hospital." The word *bless* is mild and innocuous today, but it is etymologically related to the word *blood* and evidently originally suggested bloody, primitive sacrifices. The word *sinister,* which now means "evil, adverse, ominous, threatening," originally meant merely "left, as contrasted with right." *Dexterous,* which originally meant only "right, as contrasted with left," has acquired the meaning of "clever, deft, adroit." The word *assassin* is related to the word *hashish,* "intoxicating hemp"; an Oriental secret order nerved its members to commit political murder by giving them hashish, and *assassin,* originally "hashish eater," has come to mean "political murderer." The word *pecuniary* now means "relating or pertaining to money." Its root *-pec-* is first found in the Latin word *pecus,* meaning "cow."

The words *hearse* and *rehearse* are an interesting pair, seemingly so different in meaning that there could never have been a connection between them. The noun *hearse* comes from the Old French noun *herce,* meaning "rake, harrow." It came to be used in reference to a casket frame with candleholders that looked like the teeth of a rake or harrow. Then it changed from indicating the stationary frame into meaning "vehicle designed to carry the dead." *Rehearse* comes from an Old French verb *rehercier,* meaning "to harrow or rake again." It has now come to mean "to practice or go over a role or performance a number of times until it is perfect."

Consideration of roots and affixes will supply a good many other illustrations of semantic change. The word *synagogue* analyzes into the prefix *syn-,* meaning, among other things, "together," and the root *-agog-,* meaning "lead, leader." Originally the word meant a convocation or gathering together of leaders; today it more frequently means "temple." *Salary* contains the root *-sal-* ("salt," as in *saline).* Roman soldiers were allotted special funds to buy salt, evidently a commodity not supplied by their quartermasters; from this allotment the word broadened out to indicate "wages, remuneration for work done." *Promiscuous* can be analyzed into the prefix *pro-,* the suffix *-ous,* and the root *-misc-* (meaning "mix, mixed," as in *immiscible,* which describes substances that cannot be mixed together). It has gone through semantic change to yield its present suggestion of complete lack of selectivity. The root syllable in *river* is used also in the word *arrive,* which originally meant to come to a destination by water, and in the word *rival,* originally "one living along the same stream." The word *seminary* contains the root *-semin-* or *-semen-,* meaning "seed," which one finds in *disseminate;* etymologically, the word *seminary* means something like "seedbed."

In many of the preceding illustrations the first meaning of the word in question has been completely lost: no one now speaks of *rehearsing,* that is, *re-harrowing,* a field. In many other cases the original meanings of words in question have been retained and newer meanings added. To *revoke* a statement is to call it back; the word has had this meaning for many centuries. In card games the word has acquired a new meaning—to fail, through carelessness or dishonesty, to follow suit. *Consumption* still means any process of consuming; to this has been added the specific consuming or wasting away of body tissue in advanced tuberculosis. The word *air* still indicates the atmosphere we breathe, but it has acquired the new meanings illustrated by such phrases as "singing an old-fashioned air," "with an air of complete indifference," and "traveling by air."

The frequency of semantic change means that analyzing a word into prefix, root, and suffix does not always lead to a sound conclusion about the meaning of that word in Modern English. This comment raises the question, how frequent is semantic change in the history of English words? Its frequency can be exaggerated. Many Old English words, such as *father, house, sea, horse, snow, storm,* and *oak,* mean basically what they meant twelve or fourteen centuries ago. And many words derived from Latin, such as *incline, deflect,* and *revolve,* still retain with fair fidelity the original meaning of prefix and root. But the number of changes is very great; it certainly runs into the thousands or even hundreds of thousands. Counting generously, it would not be rash to estimate one instance of semantic change for

Copyright © 1994 by Harcourt Brace & Company. All rights reserved.

every day of English history since the Battle of Hastings in 1066. If this figure seems high, check a large dictionary such as the *Oxford English Dictionary* or the Merriam-Webster *New International Dictionary,* realizing that semantic change has occurred for every word for which two or more definitions are given. These definitions will run high in the thousands.

Because of this widespread tendency of words to change their meanings, difficulties sometimes arise in understanding the literature of earlier times, as the following two lines from the first act of Shakespeare's *Hamlet* illustrate:

Hamlet: The air bites shrewdly; it is very cold.
Horatio: It is a nipping and an eager air.

If these two lines are read with their modern meanings, they may approach nonsense. Read with the meanings current in Shakespeare's day, with *shrewdly* meaning "piercingly, chillingly," not "astutely, calculatingly, craftily," and with *eager* meaning "sharp, biting, keen" (the meaning that the root has in the word *vinegar)* rather than "ardent, avid," the lines make perfect sense.

In addition to literature, the interpretation of the history and law of earlier periods is made more difficult by semantic change. From the first charter of Virginia, granted by King James in 1606, comes the following clause: "We would vouchsafe unto them our License, to make Habitation, Plantation, and to deduce a Colony of sundry of our people." We may guess that *plantation* here means the act of planting, but unless we can analyze from *deduce* the original meaning of "lead out," the passage is puzzling. From the petition of the patriotic Regulators of North Carolina in 1769 comes the following: "Lawyers, Clerks, and other petitioners, in place of being obsequious servants for the Country's use . . . ." In this passage *obsequious* has its old meaning of "devoted, zealous to please," rather than its newer uncomplimentary meaning of "fawning, unctuous." Awareness of the likelihood of semantic change is always an aid in interpreting historical materials. The *Oxford English Dictionary* and the Merriam-Webster *New International Dictionary* are both thorough in including older meanings.

Another problem brought about by semantic change concerns the interpretation of a word changing at the present time. Thirty years or more are usually required for the new meaning of a word to become completely established, that is, thoroughly familiar to almost all users of English. Often more conservative persons resist new meanings. Such persons frequently argue from etymology. Thus it is sometimes said that the word *cavalcade* should be limited to a company or column of horsemen and should not be used in reference to automobiles, since the first element of the word, *-caval-* (originally *-cabal-),* meant "horse" in later Latin. It is argued that *unique* should mean "single, sole"—as it does in the sentence "the manuscript of *Beowulf* is unique"—and not "unusual, strange, rare," as in "we scored on the most unique play of the game," because the word is derived from Latin *unicus,* related to *unus,* meaning "one." But once a word has been frequently used and understood in a certain sense, it is usually futile to object to that sense. It would be ridiculous today to maintain that inoculations had to be put only into people's eyes or that the word *vaccine* should be limited to cow serums. In the past, etymological arguments have been futilely adduced against such common usages as *nice* in the sense of "generally pleasant" and *mad* in the sense of "angry, irritated, vexed."

On the other hand, it is also true that many words acquire marginal meanings that never win complete acceptance. The word *aggravate,* for instance, was first used in the sense of "vex, annoy" more than three hundred years ago, but that sense is still objected to. When one wishes to explain, inform, or persuade by speaking or writing, one is wise to avoid any expression likely to offend or irritate if the person to whom one is speaking or writing happens to object to the usage of *lousy* in "It was a lousy movie," then it is simply common sense to avoid that turn of speech in talking to him. Such choices may be made more wisely on the basis of social utility than on arguments about linguistic philosophy. There is no sure way to know when a new usage is established, but its inclusion in a good dictionary without stigma will indicate that the editorial staff has found numerous instances of it.

 Copyright © 1994 by Harcourt Brace & Company. All rights reserved.

Writers on the history of the English language have classified eight main kinds of semantic change:

1. *Specialization*—the process whereby the meaning range of a word narrows, so that instead of referring to a wide class or group, the word becomes restricted in its use to a special subclass. *Worm* once indicated any crawling vermicular or serpentine creature from a tiny earthworm to a raging dragon; now it is of course limited to the smaller and less awesome species. See also the word *starve.*

2. *Generalization*—the process whereby the meaning range of a word widens, the opposite of specialization. Originally *barn* meant only "storage place for barley," and such usages as "horse barn" or "car barn" were impossible. Originally *box* signified "box wood," then "a container of box wood," and it would have been a semantic wrench to think of metal boxes or cardboard boxes. Proper names sometimes widen out away from reference to one particular person or family. The proper name *Caesar* gave rise to the common noun *caesar,* whence Russian *czar,* meaning "a ruler." This so-called commonization of proper names is a form of generalization.

3. *Shift from concrete to abstract*—early in its history, *humor* indicated a bodily liquid or fluid—the idea of moisture is still expressed by the word *humid,* which employs the same root—but now of course the word generally indicates an abstract quality. *Dreary* first meant "bloody, bloodstained" instead of the less tangible present-day meaning of "doleful, dismal, depressing."

4. *Shift from abstract to concrete—bead* originally indicated a prayer; it is related to the verb *to bid.* It has thus changed from indicating the relatively intangible to the relatively tangible and concrete. *Curiosity* in "buying Chinese curiosities" and *shade* in "pulling down the shades," also illustrate concretization.

5. *Weakening*—the process whereby words come to express weaker, less forceful or vivid meanings than they had previously. This may be coupled with generalization and is hard to distinguish from it. The word *fall* in "to fall sick" means little more than "to become"; *grow* in "she grew old and feeble" has lost older notions of acquiring new strength and vigor, as in "the corn is growing well." A *wonderful* time at a party is simply a very pleasant time, not a time calculated to inspire wonder.

6. *Strengthening*—the process whereby words come to express stronger, more forceful meanings than they had previously. *Hell* originally meant merely "concealed, hidden place"; its root was used in words indicating recesses, holes, and valleys.

7. *Amelioration*—the process whereby words come to have more pleasing, dignified, and lofty meanings than they had previously. *Steward,* now used of various high officials and of persons in charge of providing for the comfort of human beings, originally meant "sty warden, pig keeper." The proud words *cavalier* and *chivalry* go back to a late Latin root *-cabal-,* meaning "old horse, plug, nag" (see earlier comments on *cavalcade*). *Easter,* given lofty significance in Christianity, was originally the word for a pagan spring ceremony.

8. *Pejoration*—the process whereby words come to have less pleasing meanings, whereby originally innocent words come to indicate the objectionable, uncomplimentary, and low. The word *doom* at one time meant simply "to judge"; one might be doomed innocent, or, at doomsday, doomed to eternal life in heaven. In today's English the word *suggestive* usually means having the power not merely of suggesting but of suggesting the risqué or immoral.

Most of these illustrations show only a single change in meaning. But a common word often develops a cluster of additional meanings rather than a single new or additional meaning. *House,* originally indicating a structure intended for permanent human habitation, has acquired the additional meanings expressed in such phrases as "a chicken house," "an ice house," "the House of Representatives,"

Copyright © 1994 by Harcourt Brace & Company. All rights reserved.

"playing to a full house," "drinks on the house," and "a house of ill fame." This process whereby words acquire a number of different meanings through various kinds of semantic change is called *radiation.* Any word in your dictionary with several definitions is likely to illustrate radiation; note such entries as those for *act, advance, age, air, attack, balance, ball,* and *bank.*

There are various causes of semantic change. One is the search for euphemism, that is, the milder, more pleasant, less blunt way of expressing harsh truths and unpleasant facts. *Crazy* and *lunatic* are strong, blunt words. To express the unpleasant idea, the word *insane,* originally simply "not healthy," was pressed into service, but with time it too has become blunt and harsh. In newspaper reporting the word *rape* is sometimes regarded as offensive, and the word *attack* is substituted—with the result that *attack* itself is undergoing semantic change. Another cause for semantic change is ellipsis, the process of omitting words from commonly used expressions. Originally *meat* meant any food, as it still does in "One man's meat is another man's poison." Beef, lamb, pork, and mutton were called *flesh meat.* But in time people stopped saying the word *flesh,* and the word *meat* underwent specialization of meaning. Sometimes cultural changes have altered the meanings of words. *Pen* at one time indicated the tail plume of a goose, in earlier times the usual device for writing with ink. When other devices were substituted for goose *quills,* the word *pen* was applied to them and underwent semantic changes in the process. Perhaps the most important cause for semantic change is figurative language, the subject matter of the following chapter. From the standpoint of a text, an instructor, or a course devoted to vocabulary instruction, perhaps the most important effect of semantic change has been the introduction of an element of uncertainty in any attempt to interpret words by morphemic analysis.

Copyright © 1994 by Harcourt Brace & Company. All rights reserved.

NAME ______________________ SECTION ________ DATE ________

CHAPTER 8

EXERCISE 1: The following words are notable illustrations of semantic change. In the blank after each one, write the original meaning of the word. You will usually find this meaning given in the etymology. Sometimes the meaning will be given for a form occurring early in the English language, sometimes it will be given for a form in another language, such as Latin or Greek. If you were asked for the original meaning for *apt*, you would write "fastened" or "fasten"; check your dictionary etymology for this word. (Notice that words given after the phrase "akin to" are irrelevant to this assignment; for *apt* you would not write "reach" or "near.") You may write only key words in the blanks; you may omit prepositions, articles, and so on.

1. aegis ________
2. aisle ________
3. ambush ________
4. angel ________
5. anthracite ________
6. arctic ________
7. arena ________
8. athlete ________
9. autopsy ________
10. browse ________
11. budget ________
12. cache ________
13. cancer ________
14. caprice ________
15. challenge ________
16. chapel ________
17. check ________
18. clerk ________
19. clock ________
20. cobalt ________
21. colonel ________
22. comet ________
23. comma ________
24. companion ________
25. copy ________
26. coward ________
27. cruise ________
28. daisy ________
29. diphtheria ________
30. domino ________
31. easel ________
32. eerie ________
33. etch ________
34. farce ________
35. ferret ________
36. fiasco ________
37. foreign ________
38. fulminate ________
39. galaxy ________
40. garble ________
41. grenade ________
42. halo ________
43. imp ________
44. insect ________
45. lace ________
46. lumber ________
47. miser ________
48. muscle ________
49. parish ________
50. pedigree ________
51. pioneer ________
52. plague ________
53. psalm ________
54. pumpkin ________
55. rescue ________
56. rummage ________
57. savage ________
58. scandal ________
59. sirocco ________
60. slogan ________
61. subtle ________
62. succinct ________
63. terrier (dog) ________
64. theme ________
65. theorem ________
66. tragedy ________
67. treacle ________
68. vegetable ________
69. wench ________
70. window ________

Copyright © 1994 by Harcourt Brace & Company. All rights reserved.

EXERCISE 2: In the space after each of the following words, write the original meaning of the word, or of its root, in accordance with the directions in Exercise 1. Then indicate the kind of semantic change involved by placing one of the following numbers in the shorter blank:

1. specialization
2. generalization
3. amelioration
4. pejoration

If you look up the word *traitor,* for instance, you will find that the first meaning given in its etymology is "to give across." From this rather neutral and colorless meaning, the word has changed to indicate "one given to treason." This change certainly shows pejoration. If *traitor* were given, your answer should read as follows:

traitor	(to) give across	4
1. arson	______________	____
2. bribe	______________	____
3. constable	______________	____
4. dean	______________	____
5. demon	______________	____
6. gauche	______________	____
7. harlot	______________	____
8. jewel	______________	____
9. lunatic	______________	____
10. mansion	______________	____
11. pastor	______________	____
12. pope	______________	____
13. prostitute	______________	____
14. rape	______________	____
15. senate	______________	____
16. serpent	______________	____
17. surgery	______________	____
18. villain	______________	____
19. virago	______________	____
20. weird (adj.)	______________	____

EXERCISE 3: The following words are products of commonization; they come originally from proper nouns. All of the words in this exercise come from names of real, fictional, or mythical people or places. In the blank following each word write the proper name from which it came.

Example: 1. herculean — Hercules
2. Gretna Green — Gretna Green in Scotland

1. ammonia ______________
2. arachnid ______________
3. atlas ______________
4. attic ______________

Copyright © 1994 by Harcourt Brace & Company. All rights reserved.

NAME ______________________ SECTION __________ DATE __________

5. bloomer ______________________
6. bologna ______________________
7. boycott ______________________
8. braille ______________________
9. calico ______________________
10. champagne ______________________
11. dalmatic ______________________
12. damask ______________________
13. dunce ______________________
14. gerrymander ______________________
15. grog ______________________
16. guernsey ______________________
17. guillotine ______________________
18. homburg ______________________
19. italic ______________________
20. jeremiad ______________________
21. limousine ______________________
22. macadam ______________________
23. masochism ______________________
24. nicotine ______________________
25. ohm ______________________
26. parchment ______________________
27. sandwich ______________________
28. saxophone ______________________
29. silhouette ______________________
30. spoonerism ______________________
31. syphilis ______________________
32. tabby ______________________
33. tarantula ______________________
34. watt ______________________
35. wisteria ______________________

EXERCISE 4 : The following sentences and phrases are taken from citations in the *Oxford English Dictionary.* They illustrate usages no longer current in the English language. Such usages are italicized. Refer to the *Oxford English Dictionary,* if available, or to any other unabridged dictionary. In the blank following each sentence write the meaning of the italicized word as used in the citation.

1. Now was the sun in western *cadence* low. (Milton, 1667) ______________________
2. This pension was to be *liquidated* into an equal share with us. (Cibber, 1739) ______________________

____
3. I scorn to take up a sword against a *naked* man. (Defoe, 1727) ______________________
4. A prince of great courage and beauty, but fostered up in blood by his *naughty* father. (Sidney, 1516) ______________________

____
5. The outworks stretch a great way into the *campaign.* (Sterne, 1765) ______________________
6. Til that a *capable* and wide revenge swallow them up. (Shakespeare, 1604) ______________________

____
7. And hills of snow and *lofts* of piled thunder. (Milton, 1673) ______________________
8. A noble gentleman 'tis ... every man has his fault, and *honesty* is his. (Shakespeare, 1607) ______________________

____
9. The thread itself that they make of their flax ... is ... *nervous* also and strong. (Holland, 1601) ______________________

____
10. The letter was not *nice* but full of charge of dear import. (Shakespeare, 1592) ______________________
11. He shows himself sincere but without *candour.* (Johnson, 1751) ______________________

Copyright © 1994 by Harcourt Brace & Company. All rights reserved.

12. I beseech him not to *reprobate* his child for an aversion which it is not in her power to conquer. (Richardson, 1748)

____

13. A banquet worthy of the fame which his splendid *housekeeping* had won for him. (Macaulay, 1849) _______________

____

14. They will run against things and *huddling* forwards fall from high places. (Browne, 1646) _______________

____

15. Seeking about the troops of Aragon, for to encounter with his traitorous *niece.* (Greene, 1592) _______________

____

16. The *noise* of this intended marriage soon reached Theodosius. (Addison, 1711) _______________

____

17. The loss of that letter which Cicero expected or received from his brother Quintus, as a *resolution* of British customs. (Browne, 1658) _______________

18. Well may this palace admiration claim ... and *respondent* to the master's fame. (Pope, 1726) _______________

____

19. How much we ought to ... examine and *humiliate* ourselves [and] seek to God. (Burton, 1621) _______________

____

20. Let Lovel and me have forthwith ... the *reversion* of the port. (Scott, 1816) _______________

____

Copyright © 1994 by Harcourt Brace & Company. All rights reserved.

NAME ______________________ SECTION ________ DATE ________

CUMULATIVE TEST 5: In the blank write the number of the word or phrase that corresponds most closely to the meaning of the italicized word.

1. to *adumbrate* the sketch: 1 criticize 2 destroy 3 foreshadow 4 finish — 1. ________
2. to *amerce* the offender: 1 rebuke 2 pardon 3 fine and punish 4 execute — 2. ________
3. an *anomalous* development: 1 abnormal 2 fortunate 3 inevitable 4 final — 3. ________
4. an *aquiline* specimen: like a 1 shark 2 otter 3 eagle 4 deer — 4. ________
5. an *argosy* from the East: 1 merchant fleet 2 caravan 3 delegation 4 band of freed captives — 5. ________
6. an *attenuated* solution: 1 filtered and clear 2 strengthened 3 tested 4 thinned and diluted — 6. ________
7. reckoning the matter a *bagatelle:* 1 stroke of fortune 2 serious development 3 decisive event 4 trifle — 7. ________
8. acting with *benignity:* 1 severe authority 2 negligence 3 gracious kindliness 4 deference to authority — 8. ________
9. a *buccal* infection: affecting the 1 chest 2 ears 3 mouth 4 heart — 9. ________
10. participating in the *cabal:* 1 royal entertainment 2 tragedy 3 conspiracy 4 landowners' league — 10. ________
11. a *capricious* decision: determined by 1 financial considerations 2 momentary infatuation 3 unpredictable whim 4 family loyalties — 11. ________
12. an ornamented *cincture:* 1 headdress 2 shield 3 belt or girdle 4 jacket — 12. ________
13. acting through *coercion:* 1 enthusiastic cooperation 2 forceful threats 3 resolute determination 4 unrecognized propaganda — 13. ________
14. *cognizant* of his duties: 1 aware 2 negligent 3 uninformed 4 contemptuous — 14. ________
15. a *comatose* patient: 1 unconscious 2 complaining 3 elderly 4 neurotic — 15. ________
16. chased by *corsairs:* 1 guerrillas 2 bandits 3 pirates 4 revolutionists — 16. ________
17. a *debonair* attitude: 1 aristocratic and snobbish 2 very conservative 3 lighthearted and carefree 4 stiff and aloof — 17. ________
18. *decorous* behavior: 1 wild and unruly 2 salty and nautical 3 proper and correct 4 suspicious and unethical — 18. ________
19. *desultory* study: 1 intense and serious 2 long-continued 3 wide and varied 4 random and irregular — 19. ________
20. the speaker's *diatribe:* 1 speech in praise 2 unusual diction 3 questionable taste 4 bitter and abusive talk — 20. ________
21. *dorsal* bones: those in the 1 foot 2 back 3 chest 4 neck — 21. ________
22. an *eerie* tale: 1 ridiculous or comical 2 incoherent and rambling 3 poignant or tragic 4 weird or mysterious — 22. ________
23. helping the *emaciated* prisoners: 1 enfeebled and wasted away 2 tortured 3 extremely sick 4 blind — 23. ________
24. her policy was an *enigma:* 1 mysterious puzzle 2 surrender of national interests 3 political maneuver 4 desperate gamble — 24. ________

Copyright © 1994 by Harcourt Brace & Company. All rights reserved.

25. to *expedite* the project: 1 inspect 2 lay plans for 3 speed up 4 discontinue 25. ________

26. to *expiate* his crimes: 1 atone for 2 explain in detail 3 feel remorse for 4 take pride in 26. ________

27. a *fecund* union: having 1 much discord 2 deep affection 3 many offspring 4 mutual trust 27. ________

28. *filial* obligations: those of a 1 lieutenant 2 apprentice 3 trustee 4 son or daughter 28. ________

29. the mixture *fulminated:* 1 remained inert 2 settled into separate parts 3 exploded 4 swelled in size 29. ________

30. to *garrote* a victim: 1 kidnap 2 strangle 3 blackmail 4 knock out 30. ________

31. continental *hegemony:* 1 unity 2 preponderant control 3 discord and rivalry 4 quiet and peace 31. ________

32. *hirsute* animals: 1 readily tamed 2 shy and timid 3 nocturnal 4 roughly hairy 32. ________

33. a *histrionic* gesture: 1 cautious 2 covert or hidden 3 defiant 4 affectedly theatrical 33. ________

34. in an *inchoate* state: 1 utterly confused 2 about to expire 3 only recently begun 4 firmly established 34. ________

35. famous for his senate *jeremiads:* 1 political manipulations 2 long, complaining speeches 3 persuasive gestures 4 warlike comments 35. ________

36. a *laconic* countryman: 1 stupid and unsophisticated 2 rough and crude 3 hulking and awkward 4 terse and sparing in speech 36. ________

37. a *lacuna* in the diary: 1 mistake 2 omission or gap 3 falsehood 4 conundrum 37. ________

38. the cat's *lambent* eyes: 1 softly radiant 2 beautifully colored 3 dim and weak 4 keen at night 38. ________

39. a *litigious* neighbor: fond of 1 keeping dogs 2 starting lawsuits 3 playing loud music 4 calling frequently 39. ________

40. a *maudlin* display: 1 brave and stoical 2 thoroughly admirable 3 silly and demonstrative 4 witty and comical 40. ________

41. to *mollify* the disputants: 1 aggravate 2 reinforce 3 encourage 4 soothe and appease 41. ________

42. a *mordant* critical comment: 1 acute and penetrating 2 irrelevant 3 definitive and final 4 biting and sarcastic 42. ________

43. a *nubile* girl: 1 immigrant 2 half-breed 3 marriageable 4 unhappy 43. ________

44. *occult* lore: 1 mineralogical 2 ancient 3 secret and mysterious 4 pertaining to fraternal orders 44. ________

45. *pastoral* poetry: having to do with 1 sailors 2 missionaries 3 heroes 4 shepherds 45. ________

46. *pectoral* muscles: located in the 1 head 2 neck 3 chest 4 abdomen 46. ________

47. the *penultimate* syllable: 1 heavily accented 2 rhyming 3 next to last 4 most important 47. ________

48. a *perfervid* vow: 1 hypocritical 2 religious 3 very fervent 4 silent 48. ________

49. a *potable* concoction: 1 nourishing 2 delicious 3 capable of being drunk 4 invigorating 49. ________

50. man's *primeval* life: 1 most primitive 2 evil and sinful 3 uneconomical 4 careful and cautious 50. ________

51. the argument *ramified:* 1 branched out 2 died out 3 was continued 4 intensified 51. ________

52. in a *recumbent* position: 1 undignified 2 crouching 3 defensive 4 lying down 52. ________

 Copyright © 1994 by Harcourt Brace & Company. All rights reserved.

NAME ______________________ SECTION ________ DATE ________

53. *a sadistic* pleasure: one derived from 1 alcohol 2 narcotics 3 cruelty and suffering 4 exhibitionism 53. ________

54. a *sardonic* attitude: 1 warm and friendly 2 self-sacrificing 3 docile and obedient 4 ironic and negative 54. ________

55. a *scabrous* surface: 1 smooth 2 icy and slippery 3 rough and scaly 4 ugly and discolored 55. ________

56. a *sinuous* outline: 1 wavy and winding 2 clear and accurate 3 beautiful 4 suggestive 56. ________

57. a *soporific* dosage: 1 killing pain 2 easing a cough 3 clotting blood 4 inducing sleep 57. ________

58. a *specter* in the castle: 1 madman 2 torturer 3 ghost 4 assassin 58. ________

59. the announcer's *strident* voice: 1 harsh and grating 2 extremely loud 3 fast and staccato 4 soft and soothing 59. ________

60. one of the baron's *sycophants:* 1 medical men 2 tax collectors 3 servile flatterers 4 mounted knights 60. ________

61. a *taciturn* mountaineer: 1 rugged and hardy 2 silent and disinclined to talk 3 resourceful 4 serving as scout 61. ________

62. a *tepid* reaction to the plea: 1 enthusiastic 2 extremely hostile 3 half-hearted and indifferent 4 unpredictable 62. ________

63. the *therapy* recommended in the case: 1 remedial treatment 2 legal measures 3 detective procedures 4 moral advice 63. ________

64. a *tremulous* voice: 1 authoritative and commanding 2 timid and trembling 3 melodious 4 faint and childlike 64. ________

65. a *tumid* artery: 1 strong and healthy 2 swollen and enlarged 3 weakened 4 sutured 65. ________

66. a *venial* sin: 1 mortal or deadly 2 inspired by lust 3 minor and forgivable 4 secret and unsuspected 66. ________

67. *verbosity* of the essay: 1 style 2 wordiness 3 tone 4 focus 67. ________

68. to *vitiate* his conclusion: 1 ignore 2 dispute 3 approve 4 invalidate 68. ________

69. a *vitreous* substance: 1 clay 2 milky 3 glassy 4 black 69. ________

70. a *vitriolic* answer: 1 silly 2 pleasing 3 correct 4 caustic 70. ________

Copyright © 1994 by Harcourt Brace & Company. All rights reserved.

Language is the archives of history. . . .
Ralph Waldo Emerson

9 Figurative Language

Often in speaking and writing we use words for special effects without intending our hearers or readers to interpret them with their usual, literal meanings. When a stupid, hulking student is referred to as a "dumb ox," no one assumes that he is literally a bovine quadruped. Similarly, if another is referred to as a "mathematical shark," no one is led to think of her as a large, voracious, elasmobranch fish. So also with "a stupid ape," "a horse for work," "a bear for punishment," "a wolf," and so on. These phrases illustrate figurative language—language that communicates a meaning different from the total literal meaning of the separate words.

It is possible to compile a longer list, but eight kinds of figurative language cover most figurative uses. (1) A *simile* is an exaggerated comparison expressed with *like, as,* or, occasionally, *than:* "The child's eyes were like saucers," "His feet felt heavy as lead," "She was lighter than a feather." (2) A *metaphor* implies a comparison without using *like* or *as:* "He is a dumb ox," "The patient was burning up with fever," "the barbs of sarcastic criticism," "President Prunes Appropriations Bill," "eaten up with jealousy," "a mushroom development." (3) A *metonymy* is the expression of an idea evoked by a term designating some associated notions. In "She drank the whole bottle," *bottle* is used with figurative extension to indicate the contents. In "the chair recognizes the speaker from Iowa," *chair* is a metonymy indicating the chairperson. In "reading Shakespeare," *Shakespeare* is a metonymy for "Shakespeare's plays." (4) A *synecdoche* is a figure in which the part designates the whole or the whole a part. *Head* in "fifty head of cattle" is a synecdoche, since the expression means the whole animal, not just the head. *Hands* is a synecdoche in "a factory employing fifty hands." (5) *Irony* is figurative language in which the meaning intended is exactly the reverse of what is literally stated: "He took my car without asking me for it, wrecked it, and refused to pay for any of the repairs; *he was a fine friend."* (It is a mistake to regard *irony* as necessarily a synonym for *sarcasm.* Sarcasm often employs irony, but one can be ironic without being sarcastic. You should notice, too, that there are various kinds of irony that may be mentioned in English classes; see your dictionary for definitions of other kinds of irony. This chapter is concerned only with figurative language, and the definition given here fits in only with this consideration.) (6) A *personification* endows something inanimate and often intangible with human attributes. In "Science has not yet accepted all of her conclusions," the word *science* represents a personification, as does *destiny* in "Destiny spun an odd pattern for his life." (7) An *understatement* is the deliberate use of milder, weaker, less forceful, less sensational language than the situation requires: "The hornets came out of the broken nest in a rather vexed state"; "He felt some discomfort when the pin was jammed a half inch under his fingernail." (8) A *hyperbole* is any extreme or exaggerated figure: "as deep as the ocean," "that night was pure hell," "a story as old as time."

It is impossible to draw exact lines of differentiation among these various figures. As the illustrations for hyperbole indicate, turns of speech may be at once similes or metaphors and hyperboles. The line between synecdoche and metonymy is often difficult to draw; parts of larger things are of necessity associated with those larger things. In the illustration of personification above it may be argued that *science* is a metonymy for "scientists" rather than a personification. Fortunately, it is rarely necessary to be exact in labels.

A figurative expression is sometimes a single word. With metaphor or synecdoche, for instance, it is easy to isolate one word from a sentence and feel sure that this word has been used figuratively. A simile, however, by definition involves more than one word, and understatement and irony often depend more on the wording of the whole phrase or sentence than on an individual word. In any case, simile, understatement, hyperbole, irony, and personification apparently do not bring about as many instances of semantic change as do metaphor, synecdoche, and metonymy.

Copyright © 1994 by Harcourt Brace & Company. All rights reserved.

These three figures underline many changes in word meanings. The word *fret* originally meant "to eat up, devour voraciously, as a wild animal does." It was used metaphorically in relation to the effect of cares and worries and now has come to mean "to agitate or perturb oneself with constant worry." The original metaphorical use was repeated so often that in time people forgot that it was figurative and accepted it as literal, and the earlier meaning of the word dropped into disuse. The word *thrill* originally meant "pierce, bore, make an opening in"; it came to be used frequently as a figure to indicate tingling emotional excitement. Gradually the notion that this latter indication was figurative has died out, and *thrill* now literally indicates excited sensation. Curiously, the word *bore,* which originally expressed about the same notion as *thrill,* has changed so that it is now an antonym for *thrill.* From the literal meanings of the word parts concerned, *concur* would indicate "a running together," *confuse* "a pouring together." But only an etymologist would be likely to notice these facts, and only a person singularly vigilant about word meanings would see the figures involved in "they moved from the heart of the city to the outskirts."

When no one interprets an expression as figurative and everyone comes to accept a new meaning as literal and not metaphorical, then it may be felt that the word in question has undergone complete semantic change. *Concur, confuse,* and *outskirts* illustrate this complete change, as do *corrupt* (now not interpreted as "thoroughly broken"), *error* (now not understood to mean "a wandering"), and *flamboyant* ("florid, ornate," but with the metaphor about bearing a flame or torch now forgotten).

Many stereotyped phrases are also used without awareness of their original meaning. Few persons think of hunting with hounds when they hear the phrase "to hold at bay," of actual axes and grindstones when they hear "an ax to grind," of hoisting flags when they hear "to show one's colors." "To miss fire" is often said with no thought of old firearms; "a red herring" often inspires no thought of fish. Sometimes figurative use in phrases keeps alive words that would otherwise die out; many people know that "to be at loggerheads" means "to quarrel," but few know what a loggerhead is.

Figurative language causes few problems of either expression or interpretation. In one's own writing or speaking, perhaps the most important difficulty to guard against is mixing figures. Use of two or more different and contradictory figures in the same sentence may produce laughable results: "I smell a rat; I will nip it in the bud"; "Seated firm in the saddle, with his hand on the throttle, the President will keep us out of the ruts of depression."

As we have seen, the essence of figurative language lies in the use of an expression having something other than the everyday, commonplace, literal significance of the words used. It is unfortunate that figurative language is commonly first called to students' attention in analyses of poetry, for this procedure is likely to suggest that figurative language is lofty, literary, fancy, poetic, and dreamy—the device only of the poet and not of the majority of us. Few impressions could be more incorrect. We all use a great deal of figurative language without attempting or achieving a particularly poetic or literary effect. Think of some people you know. Make up a quick, although reasonably full, description of each of them. How many figures have you used in so doing? Read such nonliterary materials as the sports pages or the financial columns of your newspaper, noticing how much figurative language you encounter there. It will be surprising if you do not find a great deal. The general prevalence of figurative language explains why so many words undergo figurative semantic change.

Copyright © 1994 by Harcourt Brace & Company. All rights reserved.

NAME ______________________ SECTION ________ DATE ________

CHAPTER 9

EXERCISE 1: By writing the appropriate number in the blank, indicate the kind of figure illustrated by the italicized wording in the following sentences.

1. hyperbole	3. metaphor	5. personification	7. synecdoche
2. irony	4. metonymy	6. simile	8. understatement

1. The explorers were ready to brave the *myriad* dangers of the march through the jungle. _______
2. He was called *"pretty* boy"; he had cauliflower ears, beetling brows, small bloodshot eyes, a flattened nose, and badly scarred cheeks. _______
3. With five-sixths of his lungs eaten away by tuberculosis, *his chances of living another fifty years are not excellent.* _______
4. He *knifed* his way through the defensive line to score the tying points. _______
5. With the change in the interest rates, stock market prices *nose-dived.* _______
6. With as much pomp *as ever was shown by archbishop, chancellor, or regent,* the headwaiter led us to our table. _______
7. When the first *clarinet* showed up drunk, Tim had to substitute for him at the last moment. _______
8. With today's rising prices it is certainly hard for the average family to find *bread and butter* for many children. _______
9. She *spat out* a rude and defiant denial. _______
10. The child got into the barber's chair *like a patient about to have a major operation.* _______
11. In his first pitching start Farrell *machine-gunned* nineteen straight batters before allowing a hit. _______
12. But his courage began to *melt away* as he thought of the dangers he still had to face. _______
13. The near collision between the two packed jet airliners *did not make the people in the control tower happier or calmer.* _______
14. The president's *office* says that such a plan is being considered. _______
15. This development left all of their plans and hopes *in rubble.* _______
16. *A blaring radio or television set in the room next door did not add to her comfort.* _______
17. Some of the food at Harry's Restaurant is not very good, but if you always eat the *Blue Plate,* you will be all right. _______
18. At that time the *infant* science of bacteriology seemed to have the solution for such problems. _______
19. But *fame* is always fickle, and now Elwood is forgotten. _______
20. The mob went down *like tenpins* when the soldiers charged. _______
21. But some time, my people, *Freedom* will come again to extend us her blessings. _______
22. The infantry held its position, but the *horse* were slow in charging. _______
23. The company has a virtual *strangle hold* on the manufacturing of new instruments. _______
24. *The bench* was not impressed by the lawyer's plea for clemency. _______

Copyright © 1994 by Harcourt Brace & Company. All rights reserved.

EXERCISE 2: In the following selections, underline any wording that is obviously figurative.

1. I have already intimated to you the danger of parties in the State, with particular reference to the founding of them on geographical discriminations. Let me now take a more comprehensive view, and warn you in the most solemn manner against the baneful effects of the spirit of party generally . . . in governments purely elective, it is a spirit not to be encouraged. From their natural tendency it is certain there will always be enough of that spirit for every salutary purpose; and there being constant danger of excess, the effort ought to be by force of public opinion to mitigate and assuage it. A fire not to be quenched, it demands a uniform vigilance to prevent its bursting into flame, lest, instead of warning, it should consume. (George Washington, Farewell Address, September 17, 1796)

2. That is the real issue. That is the issue that will continue in this country when these poor tongues of Judge Douglas and myself shall be silent. It is the eternal struggle between these two principles—right and wrong—throughout the world. They are the two principles that have stood face to face from the beginning of time, and will ever continue to struggle. The one is the common right of humanity, and the other the divine right of kings . . . . And whenever we can get rid of the fog which obscures the real question, when we can get Judge Douglas and his friends to avow a policy looking to its perpetuation—we can get out from among that class of men and bring them to the side of those who treat it as a wrong. Then there will soon be an end of it, and that end will be its "ultimate extinction." (Abraham Lincoln, Reply to Douglas, October 15, 1858)

3. So first of all let me assert my firm belief that the only thing we have to fear is fear itself—nameless, unreasoning, unjustified terror which paralyzes needed efforts to convert retreat into advance. In every dark hour of our national life a leadership of frankness and vigor has met with that understanding and support of the people themselves which is essential to victory. I am convinced that you will again give that support to leadership in these critical days. In such a spirit on my part and on yours we face our common difficulties. They concern, thank God, only material things. Values have shrunken to fantastic levels; taxes have risen; our ability to pay has fallen, government of all kinds is faced by serious curtailment of income; the means of exchange are frozen in the currents of trade; the withered leaves of industrial enterprise lie on every side . . . . Only a foolish optimist can deny the dark realities of the moment. (Franklin D. Roosevelt, First Inaugural Address, March 4, 1933)

4. In your hands, my fellow citizens, more than in mine, will rest the final success or failure of our course. Since this country was founded, each generation has been summoned to give testimony to its national loyalty. The graves of young Americans who answered that call encircle the globe. Now the trumpet summons us again—not as a call to bear arms, though arms we need—not as a call to battle, though embattled we are—but a call to bear the burden of a long twilight struggle, year in and year out, "rejoicing in hope, patient in tribulation"—a struggle against the common enemies of man: tyranny, poverty, disease and war itself. Can we forge against these enemies a grand and global alliance, north and south, east and west, that can assure a more fruitful life for all mankind? Will you join in that historic effort? In the long history of the world, only a few generations have been granted the role of defending freedom in its hour of maximum danger. I do not shrink from this responsibility—I welcome it. I do not believe that any of us would exchange places with any other people or any other generation. The energy, the faith, and the devotion which we bring to this endeavor will light our country and all who serve it—and the glow from that fire can truly light the world. And so, my fellow Americans: Ask not what your country can do for you—ask what you can do for your country. My fellow citizens of the world: Ask not what America will do for you, but what together we can do for the freedom of man. (John F. Kennedy, Inaugural Address, January 20, 1961)

Copyright © 1994 by Harcourt Brace & Company. All rights reserved.

NAME ________________ SECTION ________ DATE ________

EXERCISE 3: Following are a number of figurative expressions containing words whose meanings are not very commonly known. In the blank after each expression, give the meaning of the italicized word.

1. to make the *welkin* ring ________________
2. to *broach* a subject ________________
3. to have one's *gorge* rise ________________
4. raising a *hue* and cry ________________
5. a pig in a *poke* ________________
6. *rack* and ruin ________________
7. to come a *cropper* ________________
8. not a *jot* or *tittle* ________________
9. shuffling off this mortal *coil* ________________
10. to run full *tilt* ________________
11. to leave in the *lurch* ________________
12. by *dint* of great sacrifice ________________
13. to take in the *toils* ________________
14. to run the *gauntlet* ________________
15. to be hoist with one's own *petard* ________________

EXERCISE 4: In the blanks following the figurative phrases below, give brief statements of their meanings.

1. to eat crow ________________
2. in sackcloth and ashes ________________
3. to cool one's heels ________________
4. between wind and water ________________
5. to have one's tongue in cheek ________________
6. to pull one's leg ________________
7. putting on side ________________
8. to pay on the nail ________________
9. under the weather ________________
10. to trim one's sails to the wind ________________
11. to send to Coventry ________________
12. three sheets in the wind ________________
13. to draw in one's horns ________________
14. to pour oil on troubled waters ________________
15. to cast pearls before swine ________________

Copyright © 1994 by Harcourt Brace & Company. All rights reserved.

Polonius: What do you read my lord?
Hamlet: Words, words, words.
William Shakespeare
Hamlet, Act II, Scene 2

10 Synonyms

Synonyms are words that have the same general meaning, words that are interchangeable in certain contexts. *Hard* and *difficult* are synonyms; one may say either "a hard job" or "a difficult job" with no change in general meaning and with little difference in suggestion. *Sickness* and *illness* are synonyms; it doesn't make much difference whether one says that a person has been absent from work because of sickness or because of illness. *Silent, quiet,* and *noiseless* are synonyms, as are *lazy, indolent,* and *slothful.* Other sets of synonyms include *formality, ceremony, ritual; student, pupil; holy, sacred, divine; gay, glad, joyous, merry; hit, strike, cuff, clout;* and *see, behold, view, observe, notice.*

Synonyms are not necessarily interchangeable in all usages. One does not say "in sick health" as well as "in ill health" or "car-ill" as well as "car-sick," although *sick* and *ill* are generally synonyms. *Capable* and *able* are synonyms in "a capable woman, an able woman," but one says "capable of doing the work" and "able to do the work." And two words may be synonymous in one sense but not in others. *Stout* and *fat* are synonyms when they indicate an excess of flesh; one may say either "a stout man" or "a fat man." *Stout* and *sturdy* are synonyms in that either will fit the blank in "the _______ defenders of the besieged fortress." But *fat* and *sturdy* are not therefore synonyms.

The English language is especially rich in synonyms, partly because of the enormous number of words we have borrowed. We had *height* in Old English and borrowed *altitude* from Latin. *Fast* is an Old English word; *rapid* is from Latin via French. *Clean* is from Old English; *sanitary* and *hygienic* are borrowings through French of Latin and Greek forms. (Other Latin borrowings have come into English from the various Romance languages, with French as the principle transmission medium, of course.) A series of synonyms such as *agitate, perturb, ruffle, fluster, fret, disturb,* and *startle* shows words of various origins. The wealth of synonyms in English affords us very exact expression but imposes on us the task of careful discrimination.

Although by definition synonyms are words that have the same meaning or denotation, it is often said that no two synonyms are interchangeable without at least some slight change in suggestion or connotation. The *denotation* of a word is its limited, explicit meaning; the *connotation* of a word is the additional suggestion that it carries with it. In denotation *seaman, sailor,* and *mariner* are often about the same. *Seaman,* however, may connote considerations of official rank, as in "able-bodied seaman" and "seaman secondclass." *Sailor* often suggests a breezy, rollicking quality absent from *seaman. Mariner,* perhaps because of Coleridge's poem "The Rime of the Ancient Mariner," may suggest the grizzled veteran of many years at sea; it may, on the other hand, connote especial competence in steering and navigation, because of its use in certain official ratings. *House* and *home* offer a very familiar illustration of differences in connotation. *House* is likely to suggest only a residential structure or building, *home* to add connotations of the warmth of family life over a long period. *Drunkard* and *alcoholic* are about the same in denotation; the former may censoriously suggest an unkempt, sleazy bum, the latter may more forgivingly connote a person who is psychologically ill.

Because of the difficulty of being dogmatic about connotations, it follows that there are likely to be exceptions to the comments made above. The notion that *home* usually connotes the warm, intimate comfort of family life and *house* does not may not apply to the reaction of a person who has grown up in a cheerless, impersonal home. To some persons today, *drunkard* may have a humorous suggestion because they associate it with nineteenth-century melodramas dealing with excessive drinking. *Loud*

Copyright © 1994 by Harcourt Brace & Company. All rights reserved.

is a general term without especial connotation; its synonym *stentorian* connotes the Homeric treatment of the Trojan War but of course does so only to persons familiar with Stentor, the character in the *Iliad* who could shout as loud as fifty other men together. Comments about connotation should never be interpreted as absolute.

The exact line of demarcation between denotation and connotation is difficult to draw. If a word strongly suggests a certain characteristic to every user of English, if the word is never uttered without that suggestion, then for all practical purposes it may be viewed as part of the denotation. The word *notorious* originally meant "famous"; in time it acquired pejorative connotations that became universally known; now the idea of an evil, criminal, or scandalous reason for being widely known is practically essential to the denotation. A connotation that is always present becomes part of the denotation.

Synonyms differ in various ways. Sometimes one synonym is more learned, dignified, or pretentious than another. *Osculate* is more learned than *kiss; domicile* than *home, residence,* or *dwelling; portal* than *door. Salt* and *salty* are everyday adjectives, but *saline* suggests a more learned context, as in "a saline solution." *Daily* is ordinary English, *diurnal* and *quotidian* learned. Sometimes one word is notably more informal than its synonym; *fiddle* is a synonym for *violin* but connotes informality. *Smidge* or *smidgeon* is synonymous with *bit* or *particle* but is unlikely to be used in a formal context. Sometimes a synonym has regional suggestions; *goober* is a synonym for *peanut,* but mainly in the South; *bobby* for *policeman,* but only in England.

Sometimes the etymologies of words affect their connotations. The word *meticulous* may suggest fear of committing an oversight, a suggestion lacking in the synonym *fastidious,* because it is derived from the Latin *meticulosis,* a derivative of *metus* "fear." Two synonyms for *explain,* the words *explicate* and *elucidate,* may suggest respectively an unfolding (or uncomplicating) and an enlightening because of their roots. *Social,* from the Latin *socius,* "a comrade," may suggest the sphere of human relations more than *gregarious,* a derivative of Latin *grex* "a herd, flock." *Unctuous* differs from *ingratiating* or *fulsome* in connoting oiliness. Words that come from proper names suggest the historical or literary characters or events from which they are derived. *Tiny* and *lilliputian* are synonyms, but in addition to indicating extreme smallness the latter is likely to recall Swift's *Gulliver's Travels* to the reader; *gargantuan* means "huge, gigantic," but also suggests the work of Rabelais.

Sometimes synonyms differ in that one is general in meaning or suggestion, others more specific. *Carry* has a rather general meaning; *ferry* indicates carrying back and forth, often over water and often on a regular schedule. *Bard* is a synonym for *poet,* but is likely to suggest mainly an ancient tribal poet. A *cynic* is a person who rejects most values; a *misogynist* is a man who is cynical about women. *Pace, amble, saunter, stroll,* and *hike* are more specific synonyms for the general term *walk. Wild* and *feral* are synonyms, but the latter is often applied to an animal that has been domesticated but has reverted to wildness, as "a cat that has gone feral." *Marital* has general reference to either the occasion or state of marriage; but *nuptial* refers primarily to the first, the wedding ceremony.

Other sets of synonyms may contrast various aspects of a general subject. *Terrestrial* stresses the notion of the earth as contrasted with other heavenly bodies, *earthy* the earth as composed of soil. *Venomous* suggests poison imparted with malignant force; *toxic,* poison or poisonous effects discovered or capable of discovery by scientific means. *Desperate* conjures up pictures of a hopelessness goading people to mad, wild effort; *forlorn* a hopelessness attended by utter dejection.

Some words express greater size, degree, or effect than their synonyms. A *cavern* is often an earth chamber larger than a cave. A *metropolis* is usually a city that has influence over a wide adjacent territory. To *smash* is not merely to break, but to break utterly. *Saccharine* indicates "extremely sweet."

Synonyms also may differ in expressing value judgments. To be *resolute* is usually considered a virtue; *determined* expresses no value judgment; *obstinate* is condemnatory. To be *pious* is usually regarded as good; to be *sanctimonious* is to take piety to insincere or unreasonable degrees.

Often a full description of differences among synonyms involves several of the considerations given above. *Prevaricate* differs from *lie* in that it is more bookish and also less condemnatory than *lie.*

Copyright © 1994 by Harcourt Brace & Company. All rights reserved.

Fib is informal and less condemnatory than either of the two synonyms; it is likely to be used of children rather than adults. *Donation* is more learned than *gift* and is more likely to be used in reference to what is given to an institution, organization, cause, or movement. *Kick* is informal and figurative; *protest* is a general term; *expostulate,* used mainly in learned contexts, may imply firm, sustained objection. Analysis of differences among synonyms is an endless, fascinating study.

We have said earlier that Old English words and words borrowed early from Scandinavian often suggest a homely, emotional quality lacking in the more literary words borrowed, directly or indirectly, from Latin or Greek. Thus *love,* an Old English word, expresses stronger emotion than *affection,* borrowed from Latin via French. The Old English word *greed* is more forceful than the Latin word *cupidity. Hearty* and *kind* are somehow more direct, frank, forceful, and natural than the borrowed words *cordial* and *benevolent.* The Old English word *forgive* is apt in situations involving deep emotion; the French synonym *pardon* suggests social etiquette or legal procedure; the Latin *excuse* may connote formal, organizational procedure such as that whereby students are excused for being absent. This difference between native and borrowed words may be overemphasized, however, for many borrowed words are now as forceful and effective as native words—*rage, brave, cruel, strange, rude, praise,* and *adore,* for example.

Careful choice of synonyms is one mark of superior writing. Notice the superiority of the words italicized in the following passages over possible alternate choices:

We the people of the United States, in order to ... insure domestic *tranquility*—Constitution of the United States	peacefulness, calmness, placidity, serenity, stillness
... hearing often times The *still,* sad music of humanity—Wordsworth	quiet, silent, noiseless, quiescent, soundless
There is, however, reason to believe that there was a small *nucleus* of truth around which this great mass of fiction gathered.—Macaulay	core, center, hub, focus, heart, middle
... her head sank deep into the pillow, taking on the majestic *pallor* and immobility of marble.—Conrad	whiteness, paleness, wanness, lividness
... the *feverish* life of gold-seeking, the recklessness engendered by sudden gain and as sudden loss ... —James Truslow Adams	hectic, wild, frantic, mad, exciting, melodramatic
Yesterday, December 7, 1941—a date which will live in *infamy* ...—Franklin D. Roosevelt	shame, ignominy, notoriety, disgrace, dishonor, obloquy
The trumpet call had let loose an *enormous* volume of noise.—George Orwell	great, huge, vast, immense, colossal, gigantic, mammoth

Dictionaries, as we have seen in Chapter 1, often include synonymies with definitions. Check in your dictionary the synonymies for *kind* and *benign, torpor* and *lethargy, work* and *labor, lean* and *gaunt, blasphemy* and *profanity. Roget's Thesaurus* gives long lists of synonyms without, however, attempting to define or illustrate them or to discriminate among them. The best-known of the more comprehensive treatments of synonyms is *Webster's Dictionary of Synonyms,* published by the G. & C. Merriam Company; this book not only lists synonyms but distinguishes among them, illustrating with quotations from well-known writers. (For this the latest edition is generally preferred to the older editions.)

The antonym of a particular word is a word with the opposite meaning. In general, *bad* is the antonym of *good, high* of *low,* and *foolish* of *wise.* Words are not necessarily antonyms in every possible use; *bad* is, of course, not the opposite of *good* in "It's a good while since I saw Joe," nor *high* the reverse of *low* in "a low, mean trick." Often full knowledge of a word comes only with knowledge

Copyright © 1994 by Harcourt Brace & Company. All rights reserved.

and appreciation of its antonyms. One is aided in mastering the word *taciturn* by realizing that *garrulous* is its antonym. Similarly with *brash* and *reticent, complex* and *simple, preoccupied* and *attentive, tractable* and *recalcitrant, amiable* and *irascible,* and *dexterous* and *clumsy.*

It would seem natural that most antonyms would be derived forms with negative affixes; *unclear* is the antonym of *clear, hopeless* of *hopeful. Intractable* and *inattentive* are satisfactory antonyms of *tractable* and *attentive.* But the English language has been subjected to so many influences that it lacks completely regular patterns of affixing. Some words do not have well-established negative derivatives; for *hard* and *obscure* we do not commonly use *unhard* and *inobscure.* Sometimes we have for one affirmative form more than one negative, with or without difference in meaning or connotation; *sanitary* is paired with both *insanitary* and *unsanitary; moral* with *immoral, amoral,* and *unmoral.* Sometimes we have for one negative two or more affirmative forms: *graceless* is an antonym for both *gracious* and *graceful.*

Homonyms are words identical or very nearly identical in pronunciation, but different in origin and meaning. They may or may not be identical in spelling. The *list* of "a laundry list" and the *list* of "a list to starboard" are homonyms, as are *mean* in "the mean actions of that little sneak" and *mean* in "the mean distance from the earth to the moon." Other homonyms are *meat* and *meet; sight, cite,* and *site; write* and *right; bear* ("animal"), *bear* ("to carry"), and *bare;* and *beet* and *beat.* Exactly which words are homonyms depends on pronunciation. Except in very precise, corrective pronunciation *compliment* and *complement, illusion* and *allusion,* and *access* and *excess* are homonymous. In dialects that do not pronounce the post-vocalic *r,* words such as *lord* and *laud* and *floor* and *flaw* are homonyms. Homonyms frequently cause problems in writing: *principal, principle; hanger, hangar; council, counsel; capitol, capital; and waver, waiver.* Similar to the problem of discerning between homonyms is that of choosing between words of closely similar form: *statue, statute, stature; precede, proceed;* and *militate, mitigate.* Keep them *straight*—not *strait.*

The following paragraph analyzes the similarities and differences between a pair of synonyms. All the material in it may be found in a desk dictionary, and it is intended to serve as a model for similar student paragraphs.

hard–adamant

Hard, a word of Old English origin, is applied generally to anything that resists being pressed in, separated, cut, or pierced. From its original meaning it has spread out to indicate "obdurate, rigid, strong, oppressive, difficult." *Adamant,* borrowed from Latin via Old French, is made up eventually of two Greek elements, the prefix *a-,* meaning "not," and the root *-dam-,* meaning "subdue," along with a suffix. Originally a noun designating the diamond or another very hard stone that resists cutting, the word has branched out into adjective use with the meaning of "very hard; resisting penetration" and by extension has acquired the meaning of "unyielding," as in the sentence "Regardless of entreaties and objections, he remained *adamant.*"

Copyright © 1994 by Harcourt Brace & Company. All rights reserved.

NAME ______________________ SECTION __________ DATE __________

CHAPTER 10

EXERCISE 1: For each of the italicized words in the following phrases, write three synonyms in the blanks.

	(1)	(2)	(3)
Example: a *dangerous* position	hazardous	perilous	precarious
1. listening with *distrust*	________	________	________
2. a thief's *furtive* approach	________	________	________
3. a *burlesque* of his speech	________	________	________
4. very *terse* answers	________	________	________
5. written in a *flowery* style	________	________	________
6. a *compendium* of longer works	________	________	________
7. on your own *volition*	________	________	________
8. *coaxed* into proceeding	________	________	________
9. a very *important* feature	________	________	________
10. *intrigues* among the nobles	________	________	________
11. *useless* attempts to escape	________	________	________
12. an *excellent* accomplishment	________	________	________
13. a *healthful* effect	________	________	________
14. *infinite* distances in space	________	________	________
15. of *transitory* interest	________	________	________
16. an unusual *event*	________	________	________
17. a *gathering* of citizens	________	________	________
18. a *blending* of elements	________	________	________
19. an *immense* statue	________	________	________
20. *turn away* from one's course	________	________	________

EXERCISE 2: In the space following each word write a simple, less learned synonym.

1. adversity ________________
2. antithesis ________________
3. aperture ________________
4. catechize ________________
5. chattels ________________
6. chicanery ________________
7. coeval ________________
8. desiccate ________________
9. encomium ________________
10. enervation ________________
11. enigmatic ________________
12. enunciate ________________
13. eschew ________________
14. execrate ________________
15. expunge ________________
16. exuberant ________________

Copyright © 1994 by Harcourt Brace & Company. All rights reserved.

EXERCISE 2—Continued

17. histrionic ______
18. idiosyncrasy ______
19. indigent ______
20. inebriation ______
21. interdict ______
22. irascibl ______
23. jocos ______
24. labyrint ______
25. mundan ______
26. obeisance ______
27. paucity ______
28. physiognomy ______
29. poignant ______
30. preceptor ______
31. precursor ______
32. residue ______
33. savant ______
34. sundry ______
35. thesaurus ______
36. trepidation ______
37. turpitude ______
38. variegated ______
39. verbiage ______
40. wraith ______

EXERCISE 3: In the space following each word write a more learned or erudite synonym.

1. accustom ______
2. black (adj.) ______
3. confine (v.) ______
4. curse (n.) ______
5. curt ______
6. decay (v.) ______
7. delay (v.) ______
8. elastic (adj.) ______
9. forgetfulness ______
10. interrupted ______
11. liar ______
12. learned (adj.) ______
13. native to (adj.) ______
14. necessary (adj.) ______
15. nickname (n.) ______
16. odd ______
17. poverty ______
18. practicable ______
19. praise (v.) ______
20. profane (adj.) ______
21. punish ______
22. repay ______
23. repeat ______
24. repentant ______
25. salt (n.) ______
26. secret (adj.) ______
27. steal (v.) ______
28. surrender (v.) ______
29. think ______
30. tickle (v.) ______
31. undress (v.) ______
32. unrelated ______
33. unsteady ______
34. warn ______
35. weary (adj.) ______

Copyright © 1994 by Harcourt Brace & Company. All rights reserved.

NAME ______________________________ SECTION __________ DATE __________

EXERCISE 4: One word in each of the following sets is not a synonym for the others. Write its number in the blank.

1. 1 inordinate 2 excessive 3 relevant 4 extravagant ________
2. 1 extract 2 imbue 3 instill 4 diffuse ________
3. 1 intricate 2 complicated 3 knotty 4 perspicuous ________
4. 1 conglomeration 2 aggregate 3 dissemination 4 amassment ________
5. 1 peculiarity 2 orthodoxy 3 idiosyncrasy 4 eccentricity ________
6. 1 evanescent 2 immutable 3 transient 4 ephemeral ________
7. 1 former 2 pristine 3 quondam 4 posterior ________
8. 1 virile 2 senile 3 decrepit 4 superannuated ________
9. 1 impending 2 inveterate 3 looming 4 imminent ________
10. 1 arable 2 barren 3 sterile 4 fallow ________
11. 1 bucolic 2 urban 3 cosmopolitan 4 metropolitan ________
12. 1 epitome 2 compendium 3 elaboration 4 summation ________
13. 1 rotund 2 asymmetrical 3 globular 4 bulbous ________
14. 1 protuberant 2 flush 3 obtruding 4 projecting ________
15. 1 mercurial 2 lethargic 3 phlegmatic 4 sluggish ________
16. 1 refection 2 collation 3 refreshment 4 reception ________
17. 1 oscillate 2 undulate 3 stabilize 4 fluctuate ________
18. 1 terrestrial 2 stellar 3 sidereal 4 astral ________
19. 1 malleable 2 adamantine 3 pliable 4 plastic ________
20. 1 perfunctory 2 hasty 3 meticulous 4 cursory ________
21. 1 specter 2 apparition 3 shade 4 monitor ________
22. 1 arboreal 2 sylvan 3 pelagic 4 wooded ________
23. 1 cauterize 2 char 3 scrutinize 4 calcine ________
24. 1 fetid 2 redolent 3 mephitic 4 noisome ________
25. 1 vermilion 2 cerulean 3 cerise 4 maroon ________
26. 1 telepathic 2 clairvoyant 3 imperceptive 4 psychic ________
27. 1 corroborate 2 impugn 3 vindicate 4 substantiate ________
28. 1 sophistry 2 quibbling 3 analysis 4 casuistry ________
29. 1 enigmatic 2 perplexing 3 cogent 4 cryptic ________
30. 1 carping 2 captious 3 benign 4 hypercritical ________
31. 1 erudite 2 recondite 3 profligate 4 learned ________
32. 1 farcical 2 sagacious 3 preposterous 4 ludicrous ________
33. 1 prescient 2 provident 3 obstinate 4 foresighted ________
34. 1 fabulous 2 chimerical 3 mundane 4 fantastical ________
35. 1 manifest 2 clandestine 3 surreptitious 4 stealthy ________

Copyright © 1994 by Harcourt Brace & Company. All rights reserved.

EXERCISE 5: By writing the appropriate number in the blank after each of the following, indicate which of the numbered words is most effective in the context.

1. a dignified, 1 *fat* 2 *portly* 3 *plump* old gentleman 1. ________
2. a hard 1 *center* 2 *core* 3 *nucleus* of party stalwarts 2. ________
3. the noise 1 *reverberating* 2 *resounding* 3 *ricocheting* through the cavern 3. ________
4. the Mongols and other 1 *roving* 2 *nomadic* 3 *vagrant* peoples 4. ________
5. a store 1 *ostracized* 2 *boycotted* 3 *avoided* because of the proprietor's stand on the matter 5. ________
6. a victim 1 *deformed* 2 *defaced* 3 *mutilated* by the insane killer 6. ________
7. the little boat 1 *revolving* 2 *spinning* 3 *rotating* in the whirlpool 7. ________
8. tired and bored, he greeted us with a 1 *flaccid* 2 *loose* 3 *lax* handshake 8. ________
9. the 1 *assassination* 2 *slaughter* 3 *killing* of Lincoln 9. ________
10. the main issue facing the 1 *folk* 2 *people* 3 *population* 10. ________
11. gasoline is highly 1 *inflammable* 2 *inflammatory* 3 *combustible* 11. ________
12. the 1 *pallid* 2 *sallow* 3 *dingy* face of the invalid 12. ________
13. no open insult or 1 *inconspicuous* 2 *covert* 3 *obscure* slight 13. ________
14. extremely 1 *prudent* 2 *wary* 3 *guarded* about maintaining an emergency fund 14. ________
15. too 1 *dogmatic* 2 *absolute* 3 *dictatorial* for a moderate discussion of religion 15. ________
16. 1 *yielding* 2 *succumbing* 3 *capitulating* to the disease 16. ________
17. a pretty new wallpaper with a 1 *florid* 2 *flowery* 3 *floral* pattern 17. ________
18. the phrase "audible to the ear" is 1 *wordy* 2 *diffuse* 3 *redundant* 18. ________
19. equipped with an 1 *accessory* 2 *subsidiary* 3 *auxiliary* engine 19. ________
20. despite the bad news they remained 1 *cheerful* 2 *blithe* 3 *debonair* 20. ________
21. 1 *primitive* 2 *barbarous* 3 *barbaric* decorations, rich and colorful 21. ________
22. 1 *raucous* 2 *harsh* 3 *strident* advertising announcements on the loudspeaker 22. ________
23. 1 *humorous* 2 *facetious* 3 *jocular* conduct out of place at such serious services 23. ________
24. jackals 1 *roaming* 2 *prowling* 3 *rambling* about outside the camp 24. ________
25. the half-starved dog ate 1 *gluttonously* 2 *ravenously* 3 *rapaciously* 25. ________
26. the 1 *weariness* 2 *torpor* 3 *lethargy* induced by the tropics 26. ________
27. the crude horseplay of the 1 *blatant* 2 *clamorous* 3 *vociferous* conventioneers 27. ________
28. the 1 *voluble* 2 *glib* 3 *fluent* spiel of the commercials 28. ________
29. such 1 *vicious* 2 *villainous* 3 *infamous* activities as peddling narcotics 29. ________
30. 1 *vain* 2 *empty* 3 *vapid* promises he had no intention of fulfilling 30. ________

Copyright © 1994 by Harcourt Brace & Company. All rights reserved.

NAME ______________________ SECTION __________ DATE __________

EXERCISE 6: After each of the following pairs of words write a brief note indicating how they differ in what they suggest to you. You may be frankly impressionistic rather than literally accurate.

1. cede–yield ______________________

2. condolence–sympathy ______________________

3. corpulent–obese ______________________

4. falter–waver ______________________

5. fickle–capricious ______________________

6. haggard–cadaverous ______________________

7. immense–monstrous ______________________

8. rustic–rural ______________________

9. savage–barbaric ______________________

10. threaten–intimidate ______________________

Copyright © 1994 by Harcourt Brace & Company. All rights reserved.

EXERCISE 7: In this exercise you are asked to write in the blank after each of the following phrases the number of the *antonym*—not the synonym—of the italicized word.

1. *avid* sports aficionado: 1 fanatic 2 earnest 3 indifferent 1. ________
2. *contingent* benefits: 1 capricious 2 unexpected 3 absolute 2. ________
3. *craven* conduct: 1 trepid 2 brash 3 intrepid 3. ________
4. to *decry* the effect of the book: 1 question 2 doubt 3 extol 4. ________
5. *delectable* food: 1 delicious 2 disgusting 3 exotic 5. ________
6. a *deleterious* drug: 1 fatal 2 sudden 3 innocuous 6. ________
7. to *demur:* 1 applaud 2 acquiesce 3 protest 7. ________
8. unwilling to *deprecate* her proposal: 1 endorse 2 applaud 3 continue 8. ________
9. a *dexterous* surgeon: 1 skillful 2 proficient 3 clumsy 9. ________
10. *diffident* in attitude: 1 cautious 2 brash 3 timid 10. ________
11. *disdained* the suggestion: 1 resented 2 ignored 3 cherished 11. ________
12. *divergence* in suggestions: 1 correspondence 2 difference 3 intensity 12. ________
13. *dubious* about the outcome: 1 mercurial 2 sanguine 3 phlegmatic 13. ________
14. an *enervating* influence: 1 depressing 2 sudden 3 invigorating 14. ________
15. an *exalted* leader: 1 debased 2 revered 3 murdered 15. ________
16. *ignominy* for his actions: 1 contempt 2 reward 3 renown 16. ________
17. a *poignant* plea: 1 impressive 2 dull 3 intense 17. ________
18. *sophisticated* people: 1 jejune 2 wise 3 refined 18. ________
19. *squalid* surroundings: 1 crowded 2 pleasant 3 immaculate 19. ________
20. of *sybaritic* inclinations: 1 immoral 2 religious 3 spartan 20. ________

EXERCISE 8: The following pairs of italicized words generally cause problems for the average writer. In the blanks provided, write the number of the *appropriate* word.

1. the 1 *affluence* 2 *effluence* from the sewer 1. ________
2. the 1 *allusions* 2 *illusions* of a paranoiac 2. ________
3. a high post to be 1 *aspired* 2 *inspired* to 3. ________
4. for 1 *aught* 2 *ought* she knows about it 4. ________
5. 1 *capitol* 2 *capital* to market the device 5. ________
6. to 1 *censor* 2 *censure* him for improprieties 6. ________
7. the American 1 *counsel's* 2 *consul's* office 7. ________
8. cheap objects 1 *deprecate* 2 *depreciate* quickly 8. ________
9. a 1 *discreet* 2 *discrete* and tactful hint 9. ________
10. feeling disaster 1 *eminent* 2 *imminent* 10. ________
11. to 1 *expiate* 2 *expatiate* her crime 11. ________
12. a zoo's polar and 1 *grizzly* 2 *grisly* bears 12. ________
13. an attractive, 1 *homey* 2 *homely* wife 13. ________

Copyright © 1994 by Harcourt Brace & Company. All rights reserved.

NAME ______________________ SECTION ________ DATE ________

14. killers 1 *illuding* 2 *eluding* the police 14. ________
15. 1 *infinite* 2 *infinitesimal* light years away 15. ________
16. treachery and other 1 *iniquities* 2 *inequities* 16. ________
17. too 1 *insensitive* 2 *insensible* to appreciate art 17. ________
18. to 1 *insight* 2 *incite* the people to read 18. ________
19. a 1 *migraine* 2 *migrant* headache 19. ________
20. guided 1 *missiles* 2 *missals* in the war 20. ________
21. 1 *momentous* 2 *momentary* steps to take 21. ________
22. the 1 *official* 2 *officious* bravery awards 22. ________
23. the major 1 *precedes* 2 *proceeds* the band 23. ________
24. a 1 *principle* 2 *principal* of $10,000 24. ________
25. a 1 *satire* 2 *satyr* on the poem 25. ________
26. a 1 *septic* 2 *skeptic* about religion 26. ________
27. the king's 1 *spectre* 2 *scepter* in his hand 27. ________
28. the floods finally 1 *subsiding* 2 *subsisting* 28. ________
29. 1 *suggestible* 2 *suggestive* and easily led 29. ________
30. her womanly 1 *tuition* 2 *intuition* 30. ________

Copyright © 1994 by Harcourt Brace & Company. All rights reserved.

Words are, of course, the most powerful drug used by mankind.
Rudyard Kipling

11 Descriptive Labels

Some words have a connotative power detached from or not closely connected with their meanings—a power to suggest a situation, occasion, place, or time with which they are particularly associated or in which they are especially likely to be used. Some may suggest social situations, especially those in which the lightness, informality, and warmth of conversation contrast with the colder formality of writing. Some words in themselves suggest the country as contrasted with the city, or particular sections of the United States as contrasted with the rest of the nation, or particular sections of the English-speaking world such as Scotland or South Africa. Other words suggest past ages. This chapter is concerned with explaining the labeling of words with such special connotations.

Labels so used are called *status labels, restrictive labels,* or *usage labels.* Different dictionaries use different terms. Desk or college dictionaries today probably differ in their labeling procedures more than in any other characteristic. What follows will certainly not be a full explanation of status labels in general, or even of status labels in any one dictionary. By all means study your own dictionary to become familiar with its procedures in connection with status labels.

Until somewhat past the middle of this century, dictionaries and handbooks on composition and rhetoric used the same procedures. The term *colloquial,* abbreviated as *colloq.* or occasionally *col.,* was frequently used. As the root *-loqu-* may suggest, *colloquial* meant "spoken, conversational," particularly in contrast to *written;* it was used to indicate turns of language more appropriate to speech than to writing. "In a bad fix" was called colloquial, in contrast to the more formal "in a quandary," "in a difficult situation," or "in a predicament." "Dead broke" was colloquial in contrast to "completely without money." But judgments about what was colloquial often represented subjective guesses; what might be labeled as colloquial by one "expert" would be left unlabeled by another and perhaps called "vulgar" by a third. And many people misunderstood the word *colloquial.* For some it became a loose synonym for "incorrect or below an approved standard." Occasionally ill-prepared teachers would say, "The dictionary says that that word is colloquial, so you should not *say* it." Others connected colloquial with *local,* interpreting it to mean regional, dialectal, or sectional. Many linguists meanwhile were maintaining that the spoken language was *the* language; strictly speaking, under these circumstances *colloquial* would mean little other than "being part of the language." Hence most modern dictionaries have given up the word. *SCD* comments in its front material as follows: "The label *Colloq.* ... is now so widely misunderstood by the public as to be no longer serviceable and is therefore not used in this dictionary." Many dictionaries simply substitute the label *informal,* applying it to words and phrases that had previously been called colloquial. Such dictionaries make clear what they mean by this term in discussions in the front material or in the definition given for *informal.* Other status labels previously used more commonly than now include the following: *Humorous—absquatulate,* "to cease squatting, to leave," and *ecdysiast,* "stripteaser"; *Poetic—harken,* as in "harken to the distant bells," and *lave,* meaning "to wash," as in "a goddess laving herself in a spring"; *Literary—foeman* for "enemy," *leal* for "loyal," *smite* for "strike, strike down"; and *Rare—forecast* as a noun, meaning "foresight," as in "a man of great forecast."

Some dictionaries still use these labels. As we have said, there are considerable differences in the status or usage labels that are employed, and few aspects of dictionary production show so much variation. The procedure used in *WNCD* is neat and orderly, and perhaps explaining it alone will be adequate for our purposes here.

Status labels in *WNCD* "are of three kinds: temporal, stylistic, and regional." Two temporal labels are used: *obs* and *archaic.* As in every other dictionary, *obs,* meaning "obsolete," indicates that certain

Copyright © 1994 by Harcourt Brace & Company. All rights reserved.

words or usages are no longer used; in *WNCD* this label indicates lack of recorded usage since 1755. *Sote,* meaning "sweet," and *secretary* in the sense of "confidant" would be labeled *obs. Archaic* means suggestive of earlier times and seeming antiquated and out of common usage. *Mayhap* and *perchance* for "perhaps" and *mauger* for "despite" are likely to be labeled *archaic.*

Stylistic labels in *WNCD* are *slang, substand,* and *nonstand.* Slang is hard to define, and the application of the term is somewhat subjective. Often slang terms mark the informal language of a closed or limited group, with implied rejection of the corresponding established, standard words used by the majority: *lush* for *drunk, ice* for *diamonds, hock* for *pawn, hoosegow* for *jail,* and *dig* for *observe* or *appreciate.* Despite the fact that new slang terms often have expressive force and color, if limited comprehensibility, the label *slang* is interpreted as involving disparagement. Faded and overworked old slang is frequently tawdry and ineffective, although many an apt slang word or expression has passed into colloquial or standard English. In *WNCD* editors are relatively sparing in their use of the label *slang,* leaving unlabeled many terms that other dictionaries stigmatize. *Substand,* meaning "substandard," is used to label words and usages common throughout the American language but, practically speaking, not used by prestige groups, by persons of upper-level standing or pretention. *Ain't,* as in "he ain't come yet," is labeled as *substandard. Nonstand,* meaning "nonstandard" and used rather sparingly in *WNCD* and elsewhere, describes some words like *irregardless* that can hardly be called substandard but that are not standard either. *WNCD* does not try to discern as many other dictionaries do between formal or standard English and informal English. It does not use labels to indicate the difference between *ghost* and *spook* or between *steal* and *swipe,* for instance.

In one way or another all regional status labels in *WNCD* involve the idea of dialect. Although there are various meanings attached to the word, *dialect* commonly indicates a form of a general language that is spoken only in a limited area. This area may be as large as the whole United States as contrasted with England or as small as one or two American states or English shires or counties, but it does not encompass the whole English-speaking world. *Kill* and *run,* localized terms, are dialect preferences for the general *brook* or *creek. Spider* for *frying pan, stoop* for *porch, red up* for *order* or *arrange, coal oil* for *kerosene,* and *light wood* for *kindling* likewise illustrate dialectal choices. A strong preference for one of the three words *spigot, tap,* or *faucet* and a discomfort in using the other two indicates a dialect preference. Like other dictionaries, *WNCD* uses the label *dial; WNCD* uses it in situations too complex for more specific labeling. Wherever possible, more specific labeling is used, such as *NewEng, Midland, South,* and *Southwest.* A word used exclusively or practically so in the United States but not in British areas is not labeled; one used in England but not elsewhere is labeled *Eng;* one used in various parts of the British Commonwealth is labeled *Brit.* A word used only in certain regions of England may be labeled *dial Eng.* A word used mainly in one area but occasionally and sporadically elsewhere may write *chiefly* in its label: *jaybird ... n, chiefly Midland.*

No status label is intended to express a judgment of rightness or wrongness; none is intended to advise against any possible use of the word in question. It is the function of the label to indicate that the word being described is likely to suggest certain contexts, certain situations, and that it may be inappropriate, even ridiculously so, when used without an awareness of this suggestion.

Copyright © 1994 by Harcourt Brace & Company. All rights reserved.

NAME ______________________________ SECTION ________ DATE __________

CHAPTER 11

EXERCISE 1: The following exercise can be used with *ACD, WNWD, SCD, RHCD,* and other dictionaries that use status labels to indicate informality or varying kinds or degrees of informality; it is not, however, recommended for use with *WNCD*, which contains few labels of that kind. Look up the italicized words in the phrases, and write in the blanks the status or usage labels given. If the dictionary that you are using does not label the sense in question, leave the blank empty.

1. *abide* at home ______________________
2. children *affrighted* ______________________
3. old cronies *argufying* ______________________
4. an old *codger* ______________________
5. *edgy* troops ______________________
6. *enthused* about classes ______________________
7. *floored* by the problem ______________________
8. a complete *flop* ______________________
9. winning on a *fluke* ______________________
10. *framed* by false evidence ______________________
11. *frazzled* nerves ______________________
12. a *gangling* adolescent ______________________
13. a *hangover* from drinking ______________________
14. *hanky-panky* at the office ______________________
15. a rude *heel* ______________________
16. *high-hatting* old friends ______________________
17. *hog* the dessert ______________________
18. a *horsy* woman ______________________
19. a playground for *kids* ______________________
20. don't *knock* the town ______________________
21. to *land* a punch ______________________
22. sailing over the *main* ______________________
23. *mayhap* it will rain ______________________
24. Mr. Smith and his *missis* ______________________
25. to *mooch* lunch ______________________
26. some *mumbo-jumbo* about the test ______________________
27. *nauseating* at the thought ______________________
28. a *newsy* letter of gossip ______________________
29. *orating* about his troubles ______________________
30. the golden *orb* of the sun ______________________
31. an *ornery* old fool ______________________

Copyright © 1994 by Harcourt Brace & Company. All rights reserved.

32. *pestiferous* children ______________________
33. a *poky* train ______________________
34. a *powerful* great number of women ______________________
35. a *ramshackle* old house ______________________
36. *rattled* by the test results ______________________
37. *reminiscing* about the past ______________________
38. *shinnying* up the tree ______________________
39. the blow was a *sockdolager* ______________________
40. the *spiel* of the barker ______________________
41. a *splendiferous* meal ______________________
42. making a *splurge* with his money ______________________
43. a *spunky* child ______________________
44. puffing on a cheap *stogie* ______________________
45. *strewing* flowers along the way ______________________

EXERCISE 2: Following are forty sets of four synonyms. After each synonym are two blanks. *In the first blank* print 1 if you would use the word in question in any situation, 2 if you would use it only in writing or in restrained formal conversation, 3 if you would use it conversationally in any except the most formal situations, 4 if you would use it conversationally but only in situations calling for a degree of force or crudity. (Leave the blanks empty after words you do not know or would never use.) *In the second blank,* print 1 if the word seems forceful; print 2 if the word seems old-fashioned or out-of-date.

1. gyp ___ ___	defraud ___ ___	bamboozle ___ ___	trick ___ ___
2. depart ___ ___	vamoose ___ ___	leave ___ ___	scram ___ ___
3. hobo ___ ___	bum ___ ___	vagrant ___ ___	bindlestiff ___ ___
4. cigarette ___ ___	fag ___ ___	butt ___ ___	coffin nail ___ ___
5. dagger ___ ___	knife ___ ___	shiv ___ ___	stiletto ___ ___
6. grass ___ ___	marihuana ___ ___	Mary Jane ___ ___	pot ___ ___
7. insane ___ ___	loony ___ ___	batty ___ ___	crazy ___ ___
8. belly ___ ___	abdomen ___ ___	gut ___ ___	stomach ___ ___
9. cheek ___ ___	effrontery ___ ___	brass ___ ___	nerve ___ ___
10. catch on ___ ___	twig ___ ___	understand ___ ___	dig ___ ___
11. complain ___ ___	bellyache ___ ___	bitch ___ ___	gripe ___ ___
12. police officer ___ ___	copper ___ ___	cop ___ ___	heat ___ ___
13. sand ___ ___	guts ___ ___	grit ___ ___	courage ___ ___
14. savvy ___ ___	knowledge ___ ___	know-how ___ ___	moxie ___ ___
15. commission ___ ___	kilter ___ ___	order ___ ___	whack ___ ___
16. bit ___ ___	particle ___ ___	pinch ___ ___	smidge ___ ___

Copyright © 1994 by Harcourt Brace & Company. All rights reserved.

NAME ______________________ SECTION __________ DATE __________

17. food	___ ___	victuals	___ ___	grub	___ ___	chow	___ ___
18. insides	___ ___	intestines	___ ___	viscera	___ ___	guts	___ ___
19. snitch	___ ___	peach	___ ___	tell	___ ___	inform	___ ___
20. togs	___ ___	duds	___ ___	garments	___ ___	clothes	___ ___
21. pokey	___ ___	jail	___ ___	hoosegow	___ ___	can	___ ___
22. clout	___ ___	hit	___ ___	larrup	___ ___	belt	___ ___
23. doohickey	___ ___	device	___ ___	gadget	___ ___	contraption	___ ___
24. irked	___ ___	burned	___ ___	peeved	___ ___	miffed	___ ___
25. novice	___ ___	rookie	___ ___	tyro	___ ___	greenhorn	___ ___
26. money	___ ___	dough	___ ___	moolah	___ ___	bread	___ ___
27. brute	___ ___	goon	___ ___	lout	___ ___	oaf	___ ___
28. timid	___ ___	chicken	___ ___	yellow	___ ___	cowardly	___ ___
29. fracas	___ ___	row	___ ___	ruckus	___ ___	rumble	___ ___
30. foreman	___ ___	boss	___ ___	chief	___ ___	big daddy	___ ___
31. hick	___ ___	rustic	___ ___	rube	___ ___	countryman	___ ___
32. taunt	___ ___	razz	___ ___	ride	___ ___	roast	___ ___
33. sissy	___ ___	milksop	___ ___	mollycoddle	___ ___	pantywaist	___ ___
34. quarters	___ ___	room	___ ___	diggings	___ ___	pad	___ ___
35. ghost	___ ___	hant	___ ___	spook	___ ___	wraith	___ ___
36. connive	___ ___	chisel	___ ___	finagle	___ ___	scheme	___ ___
37. party	___ ___	shindig	___ ___	doings	___ ___	bust	___ ___
38. loaf	___ ___	laze	___ ___	goof off	___ ___	malinger	___ ___
39. bawl out	___ ___	rebuke	___ ___	chew out	___ ___	scold	___ ___
40. big shot	___ ___	wheel	___ ___	VIP	___ ___	leader	___ ___

Copyright © 1994 by Harcourt Brace & Company. All rights reserved.

EXERCISE 3: The column of words below aims at being a representative selection of words sometimes labeled as informal, colloquial, slang, or dialectal. After each word are two blanks. In the first, indicate the label given by your dictionary. In the second, give the meaning of the word.

	Label	Definition
1. bamboozle	______________________	______________________
2. barb (nonfraternity man)	______________________	______________________
3. big daddy	______________________	______________________
4. bindlestiff	______________________	______________________
5. black out (lose consciousness)	______________________	______________________
6. clam up (become silent)	______________________	______________________
7. codger	______________________	______________________
8. coffin nail	______________________	______________________
9. doohickey	______________________	______________________
10. flabbergasted	______________________	______________________
11. gals	______________________	______________________
12. guys	______________________	______________________
13. hant	______________________	______________________
14. kids	______________________	______________________
15. limey	______________________	______________________
16. moniker	______________________	______________________
17. namby-pamby	______________________	______________________
18. perchance	______________________	______________________
19. rambunctious	______________________	______________________
20. riled up	______________________	______________________
21. rube	______________________	______________________
22. schmo	______________________	______________________
23. sing (confess)	______________________	______________________
24. stogie	______________________	______________________

Copyright © 1994 by Harcourt Brace & Company. All rights reserved.

The limits of my language are the limits of my world.
Ludwig Wittgenstein

12 Reading and Listening

In Chapter 1 we mentioned three overall procedures for learning new words and understanding their meanings. The first was the rather obvious one of looking words up in a dictionary. To be sure that you would obtain full information from this source, we explained a number of details about dictionary entries. Beginning with Chapter 2 we focused attention on another procedure—word analysis, or analysis of the morphemes of a word. In this final chapter we shall discuss briefly a third procedure—that of learning to read and hear new words more intelligently in their contexts.

A full discussion of this procedure would be a lengthy one indeed; it would include consideration of many of your learning processes and a kind of summary of all that you have learned so far and of how you learned it. We must, therefore, be content here with the barest suggestion of the main ideas.

Reading or listening to sentences and paragraphs involves much more than merely perceiving the meanings of individual words. It necessarily involves either conscious consideration, which is rare, or unconscious perception, which is inevitable and hence common, of a variety of structural devices used in the English sentence. When we read or hear something about "the effects of obnubilation," we either consciously or unconsciously realize that *obnubilation,* whatever the word may mean, may be called an object of the preposition *of* and is hence almost certainly a noun. We either consciously or unconsciously perceive the difference between the intonation or punctuation patterns when we hear or read the following: "red-haired people who are bad-tempered are ..." and "red-haired people, who are bad-tempered, are ...." There is, of course, a considerable difference between the two. Perception of such matters is a very important part of interpreting and understanding any communication.

Usually in our reading or hearing of an ordinary, although perhaps difficult, passage, we find that we know the great majority of the words. In part this is because we all have rather sizable vocabularies. In part it is because much of any communication consists of "function words," "structure words," "mechanics of language"—of such words as determiners *(the, a, these, all, three),* "auxiliaries" of verbs *(is, does, has, will, might),* prepositions, conjunctions, and so on. Once in a while we can be so unfortunate as to encounter a passage in which there are so many unfamiliar words that we feel a forlorn sense of utter helplessness.

For example, the following comes from a textbook on anaesthesiology: "Cardiac catheterisation is not devoid of risk. The tip of the catheter may dislodge thrombus from the walls of the atria, and initiate cardiac arrhythmias, of which premature ventricular beats are the most common. Fatal ventricular fibrillation has been recorded during its performance" (Wylie and Churchill-Davidson, *A Practice of Anaesthesia,* Chicago, 1966). But even with such a passage, as will be explained shortly, we need not despair.

Sometimes full interpretation of a passage depends on our finding the meaning for two or three unfamiliar words. In the article for "Ravenna," *Encyclopaedia Britannica* has the following:

> S. Apollinaire Nuovo, the most important basilica in the town, was built by Theodoric to be the largest of Arian churches. The exterior is uninteresting, and the church lost both atrium and apse in the 16th century.... The walls of the nave are adorned with mosaics of the 6th century; the scenes from the New Testament above the windows date from the time of Theodoric.

Copyright © 1994 by Harcourt Brace & Company. All rights reserved.

Although this passage is not quite so discouraging as the preceding one, it is hard to understand fully without knowing the words *basilica, atrium, apse, and nave.*

Even with their unfamiliar words, these passages will have taught us something worth noticing and remembering. There are few feasible ways whereby we could naturally meet with the passage about cardiac catheterization without knowing that anaesthesiology or at least the general field of medicine was concerned. It is not hard for us to put *cardiac, catheterization, catheter, thrombus, atria, arrhythmia, ventricular,* and *fibrillation* into the class of words used in medicine; it is inevitable that we do so. It is inevitable in connection with the Ravenna passage that we put *basilica, atrium, apse,* and *nave* into the class of words used in church architecture. In so doing we have learned a fair amount. One thing, then, that we can do is to relate unfamiliar words to certain spheres of interest or activity. This is a good first step. When you notice that the English teacher mentions *euphony* or *alliteration* or *participial,* maybe you will not know what these words mean, but you will have taken a first step toward learning their full meaning.

You should remember that there is such a thing as semantic change—specifically, that there is radiation, the process whereby a word comes to acquire a variety of meanings, radiating from one central meaning. You must never assume that a new and unfamiliar word always and necessarily suggests only one sphere of interest or activity. If in biology you learn that the word *primate* indicates an order including humans, apes and monkeys, and tarsiers, and you do not take the possibility of radiation into consideration, you may be much surprised and confused when you meet with *primate* in its meaning of "leading bishop," a bishop with precedence or priority over others. Similarly, if you learn that *Capuchin* refers to an order of friars, you should not be surprised to realize that through radiation it also indicates a genus of South American monkeys. Maybe you have noticed that the plural form *atria* was used above in the quotation from anaesthesiology and that the singular form *atrium* was used in connection with an old church in Ravenna. The word originally means "main hall"; the architectural use adheres to this meaning, but from this meaning has come an anatomical use of the word, meaning "chamber or cavity." Place the word in a general sphere, but remember that it may also be used in other spheres.

Suitability to context is the dictionary definer's main device in evolving and checking definitions, particularly if he or she has an adequate number of illustrative citations to work with. A lexicographer who is faced with the necessity of writing a definition for *parsimonious,* for instance, does not decide in advance what the word should mean. Someone who is quite familiar with the effects of semantic change is unlikely to be much swayed by a knowledge of the eventual meanings of the roots involved. Instead, the lexicographer examines a number of usages such as the following: not exactly parsimonious, but no one has ever called her generous; he has turned parsimonious in his old age and is hanging on to every cent; the parsimonious care with which his aunt saved every scrap and shred of cloth; too parsimonious to pay a decent price for repairing the roof; and a dog half-starved in such a parsimonious household. Examination of such wording is sure to lead to some such definition as "very sparing and reluctant about expenditures; showing excessive frugality." And this is the meaing of the word.

It is important in this connection to try to remember words. Let us say you read of an *arrant* coward. Can you remember having heard of an arrant traitor, an arrant liar, an arrant knave in other things that you read? If so, you are close to evolving your own definition of the word and really knowing it. If it is inconvenient to use your dictionary and if it is impossible or difficult to divide the new word into morphemes, you still may remember encountering it, and you may remember just a little of the context. Perhaps "circular memory" might enter into your conjecture wherein you recall the word *errant* rather than *arrant;* for example, "knight errant." In this case, memory becomes a useful tool, since *arrant* is a variant form of *errant,* meaning "egregious, thoroughgoing, or unmitigated." Thus, through memory and association one may be able to determine meanings of words.

Copyright © 1994 by Harcourt Brace & Company. All rights reserved.

CHAPTER 12

EXERCISES IN CONTEXT: The following passages are excerpts from works of specific interest, and are included here as a different—and perhaps more realistic—kind of exercise, one that will help you to learn words in context. Analyze the wording of these passages, following the plan used in this book.

1. Look up in your dictionary the words that you do not know or do not fully know. Can you understand—and understand at once—all that the dictionary entries tell you about these words—their syllabification, pronunciation, part of speech, variant forms, inflectional forms, etymologies, sense developments, status spheres?

2. For each uncommon, troublesome, or unusual word ask yourself the questions raised in Chapters 2 through 11 of this book: What is the etymology of the word in question? Does it have a prefix or prefixes? If so, what do the prefixes mean? Do they show assimilation? Do you know the root or roots used? Are the given meanings for the roots useful or not useful to you in trying to interpret the meanings?

Can you readily think of other words that seem to show those same elements? Are you sure that they do? Do the words offer illustrations of semantic change that might cause difficulties in interpretation? Are some of the words obviously used with figurative extensions of meaning that cause problems in understanding them? Can you comment on authors' choices among various possible synonyms? Is there anything noticeable about time, social class, or region or area suggestions of words used?

3. To what extent are "context clues" of use? Where do you find situations in which the context all but defines the word in question for you? Where are there situations in which context clues might be misleading?

And while you are answering these questions, make a mental note to continue to ask yourself and to answer such questions about anything you hear or read for the rest of your life, because this is the path that leads to a greater and expansive vocabulary.

A. Changes in Structure and Sound Pattern. For the most part, anything written within the Modern English Period, early or late, may be read and comprehended today without special training. This is not the case, however, with even such late Middle English writers as Chaucer or Gower. The reader requires some introduction to their language before he is able to strike out on his own, and the earlier the text, the more difficult it is likely to be for him. Old English has all the appearance of a foreign language. The works of Alfred and his contemporaries can be understood only after a considerable amount of preparation.

The explanation for the cumulative difficulty as we move backward in time is obvious: the sounds, the structure, and the word stock of the language become progressively different from what they are today. Since in any dictionary our principal concern will naturally be with the lexicon, we shall treat this in some detail and dismiss the structure and the sounds with a few brief generalizations.

The English philologist Henry Sweet summed up the structural changes in the language very neatly when he characterized Old English as a language of full inflections, Middle English as a language of leveled inflections, and Modern English as a language of lost inflections. Although "full" is a relative term, it is fair to say that Old English was inflected about as heavily as German is today. Nouns had four cases, and if at times nominative and accusative or genitive and dative did not have distinctive case endings, the articles ... which accompanied them did. Verbs had an array of distinctive forms for person.... Gender was grammatical instead of natural...; there was no essential connection between the sex of objects and the gender category.... Thus, a masculine knight rode a neuter horse into a feminine battle.

Marckwardt, Albert H. "A Brief History of the English Language." *Standard College Dictionary*. 1968.

B. The English language is unusually rich in synonyms and near-synonyms. This richness is due to the fact that the vocabulary of English, a language especially hospitable to loan-words, is drawn from many sources. The vocabulary of Anglo-Saxon, already containing

Copyright © 1994 by Harcourt Brace & Company. All rights reserved.

loan-words from Celtic, Latin, and Scandinavian, was just about doubled after the Norman Conquest by borrowings from French, to form the Middle English vocabulary. From the sixteenth century on, with the revival of classical learning, there was vast borrowing from Latin and Greek....

Often the borrowings were in a strict sense unnecessary; many that remain today are simply relics of the sixteenth-century fad of embellishing one's speech and writing with Latinisms. Certainly it is possible to talk about *kissing* without using the word *osculatory,* about *today* without *hodiernal,* about *walking* without *gressorial.* Nevertheless, the availability of foreign and learned vocabularies, even if they partly duplicate the native vocabulary, is a tremendous asset to any language. An advanced civilization needs, in addition to a language of everyday life (from which emerges the language of poetry), a language for law and social organization and the discussion of policy, and an even more abstract language for scientific and philosophical discourse....

Are there any *exact* synonyms? The general semanticists, who assert that "no word ever has the same meaning twice," would seem to assert that a word cannot even be synonymous with itself.... Despite Hilaire Belloc's haughty distinction, "what Anglo-Saxons call a *foreword,* but gentlemen a *preface,*" these terms are also genuinely interchangeable in most contexts. But interchangeability in certain contexts does not mean interchangeability in all. "The cast is now *complete*"—not *whole,* or *entire.* A skirmish may be a *preface* to a battle, but not a *foreword.*

Hayakawa, S. I. "Synonyms and Antonyms." *Standard College Dictionary.* 1968.

C. Change in meaning is frequently due to ethical, or moral, considerations. A word may, as it were, go downhill, or it may rise in the world; there is no way of predicting what its career may be. *Politician* has had a downhill development in American English; in British English it is still not entirely without honor. *Knave* (OE *cnafa),* which used to mean simply 'boy'—it is cognate with German *Knabe,* which retains the earlier meaning—is another example of pejorative (from Lat. *pējor* 'worse') development; it came to mean successively 'serving boy' (specialization), like that well-known knave of hearts who was given to stealing tarts, and ultimately 'bad human being,' so that we may now speak of an old knave, or conceivably even of a knavish woman. On its journey downhill this word has thus undergone both specialization and generalization. *Boor,* once meaning *peasant,* has had a similar pejorative development, as has *lewd,* earlier 'lay, as opposed to clerical,' and thereafter 'ignorant,' 'base,' and finally 'obscene,' which is the only meaning to survive. The same fate has befallen the Latin loan-word *vulgar,* ultimately from *vulgus* 'the common people'; the earlier meaning is retained in *Vulgar Latin,* the Latin which was spoken by the people up to the time of the early Middle Ages and was to develop into the various Romance languages.... *Silly* (OE *sǣlig*), earlier 'timely,' came to mean 'happy, blessed,' and subsequently 'innocent, simple'; then the simplicity, a desirable quality under most circumstances, was misunderstood (note the present ambiguity of a *simple man*), and the word took on its present meaning.

Pyles, Thomas. *The Origins and Development of the English Language.* NY: Harcourt, 1964. 308–309.

D. Normally, when a word is borrowed it is made to fit the phonological system of the borrowing language. The English word *rendezvous,* for example, was taken from French, but it obeys the phonological principles of English. It is pronounced with the English [r], not the French one; the first vowel is nonnasal, although it is nasalized in French; and so on. The reason is obvious—English speakers know English, but they do not, for the most part, know French.

Loan words are not always completely assimilated to the phonological system of the borrowing language, however. The same people who sprinkle their speech with French words for purposes of prestige may very well, for the same reason, attempt to preserve the French pronunciation. If enough people are familiar with the donor language, or if a great number of words are borrowed, the loan words may function as a phonological Trojan horse, sneaking new sounds into the inventory of sounds used in the borrowing language. As a matter of fact, the voiced fricatives [v z] worked their way into English from French in just this manner. They had occurred previously as variant phonetic manifestations of other sound types, but not as distinctive sounds. Loan words such as *very, veal, zeal,* and *zest* were responsible for their introduction....

The borrowing of lexical items, then, can have an important impact on the phonological system of a language. One can hypothesize, in fact. that this is the basic mechanism by which languages influence one another phonologically.

Langacker, Ronald W. *Language and Its Structure: Some Fundamental Linguistics Concepts.* NY: Harcourt, 1968. 180–181.

E. Leonardo was proud of his status as an engineer: he even listed half a dozen engineers of classical times, from Callius of Rhodes to Callimachus in Athens, he who was skilled in making great bronze castings, as if to establish his own place among his ancient peers. With

Copyright © 1994 by Harcourt Brace & Company. All rights reserved.

a sense of history later engineers lost, he ransacked the annals of antiquity for suggestive hints from Greek or Persian engineers.

One need not be surprised that the demand for such inventions did not come from either agriculture or handicraft industry: the stimulus to invention, if not the immediate practical support, came from the same socio-technical power complex that had produced the earliest megamachines: absolutism and war.

Similarly, Leonardo was familiar with the early German method of producing poison gas (from feathers, realgar, and sulphur) to asphyxiate a garrison: a grisly fifteenth-century invention that anticipated its first twentieth-century application by the same nation. Like other military engineers of his time, he played with the possibility of armored tanks, propelled by hand-operated cranks, to say nothing of revolving scythes, advancing in front of a horse-propelled vehicle, to mow down the enemy.

Unlike the unduly sanguine prophets of the nineteenth century, who equated mechanical invention with human improvement, Leonardo's dreams were colored by his consciousness of the spectacle of the human savagery and the murderous malice that some of his own proposed military instruments were designed to serve.

Mumford, Lewis. *The Myth of the Machine: Techniques and Human Development.* NY: Harcourt, 1967. 290–291.

F. What brings the convention to order is not the chairman's gavel, but a rendition of the national anthem by a contralto, probably a vacationing star from the Metropolitan Opera. After this comes the invocation, which often turns out to be a small sermon, complete with text, rather than a prayer. This is a feature of every session, with minister, priest, and rabbi taking turns. A short welcoming address by the mayor or governor, some "remarks" by the presiding officer, and the reading of the Call are then disposed of—against the swelling din of greetings, caucusing, and general commotion—and the convention is open for business.

The delegates skip lightly over the first day's business, and we shall do likewise. The objective is to confirm the National Committee's choice of a temporary chairman, which is quickly done, and to set up the convention's four main committees—on credentials, permanent organization, rules, and resolutions....

Members of these hard-working groups are too busy, as we shall see, even to show up at this session, so they miss the convention's first fireworks, which are touched off by the ritual of the keynote address. Delivering this ovation is usually the function of the temporary chairman. He is expected to flay the opposition alive and work up a fine spirit of unity in his own party before it proceeds to tear itself apart over the nomination. Only partisans of the deepest dye can take seriously these grandiloquent outpourings, which credit one political sect with genius, patriotism, courage, and defense of the American home while holding the other responsible for wars, crime, early frost, and the Colorado beetle....

Bendiner, Robert. *White House Fever: An Innocent's Guide to Principles and Practices, Respectable and Otherwise, Behind the Election of American Presidents.* NY: Harcourt, 1960. 70–71.

G. Except for Winfield Scott, the army personnel had from the first looked upon Davis as "their own man"; they had urged his appointment "with hearty, unanimous approval," as the American consul in Panama wrote him. In the fall of 1852, Davis's friend Robert E. Lee had been appointed superintendent of the Military Academy at West Point. The two exchanged ideas for bettering the physical plant as well as the quality of instruction. In the operations of his department, Davis infused an energy hitherto unknown. He advocated a system to improve the discipline and efficiency of officers, and raised their salaries to something more nearly commensurate with amounts men of their caliber would be receiving in civil positions.... He was vigorous in directing pending projects of harbor and river improvements. Davis's capacity for work amazed his wife and all but undid his aides. Sometimes he would forget to eat luncheon entirely, and in times of special pressure might arrive home for dinner as late as 2 A.M.

During the first year of Davis's administration the enlargement of the Capitol was actively prosecuted under his direction. His engineering department had charge of bringing an adequate supply of fresh water to Washington from the Potomac Falls through a nine-foot conduit. The great stone aqueduct with a span of 220 feet, known as John Cabin, was constructed largely under Davis's direction.

Perhaps greater than his army reforms or improvements in the capital were the series of "reconnaissances of routes" for projected railways.... In his *History of the War Department,* Ingersoll calls this work of Jefferson "the most valuable contribution to commerce and to science that had ever been prepared from actual surveys and reconnaissances in the field."

Strode, Hudson. *Jefferson Davis: American Patriot.* NY: Harcourt, 1955. 260–261.

H. After the phone rang in Faulkner's Oxford home in November, 1950, and he was informed that he had been awarded the Nobel Prize for literature, there occurred a rather ambiguous reaction on the part of the public. There was kudos abroad, kudos in New York and in

Copyright © 1994 by Harcourt Brace & Company. All rights reserved.

many another literary center, but there were loud cries of dissent from his native heath. Some parts of Mississippi, influential if in the minority, seemed almost shocked that he should receive the prize. Major Frederick Sullens, editor of the *Jackson Daily News* and acknowledged to be one of Mississippi's leading editors, wrote: "He [Faulkner] is a propagandist of degradation and properly belongs in the privy school of literature." This sentiment was echoed by a number of other Mississippi editors.

We might ask what the object of this mingled scorn and adulation was doing during this period of storm and stress. He was doing something characteristic of William Faulkner—writer, hunter and fisherman, and author of such fine hunting stories as "The Old People" and "The Bear"—he had slipped off to the Delta Bottoms near Anguilla, Mississippi, for the annual deer hunt. The deer hunting club was fifty-seven years old and a convenient place for a Nobel Prize winner to be free of importunate reporters. But even here a newspaper intruded one morning when Faulkner had the dishwashing chore. Ike Roberts, chief of the camp, read the story of the $30,000 prize and asked:

"Bill, what would you do if that ambassador walked up right now with that prize, you looking the way you do?"

Faulkner answered, "I'd hand him a drying towel."

Thus easily does genius confute its disparagers.

Campbell, Harry Modean, and Ruel E. Foster. *William Faulkner: A Critical Appraisal.* NY: Cooper Square, 1970. 3–4.

I. The moon was high and magnificent in the August night. Mrs. Morel, seared with passion, shivered to find herself out there in a great white light, that fell cold on her, and gave a shock to her inflamed soul. She stood for a few moments helplessly staring at the glistening great rhubarb leaves near the door.

She became aware of something about her. With an effort she roused herself to see what it was that penetrated her consciousness. The tall white lilies were reeling in the moonlight, and the air charged with their perfume, as with a presence. Mrs. Morel gasped slightly in fear. She touched the big, pallid flowers on their petals, then shivered. They seemed to be stretching in the moonlight. She put her hand into one white bin: the gold scarcely showed on her fingers by moonlight. She bent down to look at the binful of yellow pollen; but it only appeared dusky.

...A few whiffs of the raw, strong scent of phlox invigorated her. She passed along the path, hesitating at the white rosebush. It smelled sweet and simple. She touched the white ruffles of the roses.

...The night was very large, and very strange, stretching its hoary distances infinitely. And out of the silver-grey fog of darkness came sounds vague and hoarse: a corncrake not far off, sound of a train like a sigh, and distant shouts of men.

Lawrence, D. H. *The Penguin Great Novels of D. H. Lawrence: Sons and Lovers, The Rainbow, Women in Love.* NY: Penguin, 1984. 30–31.

J. She saw the stiffened bodies of the colliers, which seemed already enclosed in a coffin, she saw their unchanging eyes, the eyes of those who are buried alive: she saw the hard, cutting edges of the new houses, which seemed to spread over the hillside in their insentient triumph of horrible, amorphous angles and straight lines, the expression of corruption triumphant and unopposed, corruption so pure that it is hard and brittle: she saw the dun atmosphere over the blackened hills opposite, the dark blotches of houses, slate roofed and amorphous, the old church-tower standing up in hideous obsoleteness.... And then, in the blowing clouds, she saw a band of faint iridescence colouring in faint colours a portion of the hill. And forgetting, startled, she looked for the hovering colour and saw a rainbow forming itself. In one place it gleamed fiercely, and her heart anguished with hope, she sought the shadow of iris where the bow should be. Steadily the colour gathered, mysteriously, from nowhere, it took presence upon itself, there was a faint, vast rainbow. The arc bended and strengthened itself till it arched indomitable, making great architecture of light and colour and the space of heaven, its pedestals luminous in the corruption of new houses on the low hill, its arch the top of heaven.

And the rainbow stood on the earth.... She saw in the rainbow the earth's new architecture, the old, brittle corruption of houses and factories swept away, the world built up in a living fabric of Truth, fitting to the over-arching heaven.

Lawrence, D. H. *The Penguin Great Novels of D. H. Lawrence: Sons and Lovers, The Rainbow, Women in Love.* NY: Penguin, 1984. 703.

K. At last the woods rose; the rookery clustered dark; a loud cawing broke the morning stillness. Strange delight inspired me: on I hastened. Another field crossed, a lane threaded, and there was the courtyard walls, the back offices; the house itself, the rookery still hid. 'My first view of it shall be in front,' I determined, 'where its bold battlements will strike the eye nobly at one, and where I can single out my master's very window: perhaps he will be standing at it—he rises early: perhaps he is now walking in the orchard, or on the pavement in front. Could I but see him! Surely, in that case, I should not be so mad as to run to him? I cannot tell—I am not certain. And if I did what then? God bless him! What then! Who would be hurt by my once more

Copyright © 1994 by Harcourt Brace & Company. All rights reserved.

tasting the life his glance can give me? I rave: perhaps at the moment his is watching the sun rise over the Pyrenees, or on the tideless sea of the south.'

I had coasted along the lower wall of the orchard—turned its angle: there was a gate just there, opening into the meadow, between two stone pillars crowned by stone balls. From behind one pillar I could peep round quietly at the full front of the mansion. I advanced my head with precaution, desirous to ascertain if any bedroom window-blinds were yet drawn-up: battlements, windows, long front—all from this sheltered station were at my command.

The crows sailing overhead perhaps watched me while I took this survey. I wonder what they thought. They must have considered I was very careful and timid at first, and that gradually I grew very bold and reckless....

Brontë, Charlotte. *Jane Eyre*. Ed. Q. D. Leavis. NY: Penguin, 1983. 448–449.

L. I looked with timorous joy towards a stately house; I saw a blackened ruin.

No need to cower behind a gatepost, indeed!—to peep up at chamber lattices, fearing life was astir behind them! No need to listen for doors opening—to fancy steps on the pavements or the gravel walk! The lawn, the grounds were trodden and waste: the portal yawned void. The front was, as I had once seen it in a dream, but a shell-like wall, very high and very fragile-looking, perforated with paneless windows: no roof, no battlements, no chimneys—all had crashed in.

And there was the silence of death about it, the solitude of a lonesome wild. No wonder the letters addressed to people here had never received an answer: as well despatch epistles to a vault in a church aisle. The grim blackness of the stones told by what fate the Hall had fallen—by conflagration. But how kindled? What story belonged to this disaster? What loss, besides mortar and marble and woodwork had followed upon it? Had life been wrecked as well as property? If so, whose? Dreadful question: there was no one here to answer it—not even dumb sign, mute token.

In wandering round the shattered walls and through the devastated interior, I gathered evidence that the calamity was not of late occurrence. Winter snows, I thought, had drifted through that void arch, winter rains beaten in at those hollow casements; for, amidst the drenched piles of rubbish, spring had cherished vegetation: grass and weed grew here and there between the stones and fallen rafters. And oh! where meantime was the hapless owner of this wreck?

Brontë, Charlotte. *Jane Eyre*. Ed. Q. D. Leavis. NY: Penguin, 1983. 449–450.

M. As they stepped onto the door-stones, and halted to take a last look at the moon, or, more correctly, at each other, by her light, I felt irresistibly impelled to escape them again; and, pressing a remembrance into the hand of Mrs. Dean, and disregarding her expostulations at my rudeness, I vanished through the kitchen, as they opened the house-door, and so should have confirmed Joseph in his opinion of his fellow-servant's gay indiscretions, had he not, fortunately, recognised me for a respectable character by the sweet ring of a sovereign at his feet.

My walk home was lengthened by a diversion in the direction of the Kirk. When beneath its walls, I perceived decay had made progress, even in seven months: many a window showed black gaps deprived of glass; and slates jutted off, here and there, beyond the right line of the roof, to be gradually worked off in coming autumn storms.

I sought, and soon discovered, the three headstones on the slope next the moor—the middle one grey, and half buried in heath—Linton's only harmonized by the turf, and moss creeping up its foot—Heathcliff's still bare.

I lingered round them, under that benign sky; watched the moths fluttering among the heath and harebells; listened to the soft wind breathing through the grass; and wondered how any one could ever imagine unquiet slumbers for the sleepers in that quiet earth.

Brontë, Emily. *Wuthering Heights: Authoritative Text, Backgrounds, Criticism.* Third ed. Eds. William M. Sale, Jr., and Richard J. Dunn. NY: Norton, 1989. 256.

Copyright © 1994 by Harcourt Brace & Company. All rights reserved.

NAME ______________________ SECTION ________ DATE ________

CUMULATIVE TEST 6A: In the blank print the number of the word or phrase that corresponds most closely to the meaning of the italicized word.

1. an *adamantine* official: 1 incompetent and negligent 2 stern and unyielding 3 old and senile 4 wise and foresighted 1. ________
2. a language *allomorph:* 1 mispronunciation 2 dialect area 3 variant form 4 conjugation or declension 2. ________
3. *arable* land: 1 rich in minerals 2 dry and parched 3 worked out and abandoned 4 suitable for plowing 3. ________
4. a *baccate* plant: 1 strange and exotic 2 yielding berries 3 aromatic 4 valueless and detrimental 4. ________
5. *bellicose* actions: 1 greedy and gluttonous 2 charitable and kindly 3 beautifying and cosmetic 4 quarrelsome and warlike 5. ________
6. answering with *certitude:* 1 extreme politeness 2 feeling of certainty 3 extreme promptness 4 ill temper 6. ________
7. a *cerulean* tinge: 1 dark and somber 2 suggestive of disease 3 bluish 4 carefully executed 7. ________
8. a *cogent* argument: 1 forceful 2 stupid and trivial 3 bitter and sarcastic 4 long-continued 8. ________
9. a *congenital* defect: 1 trivial 2 present at birth 3 hereditary 4 unnoticed 9. ________
10. a *culpable* action: 1 blameworthy 2 charitable 3 negligent 4 unexpected 10. ________
11. *debilitating* effects: 1 trivial 2 weakening 3 encouraging 4 deadly 11. ________
12. to *decry* such teaching: 1 participate in 2 support 3 strongly disapprove of 4 prohibit 12. ________
13. a *delectable* prospect: 1 dangerous 2 delightful 3 incomprehensible 4 rare 13. ________
14. to *deprecate* her efforts: 1 belittle 2 disapprove of 3 evaluate 4 imitate 14. ________
15. *desiccated* foods: 1 lacking nutrition 2 strange and exotic 3 bland 4 dehydrated 15. ________
16. answering with *effusion:* 1 bitterness 2 tears and emotion 3 unrestrained expression 4 quiet reserve 16. ________
17. an *ellipsis* of some words: 1 repetition 2 omission 3 emphasis 4 confusion 17. ________
18. an *encomium* about the senator: 1 obituary speech 2 speech in praise 3 scandalous rumor 4 confidential report 18. ________
19. *endemic* diseases: 1 usually fatal 2 limited to one area 3 viral 4 little-known 19. ________
20. arousing *ephemeral* interest: 1 short-lived 2 scandalous 3 scientific 4 local 20. ________
21. an *epitome* of the work: 1 criticism 2 summary 3 examination 4 censorship 21. ________
22. to *execrate* his name: 1 revere 2 ignore 3 denounce as detestable 4 circulate widely 22. ________
23. to *expatiate* on the crime: 1 discuss in detail 2 propose atonement 3 gossip widely 4 investigate causes 23. ________
24. a *factitious* account: 1 scrupulously accurate 2 full and detailed 3 made up and fabricated 4 most plausible 24. ________
25. a *febrile* condition: 1 weakened 2 wildly excited 3 feverish 4 discouraging 25. ________
26. a *festal* occasion: marked by 1 sadness and sorrow 2 historical significance 3 religious importance 4 feasting and celebration 26. ________

Copyright © 1994 by Harcourt Brace & Company. All rights reserved.

27. a *fetid* atmosphere: 1 fresh and bracing 2 routine and humdrum 3 thin and rare 4 foul and stinking 27. ________

28. *halcyon* days: 1 declining 2 worrisome and anxious 3 peaceful and prosperous 4 wild and hectic 28. ________

29. the *ignominy* of this decision: 1 deep disgrace 2 surprising suddenness 3 foresight and wisdom 4 daring bravery 29. ________

30. caring for *indigent* patients: 1 badly injured 2 foreign 3 impoverished 4 emotional 30. ________

31. *indurated* materials: 1 unnecessary 2 expensive 3 explosive 4 hardened 31. ________

32. an *innocuous* substance: 1 precious 2 dangerous 3 incongruous 4 harmless 32. ________

33. a *malleable* substance: 1 easily transported 2 prohibited 3 readily shaped or fashioned 4 commonplace 33. ________

34. studying a *missal:* 1 letter 2 code book 3 mass book. 4 attendance chart 34. ________

35. a *momentous* decision: 1 significant 2 expected 3 quick 4 thrifty 35. ________

36. *mundane* considerations: 1 religious 2 everyday and practical 3 insane 4 marital 36. ________

37. at the *nadir* of her career: 1 turning point 2 apex 3 lowest point 4 successful conclusion 37. ________

38. a *nocent* drug: 1 cheap and common 2 harmful 3 anesthetic 4 habit-forming 38. ________

39. an *obelisk* in the park: 1 monolithic spire 2 equestrian statue 3 refreshment stand 4 flower collection 39. ________

40. to *ostracize* his followers: 1 hunt down and kill 2 give pensions to 3 exclude from social contacts 4 conceal 40. ________

41. a *palpable* fact: 1 hitherto unrecognized 2 readily perceptible 3 unpleasant 4 universally accepted 41. ________

42. the *paucity* of the replacements: 1 poor quality 2 abundance 3 tremendous expense 4 scarcity and dearth 42. ________

43. *pelagic* life forms: 1 microscopic 2 oceanic 3 prehistoric 4 interstellar 43. ________

44. a *petulant* child: 1 obviously favored 2 clever and talented 3 underprivileged 4 fretful and peevish 44. ________

45. a *phlegmatic* temperament: 1 constantly worried 2 wild and unpredictable 3 slow and stolid 4 inquisitive and prying 45. ________

46. a man of *prescience:* 1 ignorance and superstition 2 foresight and foreknowledge 3 courage and resolution 4 lucky intuition 46. ________

47. to *procrastinate* about the decision: 1 delay and postpone 2 regret 3 waver and doubt 4 determine resolutely 47. ________

48. *quotidian* rainfall: 1 very rare 2 extremely heavy 3 quite beneficial 4 occurring daily 48. ________

49. viewing the matter in *retrospect:* 1 fear and terror 2 wise consideration 3 contemplation of the past 4 quiet and solitude 49. ________

50. a *schismatic* notion: promoting 1 strict loyalty 2 contentious separation 3 personal self-sacrifice 4 encouragement to study 50. ________

51. a *sedulous* worker: 1 busy and diligent 2 incompetent and lazy 3 having seniority 4 incapacitated 51. ________

52. a *stentorian* voice: 1 extremely loud 2 timid and hesitant 3 distinctive 4 rough and raucous 52. ________

Copyright © 1994 by Harcourt Brace & Company. All rights reserved.

NAME ________________ SECTION ________ DATE ________

53. *stringent* regulations: 1 unfair and discriminatory 2 rigorous and severe 3 used on special occasions 4 benign and tolerant 53. ________

54. a *supercilious* smile: 1 bright and cheerful 2 friendly and encouraging 3 forced and insincere 4 haughty and scornful 54. ________

55. *supine* on the battlefield: 1 crouching 2 concealed 3 lying face up 4 suffering 55. ________

56. living a *sybaritic* life: marked by 1 daring adventure 2 poverty and hardship 3 sensuality and luxury 4 chronic ill health 56. ________

57. *tawdry* jewelry: 1 very expensive 2 simple and prim 3 showy and cheap 4 grotesque 57. ________

58. the *tractable* peasants: 1 easily controlled 2 half-starved 3 very industrious 4 impassive and silent 58. ________

59. a *transitory* condition: 1 extremely active 2 temporary and changing 3 intolerable 4 practically perpetual 59. ________

60. filled with *trepidation:* 1 assured confidence 2 wary caution 3 nonchalant indifference 4 fear and apprehension 60. ________

61. suspected of *turpitude:* 1 moral depravity 2 fraud and embezzling 3 treason 4 bribery 61. ________

62. an *undulant* effect: 1 wavy and varying 2 soothing and placating 3 dangerous 4 extremely noticeable 62. ________

63. *unkempt* person: 1 fastidious 2 showy 3 poor 4 untidy 63. ________

64. a *vacuous* remark: 1 earnest 2 snide 3 empty 4 rude 64. ________

65. *veracity* of essay: 1 truthfulness 2 clarity 3 complexity 4 weakness 65. ________

66. *verbosity* of speaker: 1 style 2 charm 3 wordiness 4 wit 66. ________

67. *vitreous* substance: 1 milky 2 glassy 3 sticky 4 oily 67. ________

68. *vitriolic* people: 1 pleasant 2 angry 3 loud 4 gentle 68. ________

69. *vivacious* dancer: 1 awkward 2 pleasant 3 lively 4 lissome 69. ________

70. *vulgate* dialects: 1 learned 2 complex 3 common 4 immoral 70. ________

Copyright © 1994 by Harcourt Brace & Company. All rights reserved.

NAME ________________________ SECTION ________ DATE ________

CUMULATIVE TEST 6B: In the blank print the number of the word or phrase that corresponds most closely to the meaning of the italicized word.

1. a person of *affluence:* 1 power and importance 2 pretense and fraud 3 wealth 4 reputation for justice 1. ________
2. an *ancillary* instrumentality: 1 irrelevant 2 tending to oppose 3 auxiliary 4 harmless 2. ________
3. to *asseverate* a claim: 1 yield and renounce 2 arbitrate and adjudge 3 reject and deny 4 maintain positively 3. ________
4. *baubles* of rank and power: 1 rights and privileges 2 showy trinkets 3 supporters 4 suppressive forces 4. ________
5. *captious* comments: 1 fault-finding and hypercritical 2 encouraging 3 slight and unimportant 4 rambling and incoherent 5. ________
6. the heroes' *cenotaph:* 1 memorial fund 2 commemorization date 3 empty tomb 4 remembrance society 6. ________
7. *coeval* events: 1 disastrous 2 unsanctioned and illegal 3 contemporary 4 strange and unexpected 7. ________
8. assuming another *cognomen:* 1 title or office 2 role in a play 3 nickname or epithet 4 attitude 8. ________
9. the *congruence* of the ideas: 1 sentimental appeal 2 universality 3 accord or agreement 4 complete contradiction 9. ________
10. a feeling of *contrition:* 1 deep horror 2 firm resolution 3 genuine repentance 4 wild happiness 10. ________
11. magnesium strips *deflagrating:* 1 discoloring 2 deteriorating 3 wearing away 4 burning brightly 11. ________
12. a *deleterious* drug: 1 beneficial 2 very expensive 3 new and untried 4 harmful 12. ________
13. totally *discrete* matters: 1 unimportant 2 secret or confidential 3 possibly detrimental 4 separate and individual 13. ________
14. the *effulgence* of the display: 1 brilliance 2 wastefulness 3 bad taste 4 popular appeal 14. ________
15. an *elasmobranch* fish: 1 prehistoric 2 flat and ray-like 3 sluggish 4 shark-like 15. ________
16. to *elucidate* a passage: 1 skip 2 explain clearly 3 object to 4 argue about 16. ________
17. aiding the *emaciated* survivors: 1 lucky 2 quietly happy 3 half-starved and enfeebled 4 panic-stricken 17. ________
18. an *enervated* patient: 1 courageous and cheerful 2 weakened 3 fretful 4 chronic 18. ________
19. an *equivocal* answer: 1 detailed 2 very satisfactory 3 unclear and ambiguous 4 quiet but determined 19. ________
20. an *erudite* subject: 1 useless 2 very learned 3 elementary 4 philosophical 20. ________
21. according to *ethnic* considerations: 1 moral 2 financial 3 racial 4 sanitary 21. ________
22. to *extirpate* those plants: 1 cultivate 2 experiment with 3 export 4 root out 22. ________
23. a *fecund* race: 1 primitive 2 suspicious 3 little-known 4 fruitful or productive 23. ________
24. a *feral* animal: 1 valuable 2 small and attractive 3 arctic 4 wild and savage 24. ________
25. believing in *flagellation:* 1 constant prayer 2 ascetic living 3 sleepless vigils 4 whipping and punishment 25. ________

Copyright © 1994 by Harcourt Brace & Company. All rights reserved.

NAME ______________________ SECTION ________ DATE ________

26. the *frugality* of the household: 1 discord 2 careful economy 3 love and amity 4 laxness and immorality 26. ________

27. bothered with *gastritis:* 1 shortness of breath 2 stomachache 3 frequent head colds 4 itching feelings 27. ________

28. to *imbue* with enthusiasm: 1 infuse with 2 deprive of 3 record 4 suspect 28. ________

29. an *impecunious* relative: 1 eccentric 2 unpopular 3 hospitable 4 impoverished 29. ________

30. an *infinitesimal* amount: 1 alarming 2 disproportionate 3 carefully measured 4 tiny 30. ________

31. an *itinerant* printer: 1 expensive 2 reliable 3 industrious 4 moving from place to place 31. ________

32. a *liaison* with the actor: 1 affair 2 argument 3 business agreement 4 quarrel 32. ________

33. a *macabre* scene: 1 usual 2 delightful 3 distant 4 gruesome 33. ________

34. *mafficking* at the news: 1 lamenting 2 thinking carefully 3 celebrating uproariously 4 being bored 34. ________

35. a *magnanimous* gesture: 1 insulting 2 generous and lofty 3 fearful 4 very conspicuous 35. ________

36. a *meretricious* display: 1 gaudily showy 2 very attractive 3 commendable 4 candid and honest 36. ________

37. written with much *metonymy:* 1 speed and verve 2 figurative language 3 careful revision 4 itemization of details 37. ________

38. a *morose* character: 1 comical 2 extremely stupid 3 very moral 4 sullen and gloomy 38. ________

39. a science classification involving *morphology:* 1 forms 2 weights 3 chemical composition 4 blood counts 39. ________

40. the role of a *mountebank:* 1 explorer 2 financial consultant 3 alpinist 4 charlatan 40. ________

41. a *neophyte* at the activity: 1 spectator 2 novice 3 veteran 4 official 41. ________

42. some *nugatory* objections: 1 determined 2 cogent 3 often repeated 4 unimportant and worthless 42. ________

43. an *oscillating* needle: 1 piercing 2 staying stationary 3 swinging back and forth 4 warning of danger 43. ________

44. much *palaver* about their rights: 1 idle speech 2 deep analysis 3 fiery agitation 4 popular sympathy 44. ________

45. his *parsimonious* attitude: 1 lavish and extravagant 2 kindly and hospitable 3 threatening and fierce 4 stingy and frugal 45. ________

46. a *perspicuous* account: 1 clear and understandable 2 complicated and involved 3 minute and detailed 4 obviously false 46. ________

47. a *pertinacious* attitude: 1 resolute and tenacious 2 devil-may-care 3 very inquisitive 4 extremely self-centered 47. ________

48. a *poignant* sight: 1 commonplace 2 exciting 3 moving and pathetic 4 hitherto unexperienced 48. ________

49. a *pragmatic* viewpoint: centered on the 1 lofty and beautiful 2 heavenly or eternal 3 ego maturity 4 factual and practical 49. ________

50. a *quondam* senator: 1 fictitious 2 powerful 3 dishonest 4 former 50. ________

51. a *ramose* chart or diagram: marked by 1 complexity 2 branching 3 diverse coloration 4 interpolated notes 51. ________

Copyright © 1994 by Harcourt Brace & Company. All rights reserved.

52. *savants* and philosophers: 1 pretenders 2 wise and learned people 3 priests 4 mystics 52. ________

53. a *scintillating* effect: 1 endangering 2 irritating 3 deadening 4 sparkling 53. ________

54. the *sophistry* of the assertion: 1 obvious falsity 2 deceptive subtlety 3 apparent sincerity 4 impudent boldness 54. ________

55. the *stringent* regulations of the prison camp: 1 barbarous and cruel 2 ineffectual 3 rigorous and severe 4 quite unenforceable 55. ________

56. *succumbing* under these threats: 1 yielding 2 going underground 3 resisting fiercely 4 becoming confused and uncertain 56. ________

57. a report marked by *supererogation:* 1 thorough research 2 fawning respectfulness 3 inclusive recommendations 4 unnecessary addition 57. ________

58. a *surreptitious* approach: 1 brave and defiant 2 stealthy and sly 3 quick and prompt 4 slow and reluctant 58. ________

59. a *sycophant* in the court: 1 plotter or intriguer 2 dashing adventurer 3 military adviser 4 servile yes-man 59. ________

60. the *torpor* of the natives: 1 fierceness and savagery 2 friendliness and kindness 3 dull inactivity 4 malnutrition and illness 60. ________

61. to *traduce* a reputation: 1 defend and protect 2 ignore or overlook 3 preserve as spotless 4 lower or defame 61. ________

62. *traumatic* effects: brought about by 1 retreat from reality 2 wounds or injuries 3 childhood fears 4 envy and jealousy 62. ________

63. in a *tremulous* voice: 1 vigorous and commanding 2 barely audible 3 timid and trembling 4 softly musical 63. ________

64. an *unctuous* greeting: 1 smug and insincere 2 loud and demonstrative 3 formal and ceremonial 4 slight and casual 64. ________

65. *vacillate* a choice: 1 determine 2 extol 3 fluctuate 4 substantiate 65. ________

66. *vernacular* wording: 1 poetic 2 colorful 3 conversational 4 political 66. ________

67. a *virulent* substance: 1 powerful 2 popular 3 poisonous 4 weak 67. ________

68. a *waif:* 1 wave 2 stray 3 wafer 4 flag 68. ________

69. a *wraith:* 1 cost 2 phantom 3 neophyte 4 child 69. ________

70. being the *zany:* 1 clown 2 coward 3 officer 4 old man 70. ________

Copyright © 1994 by Harcourt Brace & Company. All rights reserved.

NAME ______________________ SECTION __________ DATE __________

CUMULATIVE TEST 6C: The first part of this test is composed of four columns of sixty words in all. After each word is a blank. The second part of the test is composed of three columns of sixty more words. Each of these words is a synonym for one word in the first list. In the blank after each word in the first part, write the number of the synonym in the second part.

Part 1

1. aborigines ______
2. abrogate ______
3. abstruse ______
4. abysmal ______
5. acrimony ______
6. admonitory ______
7. adroit ______
8. aegis ______
9. affluence ______
10. agamic ______
11. alacrity ______
12. anthropoid ______
13. avarice ______
14. benignant ______
15. braggart ______
16. cajole ______
17. cephalic ______
18. colloquium ______
19. comestible ______
20. cruciate ______
21. dendroid ______
22. dichotomize ______
23. ebullient ______
24. ephemeral ______
25. factitious ______
26. flaccid ______
27. flamboyant ______
28. garner ______
29. heinous ______
30. homunculus ______
31. inchoate ______
32. insouciant ______
33. junta ______
34. lapidary ______
35. lenitive ______
36. macabre ______
37. mimetic ______
38. mutation ______
39. nubile ______
40. oscillate ______
41. pathogen ______
42. photic ______
43. portent ______
44. prolific ______
45. quasi ______
46. redundant ______
47. riant ______
48. salutary ______
49. scurrilous ______
50. sequester ______
51. solarium ______
52. spelunker ______
53. stultify ______
54. succinct ______
55. talisman ______
56. thalassic ______
57. travail ______
58. ubiquitous ______
59. vatic ______
60. waylay ______

Part 2

1. greediness
2. lively, exuberant
3. dwarf
4. change
5. superfluous
6. gay, laughing
7. sun room
8. prevent
9. a charm
10. sign, omen
11. short-lived
12. edible
13. tree-like
14. showy
15. gather, collect
16. boaster
17. conference
18. limp, flabby
19. beginning stages
20. imitative
21. speedy promptness
22. coax, flatter
23. of the head
24. divide in two
25. kindly, aiding
26. carefree
27. gruesome
28. marriageable
29. everywhere
30. fruitful
31. revolutionary council
32. soothing
33. swing to and fro
34. relating to light
35. cave explorer
36. terse, curt
37. of the seas
38. somewhat, seemingly
39. vulgar and abusive
40. ambush
41. made up, artificial
42. cross-shaped
43. shockingly evil
44. human-like
45. gem cutting
46. cause of disease
47. prophetic
48. toil and torment
49. healthful
50. seclude
51. wealth
52. sponsorship
53. early natives
54. cautionary
55. without sexual mating
56. complex
57. bottomless
58. dexterous
59. annul
60. animosity

Copyright © 1994 by Harcourt Brace & Company. All rights reserved.

NAME ______________________________ SECTION __________ DATE __________

CUMULATIVE TEST 6D: Following are 100 words. When you first look at them, they will seem miscellaneous and quite unrelated. These words, however, are composed of twenty sets of five synonyms apiece. On each line in the second part of the test, write a set of four synonyms selected from the first list. The first word of each set is indicated by a number, and then appears below opposite its number.

List 1

arraign	autocratic	pristine	contingent	(2) animosity
(12) fortuitous	(4) arbitrary	lucid	peremptory	germane
impervious	gross	(5) argot	(14) indict	ignominy
odium	(11) flagrant	rancor	raillery	phantasm
rank	mollify	(15) infamy	(18) primeval	(13) impassive
lingo	primordial	covetous	impeach	primitive
(20) transparent	lustrous	obstreperous	jejune	persiflage
temerity	egregious	cant	animus	apathetic
material	grasping	(7) badinage	substantiate	opprobrium
verify	incidental	avaricious	primal	stolid
wraith	propitiate	imperious	(3) apparition	(8) banal
diaphanous	(10) corroborate	vapid	clamorous	lambent
(16) luminous	vernacular	conciliate	spectre	effrontery
indifferent	(17) placate	compatible	greedy	hostility
adventitious	authenticate	obloquy	(19) relevant	incriminate
casual	accuse	(6) audacity	consonant	validate
(1) acquisitive	antipathy	phantom	appease	(9) boisterous
jargon	nefarious	gall	chaffing	dictatorial
insipid	lucent	limpid	inane	vociferous
hardihood	pellucid	banter	blatant	radiant

List 2

1	2	3	4	5
1. acquisitive	______	______	______	______
2. animosity	______	______	______	______
3. apparition	______	______	______	______
4. arbitrary	______	______	______	______
5. argot	______	______	______	______
6. audacity	______	______	______	______
7. badinage	______	______	______	______
8. banal	______	______	______	______
9. boisterous	______	______	______	______
10. corroborate	______	______	______	______
11. flagrant	______	______	______	______
12. fortuitous	______	______	______	______
13. impassive	______	______	______	______

Copyright © 1994 by Harcourt Brace & Company. All rights reserved.

NAME ______________________________ SECTION __________ DATE __________

14. indict	________	________	________	________
15. infamy	________	________	________	________
16. luminous	________	________	________	________
17. placate	________	________	________	________
18. primeval	________	________	________	________
19. relevant	________	________	________	________
20. transparent	________	________	________	________

Copyright © 1994 by Harcourt Brace & Company. All rights reserved.

Chapter Word List

The following word list includes all words found in the Preliminary Vocabulary Tests 1, 2, and 3, and also the majority of words in subsequent chapters. When words have *not* been included, an indication has been made to that effect. Chapters wherein those words appear are indicated at the beginning of each listing.

Preliminary Vocabulary Test 1

1. abstruse
2. antipathy
3. assiduous
4. benign
5. captious
6. chicanery
7. chimera
8. clandestine
9. commodious
10. coterie
11. denigrate
12. deprecate
13. dilatory
14. disparities
15. dissembling
16. effete
17. encomium
18. enervated
19. erudite
20. euphonious
21. forensic
22. hyperbole
23. imminent
24. indigent
25. innocuous
26. insentient
27. lassitude
28. mitigate
29. nemesis
30. palpable
31. panegyric
32. pernicious
33. persiflage
34. precursor
35. progeny
36. rapacious
37. salubrious
38. sententious
39. specious
40. stentorian
41. strident
42. taciturn
43. thalassic
44. torpid
45. traduce
46. trenchant
47. vagaries
48. veracity
49. vitiate
50. vitriolic

Preliminary Vocabulary Test 2

1. admonitory
2. alleviate
3. animosities
4. anomalous
5. apothegms
6. arduous
7. banality
8. coerced
9. derision
10. discrete
11. dissident
12. ebullient
13. emulous
14. enigmatic
15. ephemeral
16. eschew
17. ethnic
18. fatuity
19. inhibiting
20. integrity
21. internecine
22. intransigent
23. lucrative
24. lugubrious
25. mandatory
26. metamorphosis
27. nominal
28. occult
29. opulent
30. partisans
31. pastoral
32. peccant
33. penchant
34. proliferation
35. reiterate
36. restive
37. sinuous
38. sporadic
39. stipend
40. subliminal
41. succinct
42. sumptuous
43. sycophantic
44. tortuous
45. traumatic
46. travail
47. ubiquitous
48. unction
49. verbosity
50. vitreous

Preliminary Vocabulary Test 3

1. abdicate
2. aborigines
3. abrogated
4. accentuate
5. acrimonious
6. adroit
7. aegis
8. affluence
9. ameliorate
10. asinine
11. atrocious
12. auspicious
13. autocrats
14. belligerent
15. bestial
16. braggart
17. bucolic
18. buttress
19. buxom
20. callow
21. candor

Copyright © 1994 by Harcourt Brace & Company. All rights reserved.

22. captious
23. carmine
24. choleric
25. chromatic
26. clement
27. cogent
28. cognizant
29. colloquy
30. complaisant
31. concoct
32. conduce
33. conflagration
34. decrepit
35. desiccated
36. disruption
37. drastic
38. effusion
39. elongated
40. expedit
41. fillip
42. fiscal
43. flamboyant
44. friable
45. garbled
46. gossamer
47. habitat
48. hermetic
49. homogeneous
50. immutable
51. incarnate
52. incongruous
53. incredulity
54. indigenous
55. irascible
56. itinerary
57. lacteal
58. lexicon
59. lucidity
60. mediate
61. menial
62. mercurial
63. meretricious
64. misconstruing
65. momentous
66. monitions
67. moot
68. nefarious
69. obesity
70. obtruding
71. olfactory
72. onerous
73. orisons
74. oscillating
75. ossified
76. ostentation
77. overt
78. parrying
79. penurious
80. philology
81. pliant
82. precluding
83. pseudonym
84. rectitude
85. regress
86. renovation
87. replica
88. rigmarole
89. sacerdotal
90. scurrilous
91. senile
92. simulate
93. stultify
94. thermal
95. transcribe
96. truculent
97. turpitude
98. unkempt
99. waif
100. zany

Copyright © 1994 by Harcourt Brace & Company. All rights reserved.

Chapter 1

Exercise 1

1. abysmal
2. aquamarine
3. bestial
4. choleric
5. dais
6. dissimilar
7. hiatus
8. posthumous
9. schismatic
10. tendency

Exercise 2

1. benign
2. cadaver
3. caduceus
4. charlatan
5. contingent
6. frenetic
7. habilitate
8. mobility
9. perusal
10. sequester

Exercise 3

1. alluvial
2. corrugate
3. equilibrium
4. halcyon
5. leguminous
6. ontology
7. pragmatism
8. residuum
9. resplendent
10. surreptitious

Exercise 4

1. angst
2. April fool
3. British history
4. Indian
5. Levi's
6. literature
7. Olympic Games (games)
8. penicillin
9. Purple Heart
10. strontium

Exercise 5

1. Amazon, amazon
2. Catholic, catholic
3. Democrat, democrat
4. Exodus, exodus
5. Frank, frank
6. Hegira, hegira
7. Mandarin, mandarin
8. Messiah, messiah
9. Morocco, morocco
10. Reformation, reformation

Exercise 6

1. blitzkrieg
2. cum laude
3. gendarme
4. hoi polloi
5. hors d'oeuvre
6. kudos
7. nom de plume
8. ombudsman
9. outré
10. raison d'être

Exercise 7

1. aluminum, aluminium
2. armor, armour
3. caliber, calibre
4. check, cheque
5. cozy, cosy
6. jewelry, jewellry
7. luster, lustre
8. mayhem, maihem
9. pretense, pretence
10. wagon, waggon

Exercise 8

1. aegis, egis
2. ascent, assent
3. consul, counsel
4. discreet, discrete
5. dispatch, despatch
6. missal, missile
7. palate, palette
8. quean, queen
9. visor, vizor
10. wander, wonder

Exercise 9

1. archipelago
2. charisma
3. coruscate
4. iridescence
5. loquacious
6. lugubrious
7. onerous
8. similitude
9. sycophantic
10. thalassic

Exercise 10

1. abstruse
2. cognizant
3. fillip
4. fluoresce
5. harridan
6. indecorous
7. liaison
8. precursor
9. scurrilous
10. vagaries

Exercise 11

1. aficionado
2. blithe
3. conch
4. creek
5. duke
6. either
7. forehead
8. hegira
9. junta
10. kiln
11. neither
12. often
13. quinine
14. roof
15. root
16. schedule
17. titular
18. transient

Copyright © 1994 by Harcourt Brace & Company. All rights reserved.

Exercise 1

1. Afrikaans
2. Armenian
3. Avestan
4. Bengali
5. Breton
6. Cornish
7. Danish
8. Dutch
9. Frisian
10. Gaelic
11. German
12. Gothic
13. Greek
14. Italian
15. Low German
16. Norwegian
17. Old French
18. Old Spanish
19. Persian
20. Portuguese
21. Provençal
22. Spanish
23. Swedish
24. Vulgar Latin

Exercise 2

1. albino
2. argali
3. begum
4. boomerang
5. dinghy
6. dungaree
7. matzo
8. pogrom
9. taboo
10. totem

Exercise 3

1. aberration
2. beatitude
3. bursar
4. chimera
5. connubial
6. eschatology
7. litigate
8. repertory
9. sententious
10. uxorious

Exercise 4

1. aficionado
2. avant-garde
3. batiste
4. boudoir
5. bravado
6. consortium
7. cortege
8. crescendo
9. curé
10. de jure
11. detritus
12. exposé
13. extravaganza
14. farceur
15. fete
16. fiasco
17. gourmet
18. junta
19. maestro
20. métier
21. minutiae
22. moratorium
23. penchant
24. peyote
25. piquant
26. prognosis
27. rapport
28. roué
29. travail
30. tyro

Exercise 5

1. aggregate
2. amplitude
3. apex
4. argot
5. assiduous
6. bagatelle
7. bellicose
8. berceuse
9. bizarre
10. bounty
11. cabal
12. catacombs
13. chartreuse
14. chicanery
15. clandestine
16. connoisseur
17. criterion
18. delectable
19. demise
20. docile
21. ductile
22. equanimity
23. exigent
24. fastidious
25. flamboyant
26. fortuitous
27. genial
28. hegira
29. imperious
30. ingenuous
31. intrinsic
32. mollify
33. multifarious
34. opulent
35. pastoral
36. recalcitrant
37. reiterate
38. reverie
39. sanguine
40. scintillating
41. succinct
42. supercilious
43. surfeit
44. taciturn
45. ubiquitous

Exercise 6

1. aegis
2. archipelago
3. argot
4. automaton
5. badinage
6. berceuse
7. cabal
8. chartreuse
9. connoisseur
10. demise
11. denouement
12. dossier
13. éclat
14. ennui
15. étude
16. fiasco
17. fugue
18. gauche
19. genre
20. hauteur
21. insouciant
22. jejune
23. largesse
24. libido
25. liqueur
26. macabre
27. malaise
28. memoir
29. montage
30. née
31. pelisse
32. première
33. protégé
34. quietus
35. rebus
36. regime
37. risqué
38. saga
39. salon
40. sobriquet

Copyright © 1994 by Harcourt Brace & Company. All rights reserved.

Chapter 3

Exercise 1

1. acme
2. arid
3. bane
4. blithe
5. churl
6. droll
7. gauche
8. grist
9. gusto
10. ilk
11. kelp
12. nadir
13. niche
14. pique
15. rife
16. scion
17. shard
18. sloth
19. waif
20. wraith

Exercise 2

1. addle
2. apex
3. bauble
4. brogue
5. carp
6. chary
7. conch
8. cruet
9. dire
10. dour
11. dross
12. eschew
13. feint
14. fiat
15. frond
16. ghoul
17. gnome
18. hale
19. maim
20. mien
21. node
22. quirk
23. sleazy
24. snide
25. spoor
26. terse
27. tome
28. twit
29. wench
30. whet

Exercise 3

1. bards
2. bland
3. broach
4. buxom
5. cache
6. cant
7. con
8. coy
9. dais
10. deft
11. delve
12. despot
13. dirk
14. doff
15. dun
16. flout
17. furl
18. gamin
19. glib
20. guise
21. hone
22. lithe
23. lush
24. melee
25. neb
26. pelt
27. rue
28. ruse
29. tarn
30. trice

Exercise 4

1. ambidextrous
2. amphibious
3. deuterogamy
4. dichromatic
5. dyspepsia
6. ectoparasite
7. endocardium
8. exobiology
9. juxtapose
10. preternatural

Exercise 5

1. affiliate
2. collate
3. diffident
4. dissimilar
5. eradicate
6. innovate
7. irreligious
8. occasion
9. occlude
10. succinct

Cumulative Test 1

1. adroit
2. agamic
3. alluvial
4. ambidextrous
5. amorphous
6. ameliorate
7. animosities
8. apothegms
9. bailiwick
10. banal
11. benign
12. bestial
13. bicameral
14. bucolic
15. buxom
16. cairn
17. cant
18. carafe
19. chimeras
20. circumspect
21. clandestine
22. coagulate
23. contiguous
24. criterion
25. debilitated
26. decorous
27. delve
28. discrete
29. disseminate
30. dole
31. dour
32. dubiety
33. ebullient
34. effigy
35. elation
36. encomium
37. endemic
38. eschew
39. eulogize
40. euphonious
41. facsimile
42. fakir
43. faux pas
44. felicitate
45. furl
46. gamin
47. garbled
48. ghoul
49. glib
50. gossamer
51. hagiography
52. hegira
53. hiatus
54. intractable
55. labile
56. leery
57. lexicon
58. litigate
59. macabre
60. menial
61. mitigate
62. mollify
63. monitory
64. nadir
65. numismatic
66. obesity
67. obsolescent
68. penchant
69. perdition
70. perfidy
71. penurious
72. presage
73. primordial
74. reticent
75. salubrious
76. scintillating
77. scurrilous
78. sequestered
79. snide
80. spoor
81. stultify
82. succinct
83. surreptitious
84. taciturn
85. tarn
86. tautology
87. temerity
88. tome
89. travail
90. trolls
91. truculent
92. ubiquitous
93. ultimatum
94. ungulate
95. unkempt
96. virgules
97. vitiate
98. wraith
99. wry
100. zany

Copyright © 1994 by Harcourt Brace & Company. All rights reserved.

Chapter 4

Exercise 1

1. agamic
2. amorphous
3. anthropomorphic
4. antipathy
5. archetype
6. archon
7. asteroids
8. autonomy
9. cryptographer
10. dermatitis
11. euphony
12. genealogy
13. heterodox
14. homophones
15. monochromatic
16. Neolithic
17. polyphonic
18. psychopaths
19. pyromania
20. sophisticates

Exercise 2

1. acronymic
2. androgynous
3. autochthonous
4. cacophony
5. cytology
6. hagiographers
7. heliotropic
8. hierarchy
9. megatheres
10. neoplasia
11. nephritis
12. odometer
13. pentameter
14. phyllopod
15. polydactylous
16. polyglot
17. seismographic
18. tautological
19. thaumaturgy
20. theophany

Exercise 3

Words containing the same Greek root

1. agnosticism—gnostic
2. aphagia—esophagus
3. carcinogen—carcinoma
4. claustrophobia—agoraphobia
5. epigastrium—gastritis
6. epiphany—diaphanous
7. epode—prosody
8. gonad—archegonium
9. mastoid—mastectomy
10. megathere—theriomorphic
11. narcotism—narcosis
12. necromancy—chiromancy
13. neuralgia—neurology
14. neuritis—otitis
15. osteotomy—tomography
16. otitis—otoscope
17. pyorrhea—empyema
18. rhododendron—dendrology
19. sarcasm—sarcoma
20. toxicology—toxicosis

Exercise 4

1. androgenous—androgynous
2. anthrax—anthracite
3. autopsy—optical
4. bathyal—bathysphere
5. bibliopole—bibliotheca
6. cardiac—cardiomyopathy
7. catalepsy—epilepsy
8. chiropractor—chiropodist
9. chrysanthemum—anthology
10. cosmos—cosmonaut
11. cryogenics—cryometer
12. ethnic—ethnographer
13. euthanasia—thanatos
14. exophthalmic—ophthalmic
15. gynarchy—gynecology
16. hemiplegia—paraplegia
17. hemodialysis—hemotoma
18. hieroglyph—hierophant
19. hydrocephalous—hydrophobia
20. hydrotherapy—chemotherapy
21. iconography—iconoclast
22. idiomorphic—idiosyncrasy
23. mesentery—enteron
24. neologism—neonate
25. nephroscope—stethoscope
26. neuroblast—neurocyte
27. octopus—platypus
28. pandemic—panorama
29. pathos—pathology
30. pepsin—dyspeptic
31. phagocyte—leukocyte
32. philander—philanthropist
33. pterodactyl—dipterous
34. pyrogen—pyrophobic
35. rheumatology—rheumatism
36. rhinitis—rhinoceros
37. strophe—apostrophe
38. thermostable—thermotherapy
39. thyroid—thyroidectomy
40. xylography—xylophone

Copyright © 1994 by Harcourt Brace & Company. All rights reserved.

Exercise 1

1. abject
2. abjure
3. abscess
4. abscond
5. abstinence
6. agamic
7. alluvial
8. amorphous
9. avert
10. bicameral
11. biennial
12. bilateral
13. circumlocution
14. circumspect
15. coagulate
16. collate
17. commiseration
18. contiguous
19. contravene
20. cursory
21. demagogue
22. demigod
23. demur
24. discrete
25. dispel
26. disseminate
27. distended
28. diverse
29. divert
30. dubiosity
31. edict
32. efferent
33. effigy
34. effusion
35. encomium
36. endemic
37. euthanasia
38. exculpate
39. exogamy
40. exonerated
41. factitious
42. finite
43. geomorphic
44. infinite
45. infuse
46. intractable
47. juxtaposition
48. lectern
49. libido
50. liltigate
51. misogamy
52. misogyny
53. numismatic
54. obsolescent
55. occlude
56. perfidy
57. precursors
58. presage
59. primordial
60. progeny
61. rectitude
62. regimen
63. respiratory
64. retract
65. retrogress
66. retrospective
67. rupture
68. salubrious
69. sedentary
70. sequestered
71. subvert
72. succinct
73. supersede
74. surreptitious
75. suspensory
76. symphony
77. synchronous
78. tenable
79. tenacious
80. tenets
81. thanatopsis
82. thanatos
83. theriomorphic
84. thermophilic
85. timorous
86. tome
87. tomography
88. transient
89. truculent
90. validate
91. vitiate
92. vivacious
93. vivify
94. vivisection
95. vocation
96. vociferous
97. volition
98. voluble
99. vulgar
100. vulgate

Exercise 2

1. abstract
2. accidental
3. anticipate
4. append
5. attraction
6. complex
7. component
8. concept
9. conclusion
10. conducive
11. confine
12. correct
13. definition
14. deformity
15. different
16. difficult
17. efficient
18. ejaculate
19. expect
20. extent
21. extract
22. factor
23. imply
24. important
25. impose
26. include
27. induction
28. infinite
29. inscription
30. introduce
31. occurrence
32. opponent
33. oppose
34. perception
35. perfection
36. permissible
37. perverted
38. produce
39. proposal
40. reduce
41. resent
42. residence
43. respect
44. restrict
45. retention
46. solution
47. subject
48. subscribe
49. transmit
50. visible

Exercise 3

1. adjacent
2. agony
3. capillary
4. capon
5. cipher
6. congress
7. ducal
8. facade
9. ferocious
10. finagle
11. fustian
12. gene
13. generic
14. injunction
15. jackal
16. leghorn
17. lignite
18. mitosis
19. mitten
20. pendulous
21. poniard
22. portray
23. regard
24. rigmarole
25. session
26. spiral
27. spirit
28. tinsel
29. vertex
30. viscous

Cumulative Test 2

1. adduce
2. altercation
3. apathy
4. apostasy
5. astral
6. bizarre
7. blithe
8. bucolic
9. carcinoma
10. celibate
11. charlatan
12. clandestine
13. cliché
14. cognizance
15. comatose
16. congenital
17. contiguous
18. cornice
19. culpable
20. decorous
21. deprecate
22. desiccated
23. disheveled
24. disseminate
25. dynamic
26. éclat
27. effulgent
28. egress
29. emulous
30. epigram
31. epitome
32. eructation
33. evoke
34. exculpate
35. expedite
36. facet
37. facetious
38. febrile
39. felicitous
40. filch
41. finagle
42. flout
43. frenetic
44. fresco
45. geomorphic
46. geriatric
47. hegemony
48. hemostat
49. heterodox
50. homonyms
51. indigent
52. interdict
53. intractable
54. kudos
55. lapidary
56. liaison
57. lucrative
58. mayhem
59. mollify
60. moratorium
61. narcosis
62. necrotic
63. nonchalant
64. onerous
65. outré
66. panorama
67. patent
68. pathology
69. perfidious
70. piquant
71. podiatry
72. polychromatic
73. portend
74. portico
75. psychopath
76. ragout
77. rectitude
78. refract
79. residuum

Copyright © 1994 by Harcourt Brace & Company. All rights reserved.

80. restive
81. reticent
82. rheostat
83. schizophrenia
84. scintillate
85. scion
86. secular
87. shard
88. taciturn
89. temerity
90. theism
91. therapeutic
92. tout
93. turbid
94. turpitude
95. undulant
96. ungulate
97. vacillate
98. vitiate
99. voracious
100. whimsy

Cumulative Test 3

1. accoutrement
2. allomorph
3. amnesty
4. autonomy
5. bevel
6. camisole
7. catenation
8. charisma
9. dendroid
10. denigrate
11. dermal
12. dilation
13. dirk
14. egregious
15. epos
16. euphoria
17. flexure
18. genuflection
19. gonfalon
20. guise
21. hieroglyph
22. holocaust
23. impecunious
24. innocuous
25. intrepid
26. louver
27. mestizo
28. meticulous
29. miscible
30. monochromatic
31. morocco
32. nemesis
33. neoplasia
34. occlusion
35. ornithology
36. otitis
37. pandemic
38. pediatrician
39. pendant
40. pepsin
41. precept
42. quorum
43. regimen
44. sarcoma
45. scone
46. spleen
47. succinct
48. traumatic
49. truculent
50. viscous

Cumulative Test 4

1. amenable—preamble
2. anthropology—anthem
3. atom—tomato
4. autograph—monograph
5. bailiwick—wicked
6. banal—banner
7. barometer—barter
8. bigamy—gambler
9. bole—hyperbole
10. canton—canter
11. chimera—chimney
12. consequence—sequel
13. contiguous—tiger
14. cursive—curse
15. debilitate—billion
16. decorum—declamation
17. democrat—crater
18. dinosaur—diner
19. diverse—versify
20. dour—doughty
21. effigy—fig
22. elated—belated
23. empathy—pathfinder
24. encomium—empathy
25. epilog—depilatory
26. eschew—chew
27. expedite—peddler
28. facsimile—similar
29. felicitate—fellow
30. filibuster—filial
31. forensic—forestry
32. gallant—gall bladder
33. grammar—grampus
34. hagiology—hagridden
35. hegira—hegemony
36. hemorrhage—hemstitch
37. labile—labial
38. litigate—literate
39. macabre—macaroon
40. mastoid—mastic
41. missile—mistress
42. mitigate—emit
43. mollify—molecule
44. obese—obey
45. pantomime—pansy
46. pentameter—penthouse
47. polygon—gondola
48. postpone—postage
49. primordial—orderly
50. pyre—pyrrhic
51. scurrilous—scurry
52. specimen—speckle
53. stricture—constrict
54. subsidiary—assiduous
55. suggest—sugar
56. taboo—tabular
57. theology—theory
58. travail—travesty
59. unction—uncle
60. vitiate—vitamin

Copyright © 1994 by Harcourt Brace & Company. All rights reserved.

Chapter 6

Exercise 1

1. abrade
2. abscond
3. arrive
4. collude
5. commute
6. confute
7. conjure
8. deflate
9. exhale
10. expunge
11. imbibe
12. immune
13. indent
14. obstruct
15. perfume
16. preside
17. promote
18. relapse
19. secure
20. submerge

Exercise 2

1. abjure
2. acclamations
3. acerbity
4. acumen
5. adjudicate
6. alleviate
7. amatory
8. amity
9. attenuated
10. auriferous
11. bellicose
12. benevolent
13. carnivorous
14. commutate
15. confluence
16. corporeal
17. duress
18. efflorescence
19. errata
20. excision
21. exculpated
22. fervid
23. gregarious
24. incandescently
25. indurated
26. infirmities
27. itinerant
28. juridical
29. loquacious
30. malefactors
31. maritime
32. moribund
33. pellucid
34. piscine
35. sonorous
36. undulation
37. vacuity
38. verbiage
39. verdical
40. vulgate

Exercise 3

1. bovine
2. ursine
3. Scriptures
4. transfusion
5. adjourn
6. journey
7. medieval
8. unicorn
9. Mediterranean
10. ferric
11. ferrocyanide
12. aviary
13. apiary
14. regicide
15. fratricide
16. genuflect
17. vermiform
18. vaccinate
19. inoculate
20. insinuate
21. sinuous
22. dilapidate
23. lapidary
24. leopard
25. Lucifer
26. immaculate
27. macula
28. mellifluous
29. commensurate
30. mensuration
31. nocturne
32. sylvan
33. Pennsylvania
34. optimist
35. percussion
36. concussion
37. defunct
38. function
39. bursar
40. bursitis
41. aberration
42. errant
43. bull
44. bulletin
45. ruby
46. rubric
47. equinox
48. belligerent
49. circumlocution
50. exhume
51. humus
52. dorsal
53. endorse
54. equilibrium
55. patrician
56. patricide
57. patriotic
58. patron
59. patroon
60. Vermont
61. Florida
62. alma mater/dura mater

Exercise 4

1. abrasion—erasure
2. cadence—cadaver
3. condole—dolorous
4. conflagration—flagrant
5. conjugate—conjugal
6. denigrate—nigrescent
7. depilatory—capillary
8. dormant—dormitory
9. dorsal—endorse
10. exhume—inhume
11. expedite—biped
12. expurate—purgatory
13. frigid—refrigerator
14. incinerate—cinerous
15. incision—excision
16. jocose—jocular
17. lactation—lacteal
18. miscreant—recreant
19. nocent—innocuous
20. novice—innovation
21. resurgent—insurgent
22. salad—saline
23. sanguinary—consanguineous
24. senescent—senility
25. sublunar—lunatic

Copyright © 1994 by Harcourt Brace & Company. All rights reserved.

Exercise 1

1. beast, comrade, prince, scoundrel, wife
2. carry, cover, haul, pack, pass
3. cavern, clamor, danger, peril, poison
4. close, depart, expose, fail, proceed
5. secure, senile, similar, singular, superior
6. awe, burden, meddle, quarrel, tire
7. critic, fossil, public, satire, signal
8. assist, assure, clear, perform, sever
9. baron, brigand, orphan, peer, peon
10. budget, custom, element, honor, parliament
11. blazon, herald, jewel, mimic, revel
12. auction, ballad, engine, private, profit
13. claim, expect, inform, inhale, serve
14. betray, deny, refuse, rehearse, renew
15. athlete, period, prophet, scene, stanza
16. coarse, length, sharp, soft, white
17. decorate, possess, prohibit, relate, secrete
18. antique, benign, bestial, brutal, catholic
19. brazen, drunken, shrewd, stubborn, sudden
20. appoint, assign, divorce, employ, grant
21. clerk, friend, lord, manager, professor
22. ascertain, assess, assort, comport, deface
23. anecdote, arithmetic, artery, brute, fiction
24. earth, gold, oak, wood, wool
25. bankrupt, decent, infant, secret, vacant

Exercise 2

1. acid
2. alien
3. American
4. ample
5. beauty
6. brutal
7. caliber
8. canon
9. capital
10. central
11. civil
12. crystal
13. diverse
14. fossil
15. general
16. granule
17. human
18. ideal
19. immortal
20. italic
21. local
22. particular
23. popular
24. pure
25. tranquil

Exercise 3

1. acronym
2. algebra
3. amateur
4. arithmetic
5. autumn
6. bacteria
7. beast
8. bulb
9. caprice
10. carbon
11. circuit
12. demon
13. elephant
14. enigma
15. euphemism
16. family
17. fancy
18. harmony
19. knave
20. mountain
21. ocean
22. prince
23. residue
24. rogue
25. sloth
26. sophomore
27. stanza
28. suffice
29. suicide
30. synonym
31. territory
32. thief
33. thunder
34. tone
35. torrent
36. ulcer
37. unit
38. vigil
39. whimsy
40. zeal

Exercise 4

1. acidulous
2. Americana
3. asterisk
4. brooklet
5. darkling
6. equestrienne
7. foliaceous
8. fraudulent
9. fusillade
10. halogen
11. hillock
12. Pleistocene
13. reticule
14. spheroid
15. tonsillitis

Exercise 5

1. abhorrence
2. advisable
3. arguable
4. appearance
5. chargeable
6. concurrent
7. hardihood
8. issuance
9. juicy
10. likable, likeable
11. manliness
12. noticeable
13. perversity
14. preferred
15. prodding

Exercise 6

1. definite
2. responsible
3. antecedent
4. attendance
5. advantageous
6. insistence
7. competent
8. convenient
9. intelligence
10. indispensable
11. obedience
12. resistance
13. tendency
14. usage
15. inflexible

Exercise 7

1. abstention
2. adhesion
3. antagonism
4. appellate
5. clarity
6. cohesive
7. consumption
8. criticism
9. declension
10. demolition

Copyright © 1994 by Harcourt Brace & Company. All rights reserved.

11. diminution
12. dirigible
13. dissolution
14. emission
15. erosion
16. evolution
17. induction
18. inquisitive
19. negligent
20. obligatory
21. obtrusive
22. occupation
23. prophecy
24. redemption
25. secession
26. suspension
27. transcript
28. transmission
29. tremulous
30. union

Exercise 8

Since only suffixes are given for this exercise, obviously no words are included here.

Exercise 9

1. actor's
2. admittance
3. chieftain
4. churches
5. committed
6. cowardice
7. deducted
8. deeper
9. delightful
10. determination
11. deviation
12. empowered
13. happier
14. injuring
15. lovable
16. malicious
17. muddy
18. oxen
19. papers
20. parentage
21. payment
22. poisonous
23. referral
24. refusal
25. reliable
26. retaining
27. soonest
28. twisted
29. withdrawal
30. withering

Copyright © 1994 by Harcourt Brace & Company. All rights reserved.

Chapter 8

Exercise 1

1. aegis
2. aisle
3. ambush
4. angel
5. anthracite
6. arctic
7. arena
8. athlete
9. autopsy
10. browse
11. budget
12. cache
13. cancer
14. caprice
15. challenge
16. chapel
17. check
18. clerk
19. clock
20. cobalt
21. colonel
22. comet
23. comma
24. companion
25. copy
26. coward
27. cruise
28. daisy
29. diphtheria
30. domino
31. easel
32. eerie
33. etch
34. farce
35. ferret
36. fiasco
37. foreign
38. fulminate
39. galaxy
40. garble
41. grenade
42. halo
43. imp
44. insect
45. lace
46. lumber
47. miser
48. muscle
49. parish
50. pedigree
51. pioneer
52. plague
53. psalm
54. pumpkin
55. rescue
56. rummage
57. savage
58. scandal
59. sirocco
60. slogan
61. subtle
62. succinct
63. terrier
64. theme
65. theorem
66. tragedy
67. treacle
68. vegetable
69. wench
70. window

Exercise 2

1. arson
2. bribe
3. constable
4. dean
5. demon
6. gauche
7. harlot
8. jewel
9. lunatic
10. mansion
11. pastor
12. pope
13. prostitute
14. rape
15. senate
16. serpent
17. surgery
18. villain
19. virago
20. weird

Exercise 3

1. ammonia
2. arachnid
3. atlas
4. attic
5. bloomer
6. bologna
7. boycott
8. braille
9. calico
10. champagne
11. dalmatic
12. damask
13. dunce
14. gerrymander
15. grog
16. guernsey
17. guillotine
18. homburg
19. italic
20. jeremiad
21. limousine
22. macadam
23. masochism
24. nicotine
25. ohm
26. parchment
27. sandwich
28. saxophone
29. silhouette
30. spoonerism
31. syphilis
32. tabby (cat)
33. tarantula
34. watt
35. wisteria

Exercise 4

1. cadence
2. liquidated
3. naked
4. naughty
5. campaign
6. capable
7. lofts
8. honesty
9. nervous
10. nice
11. candour
12. reprobate
13. housekeeping
14. huddling
15. niece
16. noise
17. resolution
18. respondent
19. humiliate
20. reversion

Cumulative Test 5

1. adumbrate
2. amerce
3. anomalous
4. aquiline
5. argosy
6. attenuated
7. bagatelle
8. benignity
9. buccal
10. cabal
11. capricious
12. cincture
13. coercion
14. cognizant
15. comatose
16. corsairs
17. debonair
18. decorous
19. desultory
20. diatribe
21. dorsal
22. eerie
23. emaciate
24. enigma
25. expedite
26. expiate
27. fecund
28. filial
29. fulminated
30. garrote
31. hegemony
32. hirsute
33. histrionic
34. inchoate
35. jeremiads
36. laconic
37. lacuna
38. lambent
39. litigious
40. maudlin
41. mollify
42. mordant
43. nubile
44. occult
45. pastoral
46. pectoral
47. penultimate
48. perfervid
49. potable
50. primeval
51. ramified
52. recumbent
53. sadistic
54. sardonic
55. scabrous
56. sinuous
57. soporific
58. specter
59. strident
60. sycophants
61. taciturn
62. tepid
63. therapy
64. tremulous
65. tumid
66. venial
67. verbosity
68. vitiate
69. vitreous
70. vitriolic

Chapter 9

Figurative expressions are not included in the Chapter Word List. Thus, words are not included for Exercises 1, 2, 3, and 4.

Copyright © 1994 by Harcourt Brace & Company. All rights reserved.

Exercise 1

It was not deemed necessary to include Exercise 1 in the Chapter Word List.

Exercise 2

1. adversity
2. antithesis
3. aperture
4. catechize
5. chattels
6. chicanery
7. coeval
8. desiccate
9. encomium
10. enervation
11. enigmatic
12. enunciate
13. eschew
14. execrate
15. expunge
16. exuberant
17. histrionic
18. idiosyncrasy
19. indigent
20. inebriation
21. interdict
22. irascible
23. jocose
24. labyrinth
25. mundane
26. obeisance
27. paucity
28. physiognomy
29. poignant
30. preceptor
31. precursor
32. residue
33. savant
34. sundry
35. thesaurus
36. trepidation
37. turpitude
38. variegated
39. verbiage
40. wraith

Exercise 3

1. accustom
2. black (adj.)
3. confine (v.)
4. curse (n.)
5. curt
6. decay (v.)
7. delay (v.)
8. elastic (adj.)
9. forgetfulness
10. interrupted
11. liar
12. learned (adj.)
13. native (adj.)
14. necessary (adj.)
15. nickname (n.)
16. odd
17. poverty
18. practicable
19. praise (v.)
20. profane (adj.)
21. punish
22. repay
23. repeat
24. repentant
25. salt (n.)
26. secret (adj.)
27. steal (v.)
28. surrender (v.)
29. think
30. tickle
31. undress (v.)
32. unrelated
33. unsteady
34. warn
35. weary (adj.)

Exercise 4

1. relevant
2. extract
3. perspicuous
4. dissemination
5. orthodoxy
6. immutable
7. posterior
8. virile
9. inveterate
10. arable
11. bucolic
12. elaboration
13. asymmetrical
14. flush
15. mercurial
16. reception
17. stabilize
18. terrestrial
19. adamantine
20. meticulous
21. monitor
22. pelagic
23. scrutinize
24. redolent
25. cerulean
26. imperceptive
27. impugn
28. analysis
29. cogent
30. benign
31. profligate
32. sagacious
33. obstinate
34. mundane
35. manifest

Exercise 5

It was not deemed necessary to include Exercise 5 in the Chapter Word List.

Exercise 6

1. cede—yield
2. condolence—sympathy
3. corpulent—obese
4. falter—waver
5. fickle—capricious
6. haggard—cadaverous
7. immense—monstrous
8. rustic—rural
9. savage—barbaric
10. threaten—intimidate

Exercise 7

1. avid
2. contingent
3. craven
4. decry
5. delectable
6. deleterious
7. demur
8. deprecate
9. dexterous
10. diffident
11. disdained
12. divergence
13. dubious
14. enervating
15. exalted
16. ignominy
17. poignant
18. sophisticated
19. squalid
20. sybaritic

Exercise 8

1. affluence—effluence
2. allusions—illusions
3. aspired—inspired
4. beets—beats
5. calvary—cavalry
6. capitol—capital
7. counsel's—consul's
8. deprecate—depreciate
9. eminent—imminent
10. discreet—discrete
11. expiate—expatiate
12. grizzly—grisly
13. homey—homely
14. illuding—eluding
15. infinite—infinitesimal
16. iniquities—inequities
17. insensitive—insensible
18. insight—incite
19. migraine—migrant
20. missiles—missals
21. momentous—momentary
22. official—officious
23. precedes—proceeds
24. principle—principal
25. satire—satyr
26. septic—skeptic
27. specter—scepter
28. subsiding—subsisting
29. suggestible—suggestive
30. tuition—intuition

Copyright © 1994 by Harcourt Brace & Company. All rights reserved.

Chapter 11

Exercise 1

1. abide
2. affrighted
3. argufying
4. codger
5. edgy
6. enthused
7. floored (v.)
8. flop
9. fluke
10. framed
11. frazzled
12. gangling
13. hangover
14. hanky-panky
15. heel
16. high-hatting
17. hog (v.)
18. horsy (adj.)
19. kids (children)
20. knock (denigrate)
21. land (v.)
22. main (n.)
23. mayhap
24. missis
25. mooch
26. mumbo-jumbo
27. nauseating (v.)
28. newsy
29. orating
30. orb
31. ornery
32. pestiferous
33. poky (adj.)
34. powerful
35. ramshackle
36. rattled (adj.)
37. reminiscing
38. shinnying
39. sockdolager
40. spiel
41. splendiferous
42. splurge
43. spunky
44. stogie
45. strewing

Exercise 2

This exercise is not included in the Chapter Word List

Exercise 3

1. bamboozle
2. barb
3. big daddy
4. bindlestiff
5. black out
6. clam up
7. codger
8. coffin nail
9. doohickey
10. flabbergasted
11. gals
12. guys
13. hant
14. kids
15. limey
16. moniker
17. namby-pamby
18. perchance
19. rambunctious
20. riled up
21. rube
22. schmo
23. sing (confess)
24. stogie

Copyright © 1994 by Harcourt Brace & Company. All rights reserved.

Exercises in Context: Since student responses will vary widely, no word list is supplied for these exercises.

Cumulative Test 6A

1. adamantine
2. allomorph
3. arable
4. baccate
5. bellicose
6. certitude
7. cerulean
8. cogent
9. congenital
10. culpable
11. debilitating
12. decry
13. delectable
14. deprecate
15. desiccated
16. effusion
17. ellipsis
18. encomium
19. endemic
20. ephemeral
21. epitome
22. execrate
23. expatiate
24. factitious
25. febrile
26. festal
27. fetid
28. halcyon
29. ignominy
30. indigent
31. indurated
32. innocuous
33. malleable
34. missal
35. momentous
36. mundane
37. nadir
38. nocent
39. obelisk
40. ostracize
41. palpable
42. paucity
43. pelagic
44. petulant
45. phlegmatic
46. prescience
47. procrastinate
48. quotidian
49. retrospect
50. schismatic
51. sedulous
52. stentorian
53. stringent
54. supercilious
55. supine
56. sybaritic
57. tawdry
58. tractable
59. transitory
60. trepidation
61. turpitude
62. undulant
63. unkempt
64. vacuous
65. veracity
66. verbosity
67. vitreous
68. vitriolic
69. vivacious
70. vulgate

Cumulative Test 6B

1. affluence
2. ancillary
3. asseverate
4. baubles
5. captious
6. cenotaph
7. coeval
8. cognomen
9. congruence
10. contrition
11. deflagrating
12. deleterious
13. discrete
14. effulgence
15. elasmobranch
16. elucidate
17. emaciated
18. enervated
19. equivocal
20. erudite
21. ethnic
22. extirpate
23. fecund
24. feral
25. flagellation
26. frugality
27. gastritis
28. imbue
29. impecunious
30. infinitesimal
31. itinerant
32. liaison
33. macabre
34. mafficking
35. magnanimous
36. meretricious
37. metonymy
38. morose
39. morphology
40. mountebank
41. neophyte
42. nugatory
43. oscillating
44. palaver
45. parsimonious
46. perspicuous
47. pertinacious
48. poignant
49. pragmatic
50. quondam
51. ramose
52. savants
53. scintillating
54. sophistry
55. stringent
56. succumbing
57. supererogation
58. surreptitious
59. sycophant
60. torpor
61. traduce
62. traumatic
63. tremulous
64. unctuous
65. vacillate
66. vernacular
67. virulent
68. waif
69. wraith
70. zany

Cumulative Test 6C

1. aborigines
2. abrogate
3. abstruse
4. abysmal
5. acrimony
6. admonitory
7. adroit
8. aegis
9. affluence
10. agamic

Copyright © 1994 by Harcourt Brace & Company. All rights reserved.

11. alacrity
12. anthropoid
13. avarice
14. benignant
15. braggart
16. cajole
17. cephalic
18. colloquium
19. comestible
20. cruciate
21. dendroid
22. dichotomize
23. ebullient
24. ephemeral
25. factitious
26. flaccid
27. flamboyant
28. garner
29. heinous
30. homunculus
31. inchoate
32. insouciant
33. junta
34. lapidary
35. lenitive
36. macabre
37. mimetic
38. mutation
39. nubile
40. oscillate
41. pathogen
42. photic
43. portent
44. prolific
45. quasi
46. redundant
47. riant
48. salutary
49. scurrilous
50. sequester
51. solarium
52. spelunker
53. stultify
54. succinct
55. talisman
56. thalassic
57. travail
58. ubiquitous
59. vatic
60. waylay

Cumulative Test 6D

1. accuse
2. acquisitive
3. adventitious
4. animosity
5. animus
6. antipathy
7. apathetic
8. apparition
9. appease
10. arbitrary
11. argot
12. arraign
13. audacity
14. authenticate
15. autocratic
16. avaricious
17. badinage
18. banal
19. banter
20. boisterous
21. blatant
22. cant
23. casual
24. chaffing
25. clamorous
26. compatible
27. conciliate
28. consonant
29. contingent
30. corroborate
31. covetous
32. diaphanous
33. dictatorial
34. effrontery
35. egregious
36. flagrant
37. fortuitous
38. gall
39. germane
40. grasping
41. greedy
42. gross
43. hardihood
44. hostility
45. ignominy
46. impassive
47. impeach
48. imperious
49. impervious
50. inane
51. incidental
52. incriminate
53. indict
54. indifferent
55. infamy
56. insipid
57. jargon
58. jejune
59. lambent
60. limpid
61. lingo
62. lucent
63. lucid
64. luminous
65. lustrous
66. material (adj.)
67. mollify
68. nefarious
69. obloquy
70. obstreperous
71. odium
72. opprobrium
73. pellucid
74. peremptory
75. persiflage
76. phantasm
77. phantom
78. placate
79. primal
80. primeval
81. primitive
82. primordial
83. pristine
84. propitiate
85. radiant
86. raillery
87. relevant
88. rancor
89. rank
90. specter
91. stolid
92. substantiate
93. temerity
94. transparent
95. validate
96. vapid
97. verify
98. vernacular
99. vociferous
100. wraith

Copyright © 1994 by Harcourt Brace & Company. All rights reserved.

NAME ______________________ SECTION __________ DATE __________

VOCABULARY TEST 1: The words in the following test are "thirteenth grade" words—that is, they should be in the vocabulary of a college freshman. Choose the word or expression closest in meaning to the italicized word and print its number in the blank.

1. an *abstruse* subject: 1 unimportant 2 theological 3 complex and difficult — 1. ________
2. feelings of *antipathy:* 1 deep respect 2 piqued interest 3 dislike — 2. ________
3. an *assiduous* student: 1 affected and silly 2 careful and industrious 3 mediocre — 3. ________
4. his *benign* appearance: 1 kindly and mild 2 eccentric 3 weak and infirm — 4. ________
5. a *captious* critic: 1 fault-finding 2 quite influential 3 kind and sympathetic — 5. ________
6. a lawyer's *chicanery:* 1 trickery and fraud 2 cleverness 3 delaying tactics — 6. ________
7. a fearful *chimera:* 1 grotesque fantasy 2 cancer 3 murderous attack — 7. ________
8. a *clandestine* meeting: 1 furtively secret 2 illegal 3 unimportant — 8. ________
9. a *commodious* room: 1 littered and dirty 2 fashionable 3 ample and spacious — 9. ________
10. the surfing *coterie:* 1 closed group 2 spectators 3 opponents — 10. ________
11. to *denigrate* a reputation: 1 protect 2 blacken and defame 3 overlook — 11. ________
12. to *deprecate* her skill: 1 praise 2 try to copy 3 disapprove or slight — 12. ________
13. his *dilatory* procedures: 1 crude and insulting 2 delaying 3 scrupulous — 13. ________
14. *disparities* between stories: 1 correspondences 2 dissimilarities 3 relationships — 14. ________
15. *dissembling* her anger: 1 soothing 2 concealing 3 showing or proclaiming — 15. ________
16. an *effete* society: 1 worn out and strengthless 2 polished 3 aristocratic — 16. ________
17. an *encomium* for the chief: 1 speech of praise 2 award 3 promotion — 17. ________
18. an *enervated* patient: 1 encouraged and cheerful 2 weakened 3 chronic — 18. ________
19. an *erudite* professor: 1 very learned 2 quite dull 3 wry and sarcastic — 19. ________
20. *euphonious* sounds: 1 rough and discordant 2 imperceptible 3 pleasant — 20. ________
21. *forensic* activities: relevant to 1 sports 2 narcotics 3 speech and debate — 21. ________
22. marked by *hyperbole:* 1 grotesque curves 2 exaggeration 3 doubt and anger — 22. ________
23. an *imminent* fate: 1 impending 2 cruel 3 ironic — 23. ________
24. *indigent* applicants: 1 well-qualified 2 eagerly zealous 3 impoverished — 24. ________
25. an *innocuous* drug: 1 poisonous 2 extremely expensive 3 harmless — 25. ________
26. *insentient* things: 1 without senses or life 2 dangerous 3 expensive — 26. ________
27. tropical *lassitude:* 1 weary languor 2 discomfort 3 rich lushness — 27. ________
28. to *mitigate* the offense: 1 record 2 punish 3 lessen the seriousness of — 28. ________
29. meeting his *nemesis:* 1 faithful ally 2 agent of retribution 3 healer — 29. ________
30. a *palpable* truth: 1 recently discovered 2 quite obvious 3 immortal — 30. ________
31. delivered a *panegyric:* 1 accusation 2 eulogy 3 universal curse — 31. ________
32. a *pernicious* tendency: 1 beneficial 2 unexpectedly sudden 3 harmful — 32. ________
33. skilled at *persiflage:* 1 concealment 2 interpretation 3 light banter — 33. ________
34. a *precursor* of the new era: 1 opponent 2 forerunner 3 prophet — 34. ________

Copyright © 1994 by Harcourt Brace & Company. All rights reserved.

35. the *progeny* of the pioneers: 1 heritage 2 offspring 3 leaders 35. _________
36. a *rapacious* old man: 1 infirm 2 covetous 3 vigorous 36. _________
37. a *salubrious* climate: 1 varied 2 weakening 3 healthful 37. _________
38. a *sententious* observation: 1 profane 2 trite and puffed up 3 ungrammatical 38. _________
39. *specious* reasoning: 1 deceptively plausible 2 profound 3 inclusive 39. _________
40. a *stentorian* voice: 1 extremely loud 2 musical 3 quivering 40. _________
41. a *strident* tone: 1 harsh and shrill 2 pathetic 3 wavering 41. _________
42. a *taciturn* mountaineer: 1 daring 2 threatening 3 silent and reserved 42. _________
43. *thalassic* studies: pertaining to 1 heat energy 2 seas 3 mythology 43. _________
44. *torpid* animals: 1 diseased 2 uncommon 3 inactive and sluggish 44. _________
45. to *traduce* her character: 1 examine 2 defame 3 protect 45. _________
46. a *trenchant* comment: 1 keen and cutting 2 demanding 3 unsuitable 46. _________
47. the *vagaries* of fate: 1 whims and fancies 2 fixed decrees 3 principles 47. _________
48. a reputation for *veracity:* 1 truthfulness 2 craftiness 3 stubbornness 48. _________
49. to *vitiate* his conclusion: 1 invalidate 2 reinforce 3 ignore 49. _________
50. a *vitriolic* answer: 1 placating 2 angry and caustic 3 unnoticed 50. _________

Copyright © 1994 by Harcourt Brace & Company. All rights reserved.

NAME ______________________ SECTION ________ DATE __________

VOCABULARY TEST 2: The words in the following test have been taken from recent issues of newspapers and magazines with large national circulations. Choose the word or expression closest in meaning to the italicized word and print the number of that word or expression in the blank.

1. the dean's *admonitory* note: 1 complimentary 2 prompt 3 cautionary — 1. ________
2. to *alleviate* the distress: 1 intensify 2 ignore 3 relieve — 2. ________
3. *animosities* aroused by the talk: 1 discussions 2 enmities 3 answers — 3. ________
4. an *anomalous* development: 1 gratifying 2 abnormal 3 preliminary — 4. ________
5. *apothegms* about thrift: 1 maxims 2 precautions 3 instances of neglect — 5. ________
6. an *arduous* task: 1 laborious 2 unexpected 3 easily overlooked — 6. ________
7. the *banality* of the speech: 1 triteness 2 suitability 3 effectiveness — 7. ________
8. *coerced* to follow: 1 persuaded 2 compelled by force 3 directed — 8. ________
9. treated with *derision:* 1 veneration 2 ridicule 3 reluctant consent — 9. ________
10. into *discrete* divisions: 1 unclear 2 separate and distinct 3 uneven — 10. ________
11. opposed by the *dissident* group: 1 militant 2 dissenting 3 radical — 11. ________
12. an *ebullient* person: 1 mournful 2 unhealthy 3 enthusiastic and excited — 12. ________
13. *emulous* of his sister: 1 contemptuous 2 eager to equal or beat 3 loving — 13. ________
14. an *enigmatic* suggestion: 1 improper 2 appropriate 3 puzzling — 14. ________
15. aroused *ephemeral* interest: 1 short-lived 2 enthusiastic 3 prurient — 15. ________
16. to *eschew* more talk: 1 speed up 2 shun or avoid 3 consider — 16. ________
17. *ethnic* studies: pertaining to 1 morals 2 peoples and races 3 money — 17. ________
18. answered with *fatuity:* 1 emphasis 2 utter foolishness 3 tenderness — 18. ________
19. *inhibiting* the operations: 1 showing 2 approving 3 hindering or stopping — 19. ________
20. a person of *integrity:* 1 honest character 2 wide reputation 3 great wealth — 20. ________
21. *internecine* conflicts: 1 minor 2 covert 3 bloody or deadly — 21. ________
22. an *intransigent* enemy: 1 temporary 2 unimportant 3 uncompromising — 22. ________
23. a *lucrative* contract: 1 very profitable 2 unfortunate 3 illegal — 23. ________
24. a *lugubrious* expression: 1 laughably mournful 2 noncommittal 3 fierce — 24. ________
25. a *mandatory* order: 1 obligatory 2 trivial 3 wild and rash — 25. ________
26. the character's *metamorphosis:* 1 identity 2 complete change 3 outward appearance — 26. ________
27. a *nominal* debt: 1 trivial 2 pressing 3 legal but unjust — 27. ________
28. *occult* practices: 1 secret and supernatural 2 criminal 3 hurtful — 28. ________
29. an *opulent* display: showing 1 lavish wealth 2 bad taste 3 pitiful need — 29. ________
30. Yeltsin's *partisans:* 1 zealous followers 2 relatives 3 spies and saboteurs — 30. ________
31. a *pastoral* background: 1 religious 2 rural 3 fierce and barbarous — 31. ________
32. a *peccant* husband: 1 cruel and oppressive 2 submissive 3 sinning — 32. ________
33. a *penchant* for mathematics: 1 inability 2 liking and inclination 3 dislike — 33. ________
34. *proliferation* of taxes: 1 collection 2 rapid multiplication 3 hatred — 34. ________

Copyright © 1994 by Harcourt Brace & Company. All rights reserved.

35. to *reiterate* an objection: 1 repeat 2 withdraw 3 apologize for — 35. ________
36. *restive* natives: 1 lethargic 2 unruly 3 stupid and naive — 36. ________
37. *sinuous* motions: 1 lustful 2 difficult to see 3 winding and curving — 37. ________
38. *sporadic* cases of the disease: 1 fatal 2 unexpected 3 found here and there — 38. ________
39. a limited *stipend:* 1 grant or allowance 2 obligation 3 time limit — 39. ________
40. *subliminal* propaganda: below 1 dignity 2 conscious perception 3 truth — 40. ________
41. a *succinct* account: 1 lurid and colorful 2 terse 3 slanderous — 41. ________
42. a *sumptuous* table: 1 rich and lavish 2 bare and scant 3 mediocre — 42. ________
43. *sycophantic* followers: 1 weak and irresolute 2 flattering 3 determined — 43. ________
44. a *tortuous* path: 1 steep and narrow 2 twisting irregularly 3 almost unknown — 44. ________
45. a *traumatic* effect: marked by 1 illusion 2 misfortune 3 shock and injury — 45. ________
46. his *travail* ended: 1 toil and pain 2 voyaging 3 horseback riding — 46. ________
47. a *ubiquitous* insect: 1 dangerous 2 present everywhere 3 harmful to crops — 47. ________
48. answered with *unction:* 1 rudeness 2 oily slickness 3 self-deprecation — 48. ________
49. the *verbosity* of the essay: 1 wordiness 2 persuasiveness 3 smooth style — 49. ________
50. a *vitreous* substance: 1 glassy 2 unanalyzable 3 steely and firm — 50. ________

Copyright © 1994 by Harcourt Brace & Company. All rights reserved.

NAME ______________________________ SECTION ________ DATE __________

VOCABULARY TEST 3: The words in the following test are taken from a word frequency list. The most common are from the 10,000–11,000 bracket, the least common from the 19,000–20,000 bracket. A score of 75 might be interpreted as an indication of a vocabulary of 15,000 words (although this figure is probably low). Choose the word closest in meaning to the italicized word and print its number in the blank.

1. to *abdicate* the throne: 1 claim 2 renounce 3 occupy — 1. ________
2. the *aborigines* of the land: 1 rivers 2 natives 3 animals — 2. ________
3. a pact *abrogated* by consent: 1 drawn up 2 endorsed 3 abolished — 3. ________
4. to *accentuate* this point: 1 emphasize 2 contradict 3 consider — 4. ________
5. an *acrimonious* argument: 1 sharp and bitter 2 trivial 3 endless — 5. ________
6. an *adroit* worker: 1 bungling 2 dissatisfied 3 skillful — 6. ________
7. under the club's *aegis:* 1 protesting 2 sponsoring 3 planning — 7. ________
8. a man of *affluence:* 1 notoriety 2 position 3 wealth — 8. ________
9. to *ameliorate* conditions: 1 investigate 2 worsen 3 improve — 9. ________
10. his *asinine* comments: 1 foolish 2 sarcastic 3 determined — 10. ________
11. an *atrocious* crime: 1 mysterious 2 sordid 3 cruel and beastlike — 11. ________
12. under *auspicious* circumstances: 1 difficult 2 doubtful 3 favorable — 12. ________
13. Russian *autocrats:* 1 ideologies 2 absolute rulers 3 satellite states — 13. ________
14. *belligerent* nations: 1 bankrupt 2 densely populated 3 warlike — 14. ________
15. a *bestial* action: 1 foolhardy 2 secret 3 beastly — 15. ________
16. a foolish *braggart:* 1 fanatic 2 boaster 3 apprentice — 16. ________
17. *bucolic* surroundings: 1 frightening 2 rural 3 congested — 17. ________
18. to *buttress* an assertion: 1 support 2 explain 3 refute — 18. ________
19. a *buxom* woman: 1 fashionable 2 well-loved 3 plump — 19. ________
20. a *callow* youth: 1 immature 2 excitable 3 adventurous — 20. ________
21. the *candor* of her answer: 1 honest frankness 2 hesitation 3 abruptness — 21. ________
22. the editor's *captious* ways: 1 careful 2 faultfinding 3 angry — 22. ________
23. a *carmine* color: 1 deep 2 unattractive 3 reddish — 23. ________
24. a *choleric* temperament: 1 placid 2 dull 3 hotheaded — 24. ________
25. a *chromatic* chart: pertaining to 1 chemicals 2 colors 3 weather — 25. ________
26. a *clement* judge: 1 dishonest 2 mild and lenient 3 learned — 26. ________
27. *cogent* suggestions: 1 irrelevant 2 feeble 3 strong and convincing — 27. ________
28. *cognizant* of danger: 1 aware of 2 unhappy about 3 careless of — 28. ________
29. a *colloquy* on the question: 1 argument 2 talk 3 sudden silence — 29. ________
30. a *complaisant* welcome: 1 boisterous 2 sullen and rude 3 pleasing — 30. ________
31. to *concoct* an excuse: 1 deny 2 ignore 3 cook up, make up — 31. ________
32. to *conduce to* peace: 1 lead to 2 think about 3 work against — 32. ________

Copyright © 1994 by Harcourt Brace & Company. All rights reserved.

33. a *conflagration* downtown: 1 big fire 2 riot 3 epidemic 33. ________
34. a *decrepit* old house: 1 broken down 2 beautiful 3 cheap 34. ________
35. old and *desiccated:* 1 weakened 2 confused 3 dried out 35. ________
36. the *disruption* of his plan: 1 breaking 2 culminating 3 ending 36. ________
37. planning *drastic* measures: 1 unusual 2 routine 3 quite severe 37. ________
38. a poetic *effusion:* 1 temperament 2 vision 3 outpouring 38. ________
39. an *elongated* pattern: 1 intricate 2 lengthened 3 old-fashioned 39. ________
40. to *expedite* the deal: 1 investigate 2 cancel 3 speed up 40. ________
41. gave a *fillip* to the party: 1 pause 2 stimulus 3 alarm 41. ________
42. trained in *fiscal* matters: 1 financial 2 administrative 3 fishing 42. ________
43. the play's *flamboyant* style: 1 showy 2 baffling 3 trite and old 43. ________
44. *friable* rock: 1 volcanic 2 easily crumbled 3 multicolored 44. ________
45. a *garbled* story: 1 confused 2 prejudiced 3 very brief 45. ________
46. a *gossamer* fabric: 1 synthetic 2 rough and durable 3 filmy 46. ________
47. the *habitat* of fur-bearing animals: 1 diet 2 dwelling area 3 sanctuary 47. ________
48. a *hermetic* closure: 1 airtight 2 temporary 3 insecure 48. ________
49. sorting *homogeneous* things: 1 similar 2 miscellaneous 3 dangerous 49. ________
50. an *immutable* law: 1 extremely just 2 changeless 3 imperfect 50. ________
51. seeing the devil *incarnate:* 1 alone 2 in the flesh 3 on earth 51. ________
52. an *incongruous* costume: 1 inappropriate 2 cheap 3 modest 52. ________
53. heard the news with *incredulity:* 1 disbelief 2 calm 3 fright 53. ________
54. an *indigenous* plant: 1 edible 2 native 3 very large 54. ________
55. an *irascible* teacher: 1 angry 2 unpopular 3 severe 55. ________
56. the *itinerary* of the candidate: 1 travel route 2 endurance 3 knowledge 56. ________
57. a *lacteal* solution: 1 colorful 2 poisonous 3 milky 57. ________
58. a space-age *lexicon:* 1 education 2 outlook 3 word list 58. ________
59. explaining with *lucidity:* 1 evasion 2 lightheartedness 3 clarity 59. ________
60. to *mediate* the dispute: 1 arbitrate 2 prolong 3 intensify 60. ________
61. a *menial* position: 1 uncomfortable 2 grotesque 3 lowly and undignified 61. ________
62. a *mercurial* temperament: 1 sympathetic 2 morose 3 quickly changing 62. ________
63. *meretricious* advertising: 1 effective 2 falsely showy 3 detailed 63. ________
64. *misconstruing* his intent: 1 forgetting 2 misinterpreting 3 perceiving 64. ________
65. of *momentous* significance: 1 short-lived 2 quite important 3 uncertain 65. ________
66. *monitions* about their conduct: 1 arguments 2 hints 3 warnings 66. ________
67. a *moot* question: 1 important 2 arguable 3 ridiculous 67. ________
68. *nefarious* activities: 1 wicked 2 profitable 3 adolescent 68. ________

 Copyright © 1994 by Harcourt Brace & Company. All rights reserved.

NAME ______________________ SECTION ________ DATE __________

69. a person showing *obesity:* 1 bad manners 2 fatness 3 laziness 69. ________
70. an *obtruding* brace: 1 supporting 2 thrusting out 3 sagging 70. ________
71. the *olfactory* nerves: pertaining to 1 reflexes 2 taste 3 smell 71. ________
72. *onerous* wartime duties: 1 honorable 2 burdensome 3 secret 72. ________
73. the monks' *orisons:* 1 costumes 2 rituals 3 prayers 73. ________
74. the *oscillating* marker: 1 sinking 2 flaming 3 vibrating 74. ________
75. *ossified* tissue: 1 healed 2 turned to bone 3 deadened 75. ________
76. the *ostentation* of the display: 1 taste 2 showiness 3 smartness 76. ________
77. viewed with *overt* suspicion: 1 unjust 2 unconcealed 3 ill-based 77. ________
78. *parrying* awkward questions: 1 warding off 2 answering 3 ignoring 78. ________
79. saved by a *penurious* relative: 1 stingy 2 eccentric 3 foresighted 79. ________
80. interested in *philology:* 1 word study 2 stamp collecting 3 dramatics 80. ________
81. a *pliant* material: 1 sturdy 2 synthetic 3 flexible 81. ________
82. *precluding* any discussion: 1 waiving 2 requiring 3 shutting off 82. ________
83. taking a new *pseudonym:* 1 assumed name 2 disguise 3 assignment 83. ________
84. acting with *rectitude:* 1 rightness 2 caution 3 wide knowledge 84. ________
85. tending to *regress:* 1 stand still 2 turn aside 3 go backward 85. ________
86. a complete *renovation:* 1 abandonment 2 renewing 3 cleaning 86. ________
87. a *replica* of the ship: 1 picture 2 blueprint plan 3 copy 87. ________
88. some lengthy *rigmarole:* 1 nonsense 2 explanation 3 protest 88. ________
89. a *sacerdotal* custom: 1 primitive 2 priestly 3 harmful 89. ________
90. *scurrilous* rumors: 1 vulgar and abusive 2 widespread 3 fearful 90. ________
91. a *senile* condition: 1 convalescent 2 old and enfeebled 3 venerable 91. ________
92. to *simulate* desire: 1 pretend 2 extinguish 3 fulfill 92. ________
93. to *stultify* development: 1 quicken 2 prevent 3 await 93. ________
94. a *thermal* unit: pertaining to 1 weight 2 moisture 3 heat 94. ________
95. to *transcribe* the laws: 1 study 2 violate 3 copy 95. ________
96. a *truculent* answer: 1 fiercely assertive 2 respectful 3 candid 96. ________
97. the *turpitude* of the court: 1 extravagance 2 immorality 3 disloyalty 97. ________
98. an *unkempt* appearance: 1 fastidious 2 feverish 3 untidy 98. ________
99. the pup was a *waif:* 1 mongrel 2 stray 3 runt 99. ________
100. playing the *zany:* 1 clown 2 coward 3 lieutenant 100. ________

Copyright © 1994 by Harcourt Brace & Company. All rights reserved.